FADE IN: THE SCREENWRITING PROCESS

Robert A. Berman

Published by:
Michael Wiese Film Productions
Box 406
Westport, CT 06881
(203) 226-6979

In conjunction with:
Focal Press
A Division of Butterworth Publishers
80 Montvale Avenue
Stoneham, MA 02180

Cover design and back cover photograph by:
Peter Piik & Associates
Port Chester, NY

Printed by:
Baum-Brumfield, Inc., Ann Arbor, Michigan
Manufactured in the United States of America

First Printing, October 1988

ISBN: 0-94188-07-8

PUBLISHER'S FOREWORD

Bob Berman is a dedicated and highly disciplined writer. He is also a salesman of ideas. He sent me his "12/20 Club" screenplay and although I had dozens of other scripts piled high to read, his pure enthusiasm piqued my interest. I read it.

The script was really quite good. I was further amazed that it read so well and that it was his first screenplay. How in the world did he get his very first to be so good? After reading his two other scripts, I got to know Bob. I learned how he carefully prepared and outlined his material prior to writing, following well-defined procedures. I felt it would be valuable to share his approach with the thousands of writers who set out alone to craft their first screenplay.

True to my expectations, Bob has delivered a concise, well-organized, step-by-step guide to getting the job done. He clearly identifies the necessary steps and the thought process involved in this creative writing form. Following Bob's system, writers will stay motivated, see daily progress, and confidently complete their work with a tremendous sense of accomplishment.

Bob, thank you for making the job of writing a little easier. Now get going on your next screenplay!

Michael Wiese

For My Father
STANLEY J. BERMAN
August 15, 1909 To July 30, 1983

ACKNOWLEDGEMENTS

I am very grateful to Michael Wiese, my publisher, for providing me with this opportunity. Also, his guidance and input into fine-tuning this book was extremely helpful and greatly appreciated. From day one, this experience has been nothing but positive.

A special thanks to Peter Piik for creating the book cover design and to Lauren Schnitzer and Bernice Steckler for their proofreading assistance.

I would also like to acknowledge writers Bob Logan (Los Angeles) and Carol Ann Messecar (New York) for their advice and encouragement.

Most importantly, a very special thanks to Susan, my wife, for her continuous love, support, and understanding.

TABLE OF CONTENTS

TABLE OF CONTENTS

INTRODUCTION

INTRODUCTION

About five years ago, out of a great interest in film, I started thinking and talking about writing a screenplay. I knew that I had a good premise for "a" story -- but that was all. On a couple of occasions, I casually mentioned my idea to a few friends and business associates. Their response was usually enthusiastic. Some even prompted me to start the project, but it just never happened.

Then suddenly one day, after a twenty-year career in sales management, I made a decision to become a screenwriter and resigned. Needless to say, my family and friends were shocked and offered to drive me to a psychiatric institution for observation.

After "six hours" of carefully planning the transition to my new career, there was only one thing I was actually sure of -- I did not know anything about screenwriting. As a matter of fact, I had never previously seen or much less read a screenplay.

At the recommendation of a friend of a friend, I picked up several books on screenwriting -- although I loathe reading any kind of instructions. I simply lack the desire and the patience to muddle through these things. With three screenwriting books in hand, I spent two months reading and digesting the material as well as screenplays of successful films. At first, it was very confusing but things gradually became clearer; or so I thought. Then, basking in the warmth of my own self-confidence, I proceeded to write my first screenplay, THE 12/20 CLUB -- my original story idea.

Following the procedures outlined in these books, I struggled with my project month after month. Did I make progress? Of course. Was my "actual" first draft screenplay of THE 12/20 CLUB any good? Hardly.

My screenplay story had been completely plotted out from beginning to end so my dilemma was not one of a writer staring at a blank piece of paper. Also, having written for national magazines on diversified subjects such as music, fishing, humor, and business, I was approaching screenwriting with a basic talent for writing and a high level of confidence.

Screenwriting was my first frustrating writing experience. I thought I understood the process and, yet, there were too many days filled with apprehension and anxiety.

Proper preparation and confidence is the foundation of good writing. During the first months of screenwriting, confidence was a forced commodity -- it appeared naturally on the horizon from time to time but eventually vanished at the slightest hint of a breeze.

The first four months of screenwriting were truly painful and very frustrating. However, at the end of a year, I achieved what I thought would have been impossible from the start -- the completion of three original screenplays of which I am extremely proud.

It took me a year of struggling and suffering through the learning stages, by myself, before I assimilated and confidently understood the screenwriting process in its entirety. Having a knack for writing "how-to articles", I immediately recognized the need and value in writing a book to provide the inexperienced writer with a concise overview and understanding of the screenwriting process with an easy-to-follow method.

The screenwriting process in this book has been presented in a concise and comprehensive form and is organized into a logical sequence. Before you attempt to write your first screenplay, you must read this book until you are totally comfortable with the procedures. Then, read as many screenplays of successful films as you can. Read them until you understand each one intimately. This is part of the learning process and an absolute necessity. Any attempt to cut corners will cost you dearly when it comes time to tackle that all important first project.

It is important to have confidence in your own abilities. You must ultimately trust and rely upon your own judgment, taste, and intuition. Other opinions are sometimes valid and extremely valuable, but not always. Advice can be very helpful in the research stages and after the first draft screenplay is completed -- but not while you are actually writing.

If you receive bad advice or negative comments on what you have already completed, it can be inhibiting and have an adverse effect on your attitude and, subsequently, your writing ability. You must always approach your work from a position of confidence.

When you are tackling your first screenplay project, you may desire some input or feedback as to how to approach a given problem. If you put your faith in the screenwriting process outlined here, you will answer those questions as you complete the necessary steps.

In dealing with people inside and outside of the film industry, it is important to know and understand that very few people are qualified to accurately assess any form of creative writing and provide the writer with effective, constructive criticism; and, you are also dealing with a reader's subjective judgment as opposed to an objective evaluation.

My screenplay, THE CRIMSON MOON, is reprinted in its entirety as an integral part of the book. Since you are unfamiliar with the story, you will be able to approach the material from an objective and unbiased point of view. Also, this story illustrates the various aspects of screenwriting so there will be constant reference to the screenplay throughout the text.

I will also reference portions of my other two screenplays since all three stories are different in film genre, subject matter, and treatment. Illustrating segments of all three screenplays will be helpful in understanding the screenwriting process. In regard to the techniques applied to each story, there are strong similarities; and, at the same time, you will be exposed to those instances when "exceptions to the rule" were exercised in order to fit the needs of the story.

Of greatest importance -- don't begin to write your screenplay until you are thoroughly prepared; and once you start, don't stop to polish, correct, or rewrite until the first draft is completed.

Screenwriting is an ever-evolving process filled with challenge, mystery and exciting moments; and not unlike any other field, it is a true art form and craft mastered by a handful of talented people. Welcome to the exciting world of screenwriting.

CHAPTER 1: THE STORY

THE SCREENPLAY

Films are visions of the writer's imagination and probably the most influential medium there is in society today. While film is a collaborative art form dependent upon the skills and talents of many artists and technicians, the strength of every film project is in the screenplay.

A screenplay is a structural plan for a motion picture encompassing seven primary components -- story, plot (structure), scenes, character, dialogue, emotional action, and physical action.

When it comes to writing a novel, the author has total freedom in regard to the length and the treatment of the material. A screenwriter must adhere to the unique screenplay form, the terse style of writing, and demonstrate great precision and skill in structuring and executing the story within a specific number of pages.

As a general rule, each page of screenplay is equal to one minute of film time. This applies to both action scenes and dialogue-oriented scenes. The average feature film is two hours long which translates into approximately 120 pages of screenplay. To put length into the proper perspective--some feature films can exceed two hours while others, especially comedies, tend to run between 90 and 100 minutes. Use this as a guideline but let your story determine the final length.

The treatment of a screenplay story is totally at the discretion of the writer with every decision a matter of choice. Regardless of how interesting a story might be or how well it is structured, it is ultimately the writer's overall treatment of the material that determines the final quality of the screenplay.

While writing a screenplay requires adherence to form, there is still plenty of room for developing your own style of screenwriting. After you read a half dozen or so screenplays written by famous screenwriters, you will quickly identify the individual styles and the liberties each has taken in completing his or her work.

James L. Brooks' screenwriting style is almost that of a novelist. In TERMS OF ENDEARMENT, he describes the emotional feelings and attitudes of the characters in the scene descriptions. It greatly enhances the read and provides the actors with far more insight into the characters' roles.

Horton Foote's screenwriting style in TENDER MERCIES demonstrates tremendous skill with minimal use of scene descriptions and the most effective treatment of dialogue. In some scenes, his sporadic use of dialogue initially seems inadequate until you study it carefully. Then you realize how brilliantly it works.

THE BENEFITS OF READING SCREENPLAYS

Reading screenplays is a required step in the learning process. In form, every screenplay looks the same, but in style and treatment of the characters and subject matter, each is distinctly different. Reading screenplays of successful films gives the reader a sense of form, structure, the author's style, treatment of characters and dialogue, and provides the opportunity to compare scene descriptions as they are written in the screenplay to the way they actually look in the film.

The screenplays you acquire may be a second draft or a revised third draft, as the legend designates on the title page. In reading screenplays from successful films which are in various stages of development, you may be exposed to deleted scenes or scenes which might have been filmed but later edited out. In many instances, the deleted or edited-out scenes were excellent judgments, regardless of who made the final decision. Some scenes might have been deleted or edited out because they had no value in moving the story forward; or, quite possibly, taking a particular scene out might actually enhance the entire screenplay story.

In the second draft copy of LETHAL WEAPON, there were a lot of smart-ass wisecracks that were obviously deleted from the shooting script. The humor read well but it might have lightened things up too much. I assume that the producer and/or director wanted to keep a tight edge on the story so a lot of the humorous touches were taken out.

By reading and analyzing other screenplays, it is easy to assimilate the writing form and the intricate techniques involved.

After seeing a terrible movie, many people incorrectly assume that they can write something better. The same logic is applied to great films which often create an unrealistic impression of being rather simplistic and, therefore, easy to write. That is not the case.

Anyone who plays golf can relate to this analogy. If you have no experience with the sport, you can quickly gain a false sense of confidence by observing the ease at which a professional swings a club. Not until you actually try playing golf do you realize the great skill, technique, and timing which are involved. The correct golf swing is totally foreign to natural body rhythm making it difficult to master without instruction, a lot of practice, and hard work.

Screenwriting, like golf, may look easy, but it is not. It is a complex form of writing with many intricate details. If one of those details is not properly treated, it can unbalance the entire screenplay and significantly alter the quality of the work. Instead of having what could have been a great screenplay, you end up with something which is ultimately a disappointment.

It is important to understand the difficulties involved and yet feel confident that you now have the tools in hand and the opportunity to succeed at screenwriting.

On page 178, there is a list of stores which specialize in selling screenplays as well as film books. Read as many screenplays as you can since it will provide helpful insight into screenwriting and speed up the learning process.

The following list of screenplays are just a few of the many worth reading. Some are reasonably current while others are older classics.

Absence Of Malice
And Justice For All
Blade Runner
Body Heat
Butch Cassidy And The Sundance Kid
Chinatown
In The Heat Of The Night
The Jagged Edge
Lethal Weapon
Moonstruck
No Way Out
One Flew Over The Cuckoo's Nest
Ordinary People
Paper Chase
Stand By Me
Stake-Out
Terms Of Endearment
Tender Mercies

Thief
To Kill A Mockingbird
Top Gun
Witness

More than likely, you can find several contemporary screenplays to illustrate the treatment of subject matter you are interested in writing about. Reading those screenplays can be quite helpful in determining how scene descriptions are handled as well as how much detail is used. You will also learn when and how camera angles are used to enhance certain scenes.

FILM CRITICS AS A LEARNING TOOL

Regardless of your attitude towards film critics, their critiques of movies can provide helpful insight. While you may or may not agree with the critics' overall rating of a film, they often accurately identify flaws in a film's story as well as in the treatment of the characters.

Reading movie reviews can be extremely helpful since we learn from both the successes and failures of other people. Use film reviews as a learning tool. Read the reviews, see the films, and read the screenplays.

HOW TO READ A SCREENPLAY

Reading a screenplay for the first time can be an awkward experience. But once you understand the basic form and get by the terse style of writing, the story will propel you to the end.

Each SCENE HEADING indicates INT. (Interior) or EXT. (Exterior) LOCATION as well as time -- DAY or NIGHT. Directly below the SCENE HEADING is the SCENE DESCRIPTION where characters and/or the action of the scene is described in paragraph form.

The CHARACTER speaking is capitalized and placed in the center of the page. One space below in parentheses, STAGE DIRECTIONS are written for the character. The DIALOGUE forms a block in the center of the page under the character's name and stage directions.

Here is a brief illustration of screenplay form:

EXT. HOUSE - NIGHT

JACK BROWN walks his dog on the sidewalk. He stops in front of a house and nervously looks around.

From the bushes, JOE HANKS emerges carrying a FLASHLIGHT. He shines the flashlight on Brown. The dog BARKS. Startled, Brown reacts.

BROWN
(turning around)
Hey, what is this?

HANKS
(holding flashlight
on Brown's face)
I'm tired of you bringing your dog
to my house and having him do his
business here.

BROWN
(stammering)
Wwww well, what do you want me to do?

HANKS
(pointing)
Walk him in front of GEORGE
DUFFY'S house; I'm not too fond of
him either!

Jack Brown briskly walks his dog towards the other house. Joe Hanks turns off his flashlight and gradually walks off into the dark shadows of night.

That is it; end of scene and end of illustration.

COMMENTS ON THE READING ASSIGNMENT

It is necessary for you to read the screenplay included in this book in order to gain familiarity with the story, the structure, and the writing form. A number of screenplay terms are abbreviated so if you have any doubts, refer to SCREENPLAY TERMINOLOGY on page 84. Only for the purpose of publishing this book, all profanity in the sample screenplay has been masked. Profanity is an integral part of our language and culture. When profanity is used to duplicate real-life situations in your story, it adds a realistic dimension.

The sample screenplay, THE CRIMSON MOON, was my second original screenplay. It is a "polished" first draft in that the basic structure of the story was never altered after the first draft was completed.

In writing my screenplays, I actually visualize the characters, hear the dialogue in counterpoint, and view the action of the scene on my "mindscreen". For me, it is a very real experience like going to the movies.

After I create the main character for any of my stories, I establish a strong visual image of a known actor when writing. It helps me to focus on the development of the character and the story. Based upon his performances and screen presence in BLADE RUNNER and WITNESS, Harrison Ford was clearly my strongest impression for Matt Decker, the main character in THE CRIMSON MOON. Also, Harrison Ford perfectly matches the physical aspects as well as the age requirements for the main character; an important consideration in this story.

THE CRIMSON MOON appears in the back of the book and even though it is reduced in size, book headings and page numbers were omitted in order to preserve the look and feel of the screenplay. Please read the screenplay now in its entirety since it is an important part of the learning process. Throughout the book, the screenplay will be frequently referenced so you must be familiar with the story. I hope you enjoy THE CRIMSON MOON. After you finish, return to the next page and continue from there.

THE BASIC RULES OF DRAMATIC WRITING

Once you understand the basic rules that apply to dramatic writing, it is easy to approach screenwriting and establish your course of direction with confidence.

In any story, there can only be "one" protagonist or "one" main character; a person who has an urgent need to achieve something that is important to him or her. While there may be two characters who seemingly appear as "equals" in a story, one must clearly have a more dominant role and greater need than the other. The reason for having only one main character is to provide clarity and focus in developing your story.

For the same reason, there can only be "one" antagonist or "one" villain who will create obstacles in the path of the main character. By progressively increasing the conflict between the main character and his or her adversary, you will create a story that will sustain the audience's attention and interest. Conflict is the basis of all drama. Without conflict, there is no story.

If you choose to write a story about a man or woman battling a harsh wilderness environment or any other form of "inanimate opposition", it will not work by itself. Only when adversaries act and react through "rising human conflict" can an audience's attention and interest be sustained.

If your main character "advances" a step towards achieving his or her goal, there must be a "counterthrust" or "setback" delivered by the adversary. This is the primary essence of dramatic writing -- one person striving to achieve a goal while another attempts to defeat him or her.

The action of both the main character and the adversary must be motivated by their individual needs. Within your story, you must find a way to establish their motives with the audience.

A distinction needs to be made between the forms of human conflict, as determined by the treatment of the characters in different film stories.

Are there stories where "inanimate opposition" is the primary source of conflict? The answer is yes. But the question will always be, "how well do these stories really work?"

PLACES IN THE HEART is a moving story dramatizing the struggle of a woman trying to save her farm after the death of her husband. The harsh climate of the depression era is "the" primary force creating the conflict; which is "inanimate opposition". What is interesting and unusual about the situation is this: the bank holding the mortgage on the woman's (Sally Fields) farm was actually supportive of her, thus reducing the most obvious potential for rising human conflict. Considering the number of bank foreclosures during that period of history, I expected the bank manager to be merciless in demanding prompt payment. There are a few separate incidents where human conflict come into play but they are very minor and not continuous from a standpoint of "one" character being the primary antagonist.

ON GOLDEN POND deals with human conflict but at a different level than other stories in the traditional sense. Henry Fonda's character is struggling with himself in dealing with old age. Jane Fonda's "daughter" character struggles with the need of her father's approval. There is strong friction between these two characters until the end of the story when they really talk to each other for the first time and come to an understanding. The point is this: the conflict in ON GOLDEN POND is very dramatic within the context of this story, but less dramatic in "comparison" to those stories where the adversaries are clearly the "good" protagonist versus the "evil" antagonist.

Another example of conflict is the "antagonist within" premise which is best illustrated by two "Rocky" films, the original Rocky story, SOMEBODY UP THERE LIKES ME, about Rocky Graziano, and, of course, Sylvester Stallone's ROCKY. Both of these film stories follow the same basic premise in that the characters are born losers coming from an environment of poverty and crime. Their backgrounds are "inanimate opposition" -- the force working against them.

Their goal is to overcome those aspects of their lives which label them losers. In that respect, the stories are exactly the same. What essentially made Stallone's story different and fresh is one primary element, the story's "hook". Stallone's Rocky, an unknown fighter, is given the opportunity to fight the world champion. Overcoming the loser within himself, his self-doubt, his life of poverty and crime, is "the" primary force of conflict in both of these Rocky stories.

In a later chapter, the various forms of conflict within THE CRIMSON MOON will be illustrated. There is rising human conflict, conflict which is indigenous to the story, as well as the key character's internal conflict (antagonist within) in dealing with personal problems.

Within every story, there are major and minor conflicts, obstacles, confrontations, and struggles. These forms of conflict will vary in degrees but collectively, they provide the adhesive force sustaining the audience's attention and interest.

While film stories are similar in some respects, they are very unique within the treatment of the subject matter, characters, and all the other important elements. Read and analyze other screenplays from successful films until you clearly understand how and why each one works so well.

A LIKEABLE MAIN CHARACTER

The success of your story will also hinge upon creating a likeable main character; someone the audience can identify with, relate to, and root for. Early in your story, it is important to establish who your main character is as well as his or her likability.

Without using dialogue, you could show your main character giving assistance to a young child or possibly an elderly person. The scene can be as brief as four or five seconds but it will be long enough to immediately and effectively plant a positive character image with the audience. Most importantly, scenes like this must fit naturally into the framework of your story without appearing to be obvious.

At the same time, if your character shows any signs of being mean, nasty, or malicious, audience empathy will be lost and your story will fail right from the outset.

The emotional action and dialogue spoken by your characters must be believable. In any situation, your characters must act and react as they would in real life.

While "creative license" allows for the taking of many liberties, every story must remain within the boundaries or realities it establishes from the beginning. This applies to every story from sci-fi to serious drama. And when your story is finally resolved, nothing must be left unexplained, left "hanging", or resolved by coincidence. Everything must be tied together in one neat package.

THE STEP-BY-STEP SCREENWRITING PROCESS

When you consider the total amount of time involved in completing the actual first draft screenplay from the initial story concept, you may spend 80 percent of your time conceptualizing the story, researching the subject matter, and completing the various written exercises. Writing the actual first draft screenplay may only account for 20 percent of your total project time up to that point. (Rewriting is a separate issue.)

Those who apply themselves and follow the procedures outlined in this book can write a good, solid screenplay. Since writing is very personal and everyone has different needs, a different level of ability and skill, you will ultimately determine, through experience, what is valuable to you as far as the entire screenwriting process is concerned.

Some experienced writers may feel that certain steps, such as the scene descriptions or narrative treatment, are a waste of time. That may be true for them, but not necessarily for you. Don't let anyone else influence you in that respect. Go through all the exercises until you are experienced enough to judge the value and necessity of each step.

Each step of screenwriting is an overlapping process which gradually enhances the development and clarity of your story.

With each successive step, things gradually become easier. If you follow all the exercises, you will be surprised at how effortless it seems to write that first draft screenplay.

Taking a few shortcuts without having the experience first could set you up for disaster. Eliminating a step in the process does not save time if you end up struggling with that all important first draft screenplay.

EIGHT EXERCISES

There are eight actual exercises involved in creating a first draft screenplay from a basic story concept and they are:

1. Create a main character and then determine the character's need; that is, what does the main character want to achieve in your story.

2. Complete a character biography and outline the six aspects of good character.

3. Determine the ending of your story.

4. Outline the screenplay's structure from setup to resolution, from plot point to plot point.

5. Outline the scene descriptions.

6. Complete a narrative treatment of your story.

7. Complete the required research.*

8. Write your first draft screenplay.

*Some writers may start the screenwriting process by looking for a story through researching "subject matter". Therefore, research might be the "first" step in the process instead of the seventh.

EXERCISE TIME FACTOR

Don't set any firm time goals in regard to completing a particular screenwriting exercise because it is very difficult to predict "how much time" will be involved in finishing any step.

While it is important to follow the exercise sequence outlined, you may be able to tackle portions of a subsequent exercise if you are having difficulties with one. Sometimes, jumping to the next step might force or prompt your creative powers to resolve the uncompleted exercise. Don't become unhinged if a particular step is taking longer than anticipated -- you will find the solution.

HOW TO CREATE A SCREENPLAY STORY

Story ideas for screenplays come spontaneously for most writers. That is, a basic thought comes to mind and it is either developed or discarded. Screenplay ideas can come in two forms: SUBJECT MATTER -- what the story is about, and/or CHARACTER. Regardless of where you start, the entire process evolves from character.

Let's say you decide to start with subject matter first; something that really appeals to you like football, science, auto racing, medicine, or whatever.

What if you wanted to write a screenplay story about a group of businessmen, possibly ex-jocks, who want to put together a company football team and challenge other companies within their industry. That is fine. But remember, the process evolves from "one" character.

Once you determine who your main character will be, you then establish his or her need -- that is, what that person wants to achieve.

Your character's need will create action as well as conflict, the basis of all drama. Once you know what your main character wants to achieve, it will be easy to create obstacles that will impede your hero or heroine from reaching his or her goal.

For your football story, your main character could be Brad Reynolds, a company executive and ex-jock who never accepted the fact that his football days were well behind him. His college rival now works for a competitive company. Reynolds' need could be to put together a company football team to challenge and beat him.

Now that you know what Reynolds' goal is, you are in a position to create obstacles -- and the choices are numerous. In order to achieve his goal, it is true that Reynolds' own actions will naturally create conflict without resorting to any other human working against him; sort of the "antagonist within" premise as well as conflict which is indigenous to the story itself.

In certain stories, such as ROCKY, the "antagonist within" premise works very effectively. Another example might be an "upbeat" story where the main character fights to overcome and defeat a major physical or emotional handicap in order to achieve his or her goal.

Since Brad Reynolds is an average guy, it is necessary to create a human adversary in order to strengthen the story's conflict. Reynolds could have a tough time trying to recruit other players, difficulties at home with his family over his activities, or possibly problems with his boss who does not share his enthusiasm for sports. Those are conflicts influenced by Reynolds' own actions and inherent in the story. Therefore, having a flesh and blood adversary is an absolute necessity, and something that will strengthen the story's conflict.

What if one of his peers openly works against Reynolds achieving his goal; or possibly, behind his back? His nemesis may even benefit if he can discredit Reynolds whose actions quite possibly violate company policy or the unwritten code of acceptable behavior.

It is easy to see how rising conflict between two people can be extremely stimulating and have the strength to sustain the audience's attention and interest from the story's beginning to the end.

Your story could be a drama, a comedy, or possibly both. What if Brad Reynolds had some kind of medical problem where playing football might jeopardize his life, and he recklessly pursues his goal anyway? How and when information like that is revealed to the audience would have significant impact on the story. You make those decisions out of choice.

In developing a story idea, the process starts with CHARACTER, NEED, and SUBJECT MATTER. As concisely as possible, outline your story in no more than two or three sentences. If you titled your football story, SIX YARD PENALTY, your description would be treated like this.

> SIX YARD PENALTY is a story about Brad Reynolds, an ex-jock executive, who puts together a company football team in order to challenge and beat his college rival's company team.

That four-line sentence tells you who the main CHARACTER is (Brad Reynolds, an ex-jock executive); what the SUBJECT MATTER is (football); and the hero's NEED (he wants to put together a company football team in order to challenge and beat his college rival's company team). That description provides the focus and direction for developing the story. Everything in that story is built from that premise.

ANOTHER WAY TO CREATE A SCREENPLAY STORY

If you are not sure of what to write about, there is a simple exercise you can complete. And remember, every story begins with and evolves from character.

Select a career field that appeals to you such as teaching, medicine, science, law enforcement, aviation, etc., and determine a dramatic need for that given profession. That would stimulate the creative process leading to the next step. It is really that simple. Through bulldog determination, you can make any story work once you understand the basics of dramatic writing and screenwriting.

If you decided to write a story about a journalist, what would be the main character's need? Something really dramatic. What if the journalist wanted to interview a world-famous terrorist? Think of the possibilities; the challenge of making contact and the danger involved.

The opportunity to create action and conflict around this situation makes it potentially a great story; that is, if you can develop it.

This basic premise was just made up to illustrate a point about creating a story. Maybe you will be the first to develop it into an exciting thriller.

Make a list of various career fields. Select one which really appeals to you. Through research, reading and/or interviewing experts in that field, you might find a number of interesting elements that provide the basis for a story.

EXERCISE 1: CREATE THE MAIN CHARACTER/NEED

Create a main character and then determine the character's need; what that person wants to achieve during the course of your story. In one or two concise sentences, outline the basic premise of your story -- character, need, and subject matter.

CHAPTER 2: CHARACTER

CHARACTER, THE BASIC FACTS

How people act and react reveals a lot about their character. And, of course, if you don't know someone, it would be impossible to predict his or her behavior under any given circumstances. This same principle holds true for the main character in your story.

You must know your main character intimately so you can accurately and naturally determine how he or she will act and react to the situations you create in your story.

If you don't know your main character, you will ultimately "force" him or her to act and react. And as a result, his or her actions will come across as being contrived, unnatural, and inconsistent.

How would a stranger react to being approached by a panhandler on the street? You may know how you would respond, but how would a perfect stranger react in this situation? The hero or heroine in your story is a stranger until you define the character and establish his or her identity.

It is not enough to know how your character will react to the panhandler; but you must know how he or she will act. The primary function of the main character in any story is to act -- to take action. Therefore, you must know your main character intimately.

Creating a three-dimensional character is a major step in the screenwriting process which may seem initially unimportant. Don't make that assumption -- consider it a tool and a major asset that will contribute greatly to the development of your character and your story.

THE THREE-DIMENSIONAL CHARACTER

Human behavior -- everything we do, why we do it, how we think, and how we feel -- is strongly influenced by our three dimensions which are: PHYSIOLOGICAL, SOCIOLOGICAL and PSYCHOLOGICAL.

Our PHYSICAL make-up influences our viewpoint on life. A short person obviously sees things a lot differently than a tall person; as does someone who is fat in comparison to someone who is physically fit. Whether we are good-looking, average-looking, or homely, these are just some of the elements comprising our physical make-up which subsequently affect our viewpoints and attitudes towards life.

Our SOCIOLOGICAL background affects how a person responds to life's situations. Think of the contrast between someone growing up in poverty as opposed to wealth. Imagine life on the city streets in comparison to life at the country club. In some instances, the person growing up without material assets may be "emotionally" healthier and ultimately more successful because of that innate desire to make a better life. The basic premise of sociological background is all important in determining how a person will react to various situations.

The PSYCHOLOGICAL dimension is a combination of the first two. This element of character influences our attitudes, our degree of ambition, the level of frustration we experience and express, our complexes, and so on and so forth.

Understanding the three dimensions of character provides insight into human behavior and establishes the foundation of building a well-defined main character.

Since you make every decision concerning your main character's background, you ultimately influence "who" your character is and "how" he or she will act and react.

THE CHARACTER BIOGRAPHY BY DIMENSION

PHYSIOLOGY PROFILE

- Sex
- Age
- Height and weight
- Color of hair, eyes, skin
- General appearance (good-looking, average, homely, sloppy, neat, disheveled)
- General health
- Any abnormalities (defects)

SOCIOLOGY PROFILE

- Class b.g.: lower, middle, upper
- Home life: relationship with parents; influence of parents; parents still living; divorced; any brothers and sisters and, if so, relationship with them
- Relationships with friends (who, how long)
- Education (how much, what schools, kind of grades, likes, dislikes, aptitudes)
- Occupation: type of work, attitude towards work, basic abilities, leadership qualities
- Personal status: married, if so, how long; children, if so, how many, their ages, etc. If divorced, what is relationship with former spouse and children
- Race, nationality
- Religious beliefs, if any (what are they; and are they expressed)
- Political views, if any (what are they; and are they expressed)
- Hobbies/interests (sports, physical fitness, sailing, gardening, music, race track, gambling)

PSYCHOLOGY PROFILE

- Sex life
- Ethics, values, moral standards
- Drive, ambition
- Frustrations, disappointments
- Temperament: pessimistic, optimistic, aggressive, easygoing
- Attitude towards life: resigned, militant, defeatist
- Complexes: obsessions, inhibitions, superstitions, phobias, quirks
- Extrovert, introvert, ambivert
- Qualities: imagination, judgment, taste, poise, social graces
- I.Q.

EXERCISE 2A: THE CHARACTER BIOGRAPHY

Following the profile outlined on page 25, prepare a character biography, with as much detail as possible, on your main character and two other key characters up to the time the story actually begins. Let things flow naturally and write until you exhaust all ideas for each character. One biography may end up two pages long while another exceeds ten pages.

Many of the small biographic details will strongly influence your main character's behavior and provide a strong line of development for both character and story. As you develop your screenplay project, the value of the character biography will become very evident.

Once your main character has formed a real identity in your mind, you may only extract bits and pieces of the biographic details to enhance the character's treatment in your story. The character biography is very similar to research information in that you may only use a small portion of what you gather. But the information you use will be more meaningful to your project than you realize.

ONE MAIN CHARACTER

If your story is about four brothers, there still can be only one protagonist or one main character your story evolves from. Pick the brother with the greatest need --possibly one who is dying from a terminal illness who wants to be reunited with his brothers one last time. Or, the story could be about one brother convincing the other three that they should search for their sister who is missing and presumed dead. The possibilities are endless.

If your story was about four brothers, you would have to complete a biography on each. Your objective would be to define the different elements in each personality that would establish the right blend of those forces that would bring them close together and, at the same time, create friction and conflict.

An example. The first brother could be aggressive and domineering while the second brother is somewhat reserved and resentful. The third brother could be very "hyper" and prone to arguing at the drop of a hat. The fourth brother could be financially well off but stingy and not willing to share his good fortune with the other three.

THE MOST IMPORTANT ASPECTS OF GOOD CHARACTER

There are six individual aspects which influence the development of your character. For each aspect, the point will be illustrated by presenting my treatment of Matt Decker, the main character in THE CRIMSON MOON.

1. DRAMATIC NEED

The dramatic need of your main character provides the purpose, the focus, and the direction of your story. What does your main character want to achieve or accomplish during the course of your story?

Matt Decker wants to find his missing son -- that is his primary need. Everything else in the story evolves out of that need.

2. POINT OF VIEW

A strong character always expresses a "point of view" in how he or she sees the world.

In the scene on page 8 in the screenplay, Matt Decker expresses his point of view. When Decker is criticized by his Captain for his methods of interviewing suspects, he fires back, "Look Captain, I'm tired of our liberal judicial system that provides loopholes for criminals. I'm just trying to get the job done and balance out some of the inequities." With that statement, Decker's point of view is clearly and firmly established.

3. ATTITUDE

Every character has a basic attitude about life -- be it positive or negative, superior or inferior -- whatever trait is the most obvious.

Matt Decker has a very confident attitude about his work. His confidence is subtly expressed by the way he approaches his work and how he interacts with his subordinates, peers, and superiors.

4. CHANGE

During the course of a story, a good character must grow and go through a progressive change in accordance with his or her needs. Depending upon the character, the change could be very minor or quite significant.

Matt Decker's change is quite significant. He is transformed from being a loner to having a need to be with others -- his son, Alex, and Carol Nelson. In the first 20 pages of the screenplay, Decker is shown living a solitary existence. He is clearly a person without any emotional ties. Throughout the balance of the story, Decker gradually gets to know his son and falls in love with Carol Nelson. This type of growth evolves naturally as the story progresses.

5. WEAKNESSES - NEGATIVE TRAITS

As human beings, we all have weaknesses or some kind of negative traits that strongly influence our attitude, action, and behavior.

A negative "flaw" makes our main character far more realistic and vulnerable. It also creates internal conflict--where the main character's own action tends to work against him or her. If a person is indecisive, that negative trait might cause him to miss a great opportunity. Or, more dramatically, her indecisive behavior may hinder her from saving someone's life.

With Matt Decker, he has a problem with alcohol which he compounds by not accepting help from others. He thinks he is strong enough to handle the problem alone, but he is not. As a result, he lives on the edge, walking an emotional tightrope. Afraid of impending failure, he avoids close personal relationships with other people.

Because of his problem with alcohol, Decker feels directly responsible for the failure of his marriage and the death of his ex-partner. This always placed Decker in a position of emotional imbalance where the potential for failure, in dealing with his problem concerning alcohol, was always high.

6. MANNERISMS - HABITS

We are all creatures of habit. Certain mannerisms and habits openly reveal a lot about us. When they are properly used in dealing with your character, they can be very effective.

What is your impression of a man who smokes a cigarette and complains about his hacking cough or reddened eyes irritated by smoke? What about a man who taps a pencil on a desk or a woman who twists rubber bands in her fingers?

Under stress, Matt Decker has a habit of rubbing the back of his neck with his right hand. This mannerism was created out of a personal experience. Not too many years ago, I became consciously aware of rubbing the back of my neck to relieve tension. Given Decker's profession and emotional state, where he is very susceptible to tension, this mannerism is both realistic and effective.

EXERCISE 2B: THE SIX ASPECTS OF GOOD CHARACTER

Clearly define the six aspects of good character using no more than two or three sentences to describe each.

Once you complete the biography and outline the important aspects of good character, your character's actions will be spontaneous and natural. Early in your story, it is important for the audience to "know" your main character and form an empathetic bond with him or her. Create good characters and they will make the job of telling your story much easier.

EMOTIONAL EXPRESSION

If the proper circumstances are created, a character will have the opportunity to display a wide range of emotional expressions. However, those emotional expressions should accurately depict the character's behavior, attitude, emotional state, and circumstances, which must appear to be natural, not forced.

In a drama-based story, the primary emotional expression of the main character usually follows one strong plane. If the character is confined to playing at the same emotional level, such as always being serious, the performance, no matter how talented the actor, will come across as being dull. What about combining other elements of emotional expression such as love, humor, conflict, anger, outrage, pity, etc.? During the course of a day, how many ways do you express yourself emotionally and what are the circumstances?

Throughout THE CRIMSON MOON, Matt Decker is given the opportunity to display many emotional expressions. He displays "controlled anger" in admonishing a rookie detective; he experiences "frustration" in dealing with his Captain; he demonstrates "concern" for the wounded officers; he reveals his "sense of humor" in handling the blind date; he is "indifferent" in his relationship with Nancy Todd; he reacts "impassively" to the psychologist; and so on and so forth.

Some of these emotional expressions are very low-keyed while others are more striking. Any emotional expression should appear to be natural and believable under the specific circumstances.

In developing your story, you can utilize the contrast between the various emotional expressions to create or release tension. A bitter argument can evolve into a tender love scene or vice versa.

REVEALING CHARACTER

Character can be revealed visually and through dialogue.

Visual impressions are very effective because they register immediately with the audience. In using visual techniques to reveal character, your approach can be subtle or very dramatic.

People visually display their personality through body language -- the way they carry themselves. An individual can be outgoing, confident, shy, serious, witty, sloppy, aggressive, unsophisticated, etc.

Would you bend over to pick up a dime on the street? If so, would your action be spontaneous or would you look to see if anyone is observing you first? Or, would you look at the dime and just walk away? No matter which way you react in that situation, it reveals something about your character.

Through visual techniques, you can reveal everything about a character from personality quirks to attitude. Whenever possible, as it applies to everything in your story, don't say what you can show.

While gassing up my car, I watched a man "jaywalk" across the street. He brazenly stopped in the middle of the road, blocking traffic, to light up a cigarette. When one vehicle honked at him, he made an obscene gesture to the driver and then slowly strutted out of the way. It does not take much of an imagination to figure out this character's attitude. Make every effort to utilize visual techniques in revealing character.

Character is best revealed under pressure. Does your character excite easily or remain calm and composed under pressure? Think of ways of visually expressing your main character's action in a crisis situation.

Revealing character through dialogue can be handled the same as the visual techniques -- subtly or dramatically. In film stories, as in real life, impressions are quickly formed about people by what they say and how they say it.

One statement can immediately reveal a person's character and attitude. One individual might say, "While I enjoy listening to jazz, I really prefer classical music." Another person might respond, "Oh yeah, heavy metal is the only music worth listening to, everything else sucks!"

From their dialogue, it would not be difficult to make up a character biography outlining each person's background including a physical description.

This is another method of creating character by working backwards from a key element of character. If you know a person's attitude or point of view, it would not be too difficult to determine other things about him or her.

THE FOUR FUNCTIONS OF DIALOGUE

On the subject of dialogue, a few comments are in order. As we all know, in real life, people talk in run-on sentences expressing fragmented thoughts, etc.

Dialogue is not elegant prose, it is functional and it has four primary purposes in your story.

o To reveal character.
o To reveal the character's emotional state.
o To communicate information to your audience.
o To move the story forward.

For most inexperienced writers, dialogue is the most difficult part of writing. Initially, your dialogue will probably be awkward, trite, clumsy, stilted, etc. But it significantly improves with rewriting.

Writing good dialogue is also a skill you develop and fine-tune with experience. When it comes time to write that all important first draft screenplay, let the dialogue flow without prejudging it. Just tell your story. During the rewriting stage, you will cut, condense, refine, and polish your dialogue until it flows naturally.

CHARACTER DESCRIPTIONS

In describing your main character and other characters, treat them "generically". That is, make the description very basic so it can apply to many people.

If you describe your main character as someone who is 6'4" tall with wide shoulders and narrow hips, etc., you are dead. Unless, of course, you are writing a story for someone like Arnold Schwarzenegger or a bit part like Sly Rankin on page 114 in THE CRIMSON MOON.

Matt Decker's description appears on page one of the screenplay and it is very basic: "About forty, he is rugged-looking with a quiet air of confidence about him. He is somewhat cynical and someone who delicately walks an emotional tightrope." Physically, there are only two requirements in that description -- someone who "looks" about forty years old and has rugged features. That description could apply to a number of major actors.

Try to treat character descriptions with as much brevity as possible while emphasizing the character's physical aspects and/or basic personality.

CHAPTER 3: THE SCREENPLAY

STRUCTURING YOUR STORY

After you determine who your main character is, as well as his or her need, and complete the biographic exercises, you are ready to begin the process of structuring your story. Where do you begin? You begin with the ending.

By knowing the ending of your story, you have a straight line of development to follow from the beginning to the resolution.

You would no sooner get into a car and start driving without having a specific destination in mind. This same logic applies to your story -- at all times, you must know where you are going.

If you attempt to "make up" your story as you go along, you will either run out of steam or force things to happen. As a result, your story will be contrived and trite. You might be able to make up a story as you go along, but I strongly doubt that it will be any good when it is finished.

Knowing the ending of your story allows you to work from two directions at the same time -- forwards and backwards. Working from the beginning, you create all the necessary scenes that will take you to the resolution of your story that you have already predetermined. That is simply called forward motion.

Knowing the ending of your story points out the necessity to go back and create scenes that are needed to justify the resolution. An example. Decker literally "blows up" the villain at the end of story. Therefore, I had to go back and create scenes in order to establish his expertise with explosives.

If Decker just showed up at the quarry with dynamite and blew up the villain without "first" establishing his expertise with explosives, as well as how he acquires the explosives, it would have been pretty contrived. The first five pages of THE CRIMSON MOON were entirely determined by the ending of the story.

As another illustration about knowing your ending and working backwards, I decided that Alex would be kidnaped as the reason for bringing Decker and the villain together at the end.

Therefore, I had to go back and create a scene either showing the actual kidnaping or handling it through exposition -- the latter being my final choice. (The meaning and use of exposition, as well as my motives for using it in the above mentioned scene, are explained on pages 73-75 in the chapter on SCREENWRITING TECHNIQUES.)

All the interim action between the beginning of the story and the resolution is related and tied together by both forward and backward motion. To make the kidnaping and the ending more dramatic, the characters had to have time together so they could get to know each other and form an emotional bond because the audience reacts emotionally, not intellectually, to a film story.

So, if Alex was missing when Decker arrived in New Hampshire, he had to be found by Decker first, before he could be kidnaped by the villain. Finding Alex required another scene. Also, what about all the scenes that take place between Decker and Alex forming their relationship from the time they first meet until Alex is kidnaped? That required three more scenes.

All these scenes, plus many more, were created by knowing the ending to the story first. To reinforce the point -- all the above mentioned scenes were determined by working "backwards" from the ending.

Defining the needs of your main character ultimately provides you with the ending of your story. In THE CRIMSON MOON, Decker's need is to find his missing son. To make the story dramatic, Decker's son is kidnaped by the villain which obviously sets up the ending. It then becomes an exercise of "fleshing out" all of the details.

EXERCISE 3: DETERMINE THE ENDING TO YOUR STORY

Determine the ending to your story with as much detail as possible. Once you clearly figure out how your story will end and the various details, you basically fill in the space between the beginning and the resolution by working from two directions.

STORY LENGTH

Standard screenplay length is 120 pages which converts into a two-hour film. This is just a guideline or target you can use for developing your story; it is not a rule.

Your story will ultimately determine the actual length. Just write your story as it comes out but keep one thing in mind: it is a lot easier to "cut back" excess scenes rather than "add" new ones later.

STORY TIME PERIOD

Each screenplay story covers a specific amount of time in the main character's life. It could be "two hours", the actual length of the film, or two days, three weeks, or possibly a lifetime from childhood to old age.

In planning your project, it helps to define the exact time period your story will cover even though you may not make it known to the audience. Knowing your story's time period will significantly aid you in determining how you treat the development of your main character and the progressive change he or she goes through.

As long as your story "moves forward" following a straight line of development from beginning to end, there are no requirements in regard to any time factors other than what common sense dictates. This applies to the length of scenes, the transition of day from night, days from days, etc. In other words, you have total freedom in jumping from one scene to another. In your story, one character tells another that they will meet in two days. Without accounting for the in-between time, the next scene could be those characters actually meeting.

By defining the amount of time your story will cover, it makes the entire screenwriting process much easier. You know how much space there will be, in story time, between the beginning and the resolution.

TIME DEADLINE

If a "deadline" is established where a predetermined action will take place at a specific time, it can effectively create additional tension and suspense. A deadline intensifies a sense of urgency.

As an example, if the main character does not discover the antidote for a poison in the next 24 hours, 300,000 people will die.

A time deadline is just one facet or tool of dramatic writing. It should only be used if it fits naturally into your story without creating the impression of being forced or contrived.

The single most important element in writing a good screenplay is SCREENPLAY STRUCTURE because it insures and effectively controls a smooth and even development of your story from beginning to end.

Each phase of handling screenplay structure will be introduced gradually in order to maintain the highest degree of clarity. If a picture is worth a thousand words, then the following concise overview of screenplay structure in its entirety is the best illustration of that point.

SCREENPLAY STRUCTURE

Page(s)	Description Of Action
1-30	Act I (Setting up the story)
1-10	Introduce the main character, establish the premise of the story, what it is about, and the dramatic circumstances surrounding the action.
11-20	Focus on the main character
23-25	Introduce The First Major Plot Point
30	END OF ACT I
31-90	Act II (Confrontations/Obstacles)
45	Introduce another plot point
60	Introduce mid-point plot scene
75	Introduce another plot point
85-87	Introduce The Second Major Plot Point
90	END OF ACT II
91-120	Act III (The Resolution)
105	Introduce another plot point
115-120	Resolution of story
120	THE END

SCREENPLAY STRUCTURE - AN OVERVIEW

As previously established, each page of screenplay is equal to one minute of film time. Therefore, the positioning of various elements within the screenplay's structure (setting up the story, the plot points, and the resolution) at "specific intervals", insures a smooth development and even pacing of the story.

THE CRIMSON MOON SCREENPLAY STRUCTURE

THE CRIMSON MOON will be used to illustrate screenplay structure from the story's setup to the resolution. The story will be referenced to either the reader of the screenplay or, as if it were a film, to someone in the audience -- whichever example is more effective.

THE SETUP

You can do it in less, but you have ten pages or ten minutes to set up your story. And that is to:

1. Introduce the main character.
2. Establish what the story is about.
3. And establish the dramatic circumstances surrounding the action.

THE CRIMSON MOON SETUP

On pages 1 and 2, Matt Decker is introduced in his apartment. His gun and a badge are on the kitchen table identifying him as a Lieutenant Detective, NYPD. On page 9, Decker is told by his Captain that his ex-wife, whom he has not seen or heard from in 19 years, has been killed in an automobile accident in New Hampshire. From this setup, we understand three things...

1. Matt Decker is the main character.
2. The story is about the accidental death of Decker's ex-wife.
3. The fact that Decker is a detective for the NYPD establishes the dramatic circumstances surrounding the action.

FOCUSING ON THE MAIN CHARACTER - PAGES 11 TO 20

The next ten pages focus on the main character and the development of the story. In this segment, the goal is to reveal more information about the character, visually and through dialogue, while moving the story forward.

On page 11, Decker is at home looking at an old photograph of his ex-wife. His eyes are then drawn to that dusty bottle of Scotch resting on the hutch. At this point, the audience is not sure of its significance but they can probably guess.

On page 12, Decker meets one of his few close friends, Ron Mizak. Between pages 13 and 15, we learn that Decker does not drink alcohol. Decker's sense of humor is also revealed as he drives the "unwanted" blind date right out the door and out of his life. Through this action, he reinforces to his friends, Ron and Linda Mizak, that his personal life is his own.

Between pages 15 and 17, we learn that Decker has no emotional ties to anyone. He ultimately destroys a relationship that he has with Nancy Todd and yet, we know he is not totally insensitive or uncaring. In three earlier scenes, he follows the progress of the two wounded officers and visits them in the hospital.

From pages 19 to 21, Decker meets with a psychologist. He is obviously reluctant to be there, totally impassive, and extremely uncooperative. We learn that he is fighting a problem with alcohol "his way" and that a former partner died 15 years earlier. We don't know "how" his partner died or what Decker's involvement was, but one thing is clear, he refuses to discuss it.

In these second ten pages of the screenplay, Matt Decker is revealed both visually and through dialogue. He is a strong character who is very competent in his work which is the focus of his life. And yet, like everyone else, he has problems.

PLOT POINTS

Between pages 23 and 25, you introduce the <u>first major plot point</u>. What is a <u>plot point</u>? <u>It is a significant event or incident that propels the story forward; a segment of dramatic action</u>.

The function of the first major plot point is to spin the story around and really grab the reader's or audience's attention and interest. On page 9, you learned that Decker's ex-wife was killed in an automobile "accident". Decker goes to New Hampshire to settle her affairs which sets up the introduction of the first major plot point.

On page 23, when Decker arrives in New Hampshire, he is informed by the state police that his ex-wife was actually "murdered". Then, an additional twist is added to really propel the story forward. On the same page, Decker learns, for the first time, that he has an 18-year-old son named Alex who has been missing since his mother's murder.

The thought of having a son is totally mind-boggling to him. Nothing in his life ever prepared him for that moment. A man without any emotional ties now faces the uncertainty of actually being a father. Decker's reaction to this news is mixed. He is both angry in not knowing about his son sooner, as well as afraid of facing the situation and the responsibility.

The fact that Decker's son disappeared the day of his ex-wife's murder establishes Decker's primary need. With relentless determination, Decker is going to find his son and subsequently search for his ex-wife's killer. From page 25, that is Decker's goal and the line of direction leading to the story's resolution on page 131. The first major plot point between pages 23 and 25 sets up the story by defining Decker's need and establishes the course of direction and thrust for Act II, the next 60 pages.

If you look at the screenplay structure on page 38, you will see that the plot points fall, after the first major plot point, at intervals of every 15 pages or, in film time, every 15 minutes.

Are plot points flexible? Can they be moved? Yes, but judiciously. With the first major plot point, I would have no trouble in moving it "up" from page 23 to page 20. On the other hand, I would be hard-pressed to move it back to page 30. Of course, a lot will depend upon your story and how strong the first 20 pages are.

If you wait until page 30 to introduce your hook (the first major plot point), the rhythm, tempo, and pacing of your story might start to drag. At that point, your audience may be squirming in their seats and prone to bouncing their popcorn containers off the person's head in front of them.

<u>Screenplay structure outlines the "ideal" arrangement of the plot points, so don't worry about being totally precise in hitting the specific page numbers</u>. As you will learn from my analysis of THE CRIMSON MOON and other screenplays, the plot points don't fall exactly on those pages as outlined in screenplay structure.

Can you have more plot points than outlined in screenplay structure? Of course. Your story will determine how many and how significant each one actually is. Can you have less plot points than outlined in screenplay structure? Yes. But again, great care must be taken if you use "wide intervals" in the placement of plot points.

A story that "drags" or has long sections of "dead space" lacks proper structure. Without a strong story and the proper placement of plot points, it cannot move forward. A fast-paced action film with guns blasting away, tires screeching, people being thrown off rooftops, etc., lends itself to fewer plot points because the "action" maintains the audience's attention and interest -- but only to a point, of course.

The first major plot point between pages 23 and 25 is designed to set up Act II which is 60 pages long. The focus of Act II is to create confrontations and obstacles that will slow down or temporarily stop your hero or heroine from achieving his or her goal. From these confrontations and obstacles, conflict is created; the basis of all drama. Conflict is the force that holds and sustains the audience's attention and interest throughout your story. Characters shown in conflict with themselves and their adversaries are the focus of Act II.

Back to the analysis of THE CRIMSON MOON. On page 23, it was established that Matt Decker's need or goal is to find his missing son which is the thrust and focus of Act II. This is what ultimately involves him in investigating and solving his ex-wife's murder as well as the 50-year-old mystery involving the three million dollars buried in New Hampshire by a 1930s gangster.

On page 27, there is another plot point. Decker sees a local television news bulletin covering a holdup spree perpetrated by two men around the State of New Hampshire. The description of their car matches the type of vehicle involved in the murder of his ex-wife. Could there be a tie-in? This propels the story forward.

The plot point on page 48 establishes the possible motive behind the murder of Decker's ex-wife. Decker discovers a tie-in between his ex-wife's murder and an old steamship trunk she bought. The trunk was once owned by a 1930s gangster who supposedly buried three million dollars somewhere in Willshire County, New Hampshire. Decker reasons that searching for the money will eventually lead him to Nora's killer.

On page 58, the "mid-point" plot scene is introduced. In a 120-page screenplay, page "60" or so represents the mid-point plot scene -- the point at which you are halfway through your story. In this scene, Decker recovers the steamship trunk from a storage rental facility. And, immediately after leaving the facility, he is pursued by the black, late-model Trans Am -- the car fitting the description of the one involved in his ex-wife's murder as well as the holdup spree.

In the plot point on page 65, Decker finds and meets his 18-year-old son for the first time. Since Alex rejects Decker, it is a traumatic experience and one that leaves him feeling empty.

The story takes another leap forward on page 68. In this plot point, Decker discovers a map in the binding of a book that was in the old steamship trunk. But he soon learns that the map has no starting point, making it temporarily useless.

On page 70, Decker stops the two punks after they hold up a convenience store in town. At first, because their car is a black, late-model Trans Am, Decker assumes it might be the killers of his ex-wife. But the description of the vehicle involved in his ex-wife's murder had "tinted glass"; their Trans Am does not. The two punks are then ruled out as suspects in his ex-wife's murder.

On page 84, Decker finally determines the map's starting point so he can search for the missing money. This is the second major plot point which is designed to set up the action for Act III, the resolution of the story.

The story moves forward on page 101 with another plot point. The killer kidnaps Alex and holds him for ransom--the three million dollars buried by the 1930s gangster. The killer assumes that Decker has or will soon have the money since he found the steamship trunk.

The plot point on page 108 is another significant incident moving the story forward. Decker confronts Judge Tyler and tells him that he is the "unknown accomplice" who assisted "Cockeye" Eddie Malone in stealing the three million dollars fifty years earlier. He also suspects the Judge of being the person behind his ex-wife's murder and the kidnaping of his son. However, you soon learn that while the Judge was the unknown accomplice, he had nothing to do with the murder of Decker's ex-wife and the kidnaping of his son.

All the action between pages 108 and 125 leads to the final climax and the resolution of the story between pages 126 and 131. From page 126 to the end, Decker meets and literally "blows up" the killer of his ex-wife, saves his son's life, recovers one-and-a-half million dollars, gets the girl, and walks off into the sunset.

With an understanding of screenplay structure, you will never see another film or read a screenplay the same way again. You will consciously look for and try to identify the plot points that move the story forward. Once you understand this phase of screenwriting, it is a tremendous step forward in developing good screenwriting skills.

The screenplay structure for my other two original screenplays will now be outlined so you can see exactly how much detail is involved in this step. The exact "page" placement of the plot points as they appear in the first draft screenplay will also be indicated. This will give you a firm understanding of how the plot point intervals vary from project to project.

In reading the screenplay structure for THE 12/20 CLUB, you will note a strong similarity to the premise of my earlier illustration, SIX YARD PENALTY. I applied the basic story concept of THE 12/20 CLUB to SIX YARD PENALTY for a very specific reason.

It is possible to duplicate a basic story premise without the stories appearing to be similar. It is accomplished by using different subject matter as well as altering the treatment of characters and modifying the story's (screenplay) structure.

I certainly would not use the exact same plot points from THE 12/20 CLUB, but the basic premise of the story could remain intact and be applied to different subject matter.

Most stories are a rehash of something which has already been done. What makes any story appear fresh and original is the writer's point of view in the way the characters and the material are treated.

Here is a brief description of THE 12/20 CLUB.

> THE 12/20 CLUB is a mid-life crisis story about Brian Hill, a successful 38-year-old businessman, who creates conflict at home with his wife and two teenage children and his employer when he puts together his old high school rock 'n roll band and starts playing nightclubs again.

THE 12/20 CLUB SCREENPLAY STRUCTURE

The Setup - Pages 1-10

On page 1, after being promoted by his company, Brian Hill and his family have just moved back to New York after a 12-year absence. On page 2, Brian is seen setting up his guitars and music equipment in his den.

On page 5, Brian's best friend and former band member, Ned Taylor, stops by the house. They have an impromptu jam session. On page 6, later that night, Ned tells Brian that he has planned a reunion party for their high school rock 'n roll band.

The First Major Plot Point - Page 25

Brian tells Ann, his wife, that his old high school rock 'n roll band will be playing nightclubs again.

Plot Point - Page 45

Brian tells Ann about making a complete career change from business to music.

Mid-Point Plot Scene - Page 61

Brian learns that he is eligible for a major promotion with his company.

Plot Point - Page 78

Brian's nemesis at work finds out about his music activities.

The Second Major Plot Point - Page 89

Brian is confronted by his boss and told that his music activities will jeopardize both his position with the company as well as any consideration for the major promotion.

Plot Point - Page 106

Brian tells Ann that he has decided to keep music a hobby and focus his energies on his business career.

The Resolution - Pages 119-126

On page 119, Brian's adversary is promoted and becomes his boss. Brian is then terminated for "conflict of interests".

On page 126, on the same day, Brian comes home from a mysterious late night meeting and tells Ann that he has accepted a position of "Vice President" with a major competitive company.

That is the complete screenplay structure for THE 12/20 CLUB, connected from plot point to plot point. Even without knowing all the supporting details and interim action, the story and the line of development from setup to resolution are very clear. The resolution of this story is rationally and logically resolved without resorting to coincidence.

In the chapter covering the writing of the first draft screenplay, all the details concerning the treatment of each story's resolution are fully explained.

DOES SCREENPLAY STRUCTURE APPLY TO COMEDY?

Screenplay structure applies to every film genre without exception. A story must progressively move forward at regular intervals (plot points) or it will bog down and stall.

Even if the humor is good, a comedy will ultimately fail without the proper screenplay structure to move the story forward as well as an antagonist creating obstacles (conflict) in the path of the main character.

COMMENTS ON COMEDY

The only real difference among comedy writers is how each individual views the world. Some see humor in everything, including tragic events and the most inane situations.

When it comes to writing comedy, there is only one basic rule: place your characters into situations and let them act and react naturally. If you force things to happen, it simply will not work.

Comedy is totally subjective and reactionary; you either like something or you don't. Therefore, of all the film genres, comedy projects have to be treated with the highest degree of selectivity by people in the film industry. How could a producer and a director get involved with a comedy that does not appeal to them?

From all the books I have read on film, the greatest percentage of successful comedies have been turned down initially by every studio. And then, someone "identified with the humor" and recognized the potential of the project. Through a lot of conviction and tenacity, that person, often a producer, pushed hard to make it happen.

Unless a studio or producer is dealing with an already proven comedy writer, all newcomers are viewed with even greater skepticism and uncertainty than writers of other genres. While every film project carries a high risk status, comedy is probably perceived as the highest risk category within the industry. I have to believe that more people could identify with a well-written dramatic story than most comedies.

Having worked as an "outdoor writer", I knew that I would one day write a comedy using fishing as a story backdrop. So when I decided to write THE FISHIN' SHACK, my first step was to create a dramatic story and then outline the screenplay structure.

As I started working on THE FISHIN' SHACK, I was not sure if I could write a comedy by myself. Also, I did not know if I could come up with at least 90 pages -- the average length of most comedy features. But once the project got underway, I was amazed at what I was able to write. The screenplay is 125 pages long and comprises about 65 percent comedy to 35 percent drama. On and above the humorous dialogue, gags, stunts, and the colorful characters, THE FISHIN' SHACK moves forward, following a well-defined dramatic story.

The comedy pace is not only maintained from beginning to end, but gradually improves and sustains longer segments of running time as the story progresses. Of course, people reading THE FISHIN' SHACK will either like it or not--that is comedy. Let's take a look at the story synopsis and then the screenplay structure.

> THE FISHIN' SHACK is a comedy that unfolds around Billy Tyler, a 19-year-old bass-fishing expert, who attempts to save the family business by winning a major fishing contest.

While Billy Tyler is the main character and the focus of the dramatic story, the humor is handled by a bunch of colorful characters that belong to Billy's bass club. Therefore, the screenplay structure you are about to review only deals with the dramatic elements of the story; the elements creating conflict which holds the audience's attention and interest.

In order to clarify the story, a few additional comments are presented in parentheses.

THE FISHIN' SHACK SCREENPLAY STRUCTURE

<u>The Setup - Pages 1-10</u>

On pages 1-3, Billy Tyler, fishing with his bass club, wins his seventh "big bass" tournament putting himself three wins ahead of his adversary, Blake Hunter.

On page 5, working at the family's general store, Billy's father, Henry, tells him that he cannot afford to send him to college in the fall, because of a problem with a second mortgage which threatens the family business.

<u>The First Major Plot Point - Pages 24-25</u>

Billy's father meets with the bank president and is informed that the second mortgage on the store must be paid off by the 31st or the bank will be forced to take over the business.

<u>Plot Point - Page 31</u>

Blake Hunter, Billy's adversary, informs the son of a wealthy department store king about the Tylers' problem with their second mortgage.

Plot Point - Pages 50-51

At dinner, Henry Tyler tells his family that W.T. Hendricks, a department store king and shopping center developer, wants to meet with him and possibly offer to buy the family's business.

Mid-Point Plot Scene - Page 64

Henry Tyler meets with W.T. Hendricks and listens to his offer. Henry is given three days to think over Hendricks' proposal and get back to him.

The Second Major Plot Point - Page 71

An outboard motor company announces a "big bass" fishing contest with a $50,000 first place prize. Billy convinces his father to refuse Hendricks' offer since he has a good chance of winning the contest.

Plot Point - Page 101

The morning of the contest, Pine Creek Bog is announced as the tournament site -- a body of water where the bass have been affected by a personality-altering drug which leaked in from an experimental laboratory upstream.

(The dramatic conclusion of the story, as well as the continuation and enhancement of the humor, begins from this point.)

Plot Point - Page 103

Just prior to the "qualifying" round of competition, Blake Hunter tampers with the fishing line on Billy's three fishing rods. (Hunter is ultimately foiled when his own fishing line breaks and, as a result, he fails to qualify for the final round of competition.)

Plot Point - Page 109

Billy's fishing line snaps twice before he realizes that someone tampered with it. (The scene ends where the audience is not sure if Billy will catch a bass and qualify for the final round of competition, so he can compete for the $50,000 first place prize he so desperately needs to win.)

<u>Plot Point - Page 118</u>

Billy qualifies for the final round of competition.

<u>Plot Point - Page 120</u>

Billy loses the big bass tournament by "two ounces".

<u>Resolution - Pages 122-123</u>

That night, an executive from a fishing tackle company shows up at Billy's home. The man offers to buy the manufacturing rights to Billy's custom-made lure which a national pro used to win the big bass contest. Billy is given an advance check so he can pay off the mortgage.

There are fewer plot points in THE FISHIN' SHACK and they don't fall exactly as outlined in screenplay structure. Also, the interval between the second major plot point on page 71 to the next plot point on page 101, is exceptionally wide, so a few comments are in order.

Since the comedy progressively improves as the story develops and the humor dominates longer segments in the last 50 pages, the story moves swiftly with no "dead space". Also, the rising conflict between Billy and his adversary is dramatically heightened during the last act.

Many stories "work" even though they take great liberties in not strictly adhering to the basic rules and guidelines governing dramatic writing and screenwriting.

EXERCISE 4: OUTLINING SCREENPLAY STRUCTURE

Once you have determined the ending to your story, develop the screenplay structure by outlining all the plot points from beginning to end.

It is not necessary to use a lot of "details" but just enough information to understand the purpose of each plot point. By reading just the plot points, you should have a clear and concise synopsis of your story that can be easily understood from setup to resolution.

Don't be too concerned if you have fewer plot points than those illustrated in the screenplay structure on page 38. It is quite possible that your story, like THE FISHIN' SHACK, may lend itself to fewer plot points. Also, the significance of each plot point will vary within each story.

In evaluating all of the plot points from my original screenplays, some are quite dramatic while others seem less important. However, within the context and framework of the story, they collectively share equal importance in moving the story forward.

It could take you two days, two weeks, or longer to complete the screenplay structure to your story. The more you think about it, the easier it gets. All of a sudden, ideas start to formulate and things fall into place, piece by piece, until your story is entirely structured. But before you start, you must first know your ending.

SCENE DESCRIPTIONS

A scene is best defined as a specific segment of dramatic action. Every scene in your story has to have a purpose: to reveal character, information about the plot, and, most importantly, to move the story forward. Most scenes very rarely accomplish more than one function. Outlining scene descriptions is a step designed to "fill in" more details about your story.

Scene length will vary from possibly one brief sentence to three pages and there is no required number of scenes in any screenplay. Your story will determine how many scenes you need as you write the first draft. However, in the planning stages, it is important to outline a number of scenes as a guideline to develop your story.

In outlining the scene descriptions, figure on two pages for every scene, as a rough average. Therefore, for each 30-page segment, outline 15 scenes. How many you use later is immaterial. Scenes will be deleted, added, rewritten, moved to other areas, or combined.

The exercise for outlining scene descriptions is broken down into four 30-page segments which look like this:

Act I runs from page 1 to page 30; from story setup to the first major plot point.

Act II, the first half, runs from page 31 to page 60; to the mid-point plot scene.

Act II, the second half, runs from page 61 to page 90; to the second major plot point.

Act III runs from page 91 to page 120; to the story's resolution.

Here are the actual scene descriptions and the sequence used for planning Act I of THE CRIMSON MOON. Very little detail has been used to outline each scene. The description of each scene is only a reference point; it does not necessarily define the exact purpose of the scene to someone other than the author.

Scene descriptions are much like a shopping list where you identify something you need without detail. You may write down "dog food" as a reminder, but when you get to the supermarket, you know you will be reaching for a 16-ounce can of pizza-flavored Alpo.

SCENE DESCRIPTION SAMPLES
ACT I - THE CRIMSON MOON

1. Establishing shot of Brooklyn - inside Decker's apartment.

2. Surveillance of suspects.

3. Decker arrests suspects.

4. Captain informs Decker that his ex-wife was killed in an automobile accident.

5. Detective's squad room (humor).

6. Dinner at Ron and Linda's -- blind date.

7. Questioning suspects.

8. Decker visits former partner's father.

9. Decker at restaurant.

10. Captain chews Decker out for his technique in questioning suspects.

11. Decker arrives in New Hampshire and meets Lt. Belleteau.

12. Decker learns that his ex-wife was killed and that he has a son.

13. Decker visits a woman who knew his ex-wife and son.

14. Decker checks into motel.

15. Breakfast at diner -- TV program on gangster story.

It is interesting to note a few things about the scene descriptions for Act I of THE CRIMSON MOON.

- o Most of the scene descriptions outlined were actually used and developed as planned.
- o Scene no. 8 was discarded because it was not important enough to keep.
- o The sequence of scenes nos. 13, 14, and 15 was changed around in order to follow a more logical line of development for the story.
- o A scene was added involving Decker meeting with the psychologist, in order to reveal more details about the character and his problems.
- o The purpose of scene no. 13 was altered significantly. Instead of Decker meeting with a woman who knew his ex-wife and his son, he ends up meeting with the woman who witnessed his ex-wife's murder.
- o The character's name in scene no. 11 was changed from Belleteau to Branford.

All the scene changes were made spontaneously while writing the first draft screenplay. As your project develops, you acquire a greater sense of clarity so it becomes easier to identify those changes that will enhance the development of your story. Most of the time, you are only adjusting minor details.

EXERCISE 5: OUTLINING SCENE DESCRIPTIONS

Using the completed screenplay structure for your story as a guideline, outline the scene descriptions. Remember, each scene from the beginning of your story to the end has to have a specific function -- to reveal information about your character, the plot, and to move the story forward to its resolution. Scene descriptions should be brief and to the point as illustrated for Act I of THE CRIMSON MOON. Outlining scenes, one at a time, on 3 X 5 index cards is extremely practical. When you have finished outlining each 30-page segment, you can then rotate the scene cards and organize them into the most logical sequence.

Since the plot points should be positioned at the proper intervals (on specific pages) whenever possible, you can automatically determine their sequence in the process of outlining the scene descriptions.

As an example, the first major plot point should fall between pages 23 and 25. Therefore, using the guideline of two pages per scene, the first major plot point should be the 12th scene description.

In THE CRIMSON MOON, the first major plot point is listed as the 12th scene description. In the screenplay, the first major plot point falls on page 23. In most instances, this procedure will be very accurate. In the rewriting stages, you can always adjust your screenplay text to better align the plot points if it is really necessary.

Once the 15-scene sequence has been determined, type up the list for each 30 pages and use that as a guideline when writing the first draft screenplay.

THE NARRATIVE TREATMENT

Having completed all the previous exercises, you are now ready to address one of the most important steps, before tackling the first draft screenplay -- the narrative treatment. The purpose of this procedure is to expand, elaborate, and clarify your story from beginning to end.

When writing your narrative treatment, just let it flow naturally. As far as length is concerned, you need at least four pages to properly lay out your story but you could end up with ten times as many.

Some writers feel that a narrative treatment exceeding 20 pages is totally unnecessary. It is my feeling that a narrative treatment which naturally develops into 30, 40, or 50 pages, following the guidelines outlined, is extremely helpful to the writer. Each project requires a different volume of narrative treatment depending upon the story and how complicated the plot might be.

The narrative treatment for THE 12/20 CLUB was nine pages long while THE FISHIN' SHACK was completed in four pages. On the other hand, the narrative treatment of THE CRIMSON MOON was 54 pages. When it came time for me to tackle the first draft screenplay, my intimate knowledge of the story stimulated my creative energy and allowed me to proceed with incredible confidence and speed. Every single day, I averaged "ten pages" of screenplay in three hours. It took me less than two weeks to complete the first draft screenplay.

From my narrative treatment of THE CRIMSON MOON, I was able to extract, word for word, many things from scene descriptions to character descriptions. But most importantly, my story line was fully developed with every plot point linked together from setup to resolution.

On the next page, there is a one-page sample of narrative treatment from THE CRIMSON MOON. In view of the importance of the first ten pages, setting up the story, I use a little more detail than what is necessary. After that point, I confine my treatment to only the essential elements of the story, as outlined in the exercise procedure on page 57.

NARRATIVE TREATMENT SAMPLE

THE CRIMSON MOON

FADE IN:

Brooklyn, at dawn. For a man who lives alone, his apartment is comfortable looking and surprisingly neat. On the living room hutch, no family photographs; just a few photos from Vietnam of young soldiers standing around crates of military explosives.

Dressed in a suit, MATT DECKER enters the kitchen. About forty, he is rugged-looking with a quiet air of confidence about him. On the table, a holstered handgun and a badge. The I.D. card identifies the owner as a Lieutenant Detective, NYPD, Robbery/Homicide. Decker stares at his equipment and then picks it up.

Descending the apartment stairs, Decker is greeted by ANNIE McDOUGAL. She is a portly woman about seventy with a slight Irish brogue, who has maternal feelings for him. She thanks Decker for helping her with a problem. He smiles and continues on his way. At the curb, Decker is picked up in an unmarked police car. Behind the wheel, T.J. TYNER, a competent, black rookie detective; in the back seat, JOHNNY PELLARONI, another rookie, another story.

In lower Manhattan, Decker and the two rookie detectives walk briskly towards an apartment building. Across the street, on the third floor, a young man sits with his elbows resting on the window sill. He observes the street much like a person watching a parade. A rooftop door slowly opens. Decker and the two rookie detectives appear. Decker's two-way radio squawks and crackles. Then, a youthful voice, somewhat excited, informs Decker that the suspect has just entered the building. Decker issues instructions to all units and signals for the two rookies to follow him in silence.

A dark and dingy hallway. Early morning sounds. Infants crying. Radios playing too loud. Decker and his back-up team cautiously enter the hallway from a stairwell. Quietly, Decker approaches a door fortified with steel plates and heavy-duty security locks. He rubs the back of his neck with his hand. He looks tense. Decker gestures to two uniformed policemen at the end of the hallway to bring him the explosives.

EXERCISE 6: THE NARRATIVE TREATMENT

Your objective in writing the narrative treatment is to concentrate on the development of your main character and your story moving from plot point to plot point, from setup to resolution. Take no detours. That is, don't attempt to fill in any unnecessary details.

Use of dialogue in your treatment is optional. However, it is advised that if you do use dialogue, keep it brief. From a standpoint of being practical, it is best to save dialogue for your script. Without using extensive details, describe the visual aspects of key scenes as you see them on your "mindscreen".

Novels and short stories are written in the past tense such as, "John ran down the street and stopped next to the telephone booth." Since screenplays are written in the present tense, so should your narrative treatment. Thus, the description above is presented as, "John runs down the street and stops next to the telephone booth."

While you are writing the narrative treatment in prose style, don't get fancy; your writing is purely functional. It should not be an attempt to gain literary recognition; you are just telling your story.

Unlike all the previous steps, <u>the narrative treatment provides the broadest expansion of your story because it combines and links all the separate elements together: character, screenplay structure, plot points, and scene descriptions.</u>

It is quite possible that your story might make a fabulous novel. If that is the case, you could change your course of direction.

Of my three original screenplays, I feel that THE CRIMSON MOON would make a good novel. At one point, I seriously considered writing a novel but realized it would be impractical at this time; it would only dilute my attention from my primary goal of "establishing" my career as a screenwriter.

RESEARCH

Research is required whenever you are unfamiliar with the subject matter you are using in your story. In certain stories, "technical" or "procedural" research is an absolute necessity if credibility is to be established. Try writing a story about medicine, law, or science without knowledge of the subject matter and the benefit of research. It is impossible. Technical or procedural inaccuracies ultimately damage a good story.

Some writers spend months researching and conceptualizing a project before they put a word on paper. Unfortunately, many inexperienced writers incorrectly assume that if they are not actually writing, they are being unproductive. Nothing could be further from the truth. Research is a tool of good writing so don't make the mistake of considering it a burden or inconvenience.

Research opens the door of opportunity because it often uncovers information that you could have only discovered through the process itself.

You may be looking for one specific fact but ultimately find other information that is more meaningful. Through research, you are then in a position of exercising greater choices of what you use.

The type of research you do will vary from project to project. You could be looking for technical or procedural facts; or bits of esoteric information. You might be able to find everything you need at the public library. Or sometimes, a newspaper or magazine article might provide all the information you require.

Interviewing "experts" in a given field is probably the most valuable type of research you can complete. Since "one-on-one" interviews are spontaneous, they are often extremely effective. An answer to one question may prompt another question. In the end, more insightful information can be acquired with far greater depth and understanding.

While research is listed as the seventh step in the screenwriting process, it might be your starting point. It is quite possible to develop a story out of researching unfamiliar subject matter. Elements within the subject matter may have a certain appeal which sparks the creative juices. Next thing you know, you are developing a story line and sketching out a main character.

With THE CRIMSON MOON, "book research" and "location scouting" were significant to the development of this project. The details are explained on page 163 in the chapter covering the initial creative steps as they were applied to THE CRIMSON MOON story.

EXERCISE 7: RESEARCH

If you are writing about unfamiliar subject matter, you must take the time to research it properly. Start at the public library. If you cannot find the right kind of information there, the librarian can probably direct you to alternative sources.

Interviewing an expert in the specific field is enormously helpful. Regardless of the subject matter, through a little detective work, you can more than likely find someone in your immediate area who is both qualified and willing to help you out.

CHAPTER 4: SCREENPLAY FORM

SCREENPLAY FORM

Having completed the first seven exercises, you should be very eager to write your first draft screenplay. But before you do, you need to understand and be familiar with SCREENPLAY FORM as well as SCREENWRITING TECHNIQUES and TERMINOLOGY.

There are a number of software programs available for formatting screenplays. The most popular are SCRIPTOR for IBM and SCRIPTWRITER for Macintosh as listed on page 179 along with other writing programs. To find a program compatible with your equipment, check with your local computer store.

Since there is no uniformity in measuring space on a page between the various brands of typewriters and computers, screenplay margins and spacings will be outlined using ruler measurements. From there, it will be very easy to determine the proper settings on your own equipment. Use 8 1/2 x 11 inch paper for your screenplay.

o Each screenplay page should begin 3/4" from the top of the paper. Using a page length of 58 single spaces, that should give you about 3/4" at the bottom of the page. Some pages may be shorter, but the maximum length from the top is 58 single spaces starting from the screenplay "page number".

On the next page, the exact layout of a screenplay page is illustrated. Keep in mind that figure A, the line where the screenplay "page number" appears, represents the top of the screenplay page which is 3/4" from the top of the paper.

A. (top of page, 3/4" from top of paper) 1.

B. EXT. STREET - DAY

C. A black sedan turns onto a residential street and parks in front of a station wagon. Children run down the street playing tag. In the b.g., we HEAR the SOUND of a GARBAGE TRUCK making a pickup.

GEORGE HOWARD gets out of the black sedan and stands next to it. About thirty-five, he is fairly average-looking. He cautiously looks around and smiles at someone in the station wagon.

ANGLE ON ANN PARKER

as she gets out of the station wagon. In her early thirties, she is rather attractive with long, shapely legs. She slowly walks up to George and kisses him passionately.

As they break their embrace.

D. GEORGE
E. (smiling at Ann)
F. You look terrific!

ANN
I know.

G. (Bottom of page 1) (CONTINUED)

(Top of next page) 2.

H. CONTINUED:

GEORGE
What's Bill doing today?

ANN
He's working in New Jersey.

GEORGE
Well then -- let's not waste any more time.

George and Ann drive off together in his car.

A. The PAGE NUMBER appears in the top right-hand corner approximately 3/4" from the top of the paper with a 1 1/4" right-hand margin. The page length of 58 single spaces begins on this line.

B. The SCENE HEADING is two single spaces below the page number. The SCENE HEADING indicates either INT. (Interior) or EXT. (Exterior) LOCATION and TIME -- either DAY or NIGHT. Use a 1 3/4" margin on the left side of the page with a 1 1/4" margin on the right.

C. The SCENE DESCRIPTION appears two single spaces below the SCENE HEADING. This area is used to outline the visual aspects of the scene, single-spaced, in lowercase letters. Anything pertaining to SOUND is CAPITALIZED as illustrated. Character descriptions are also presented in the scene description section. Anytime a character appears for the "first" time in the screenplay, the character's name is CAPITALIZED.

   The SCENE DESCRIPTIONS should be as brief as possible. If a lot of detail is required, write two or three short paragraphs as opposed to one long one -- it is a lot easier to read. The SCENE DESCRIPTION margin is the same as the SCENE HEADING.

D. The CHARACTER speaking appears in CAPITAL LETTERS in the center of the page, starting 4 1/4" from the left-hand side of the page; two single spaces below the ending of the SCENE DESCRIPTION.

E. STAGE DIRECTIONS appear one single space below the CHARACTER'S NAME in "parentheses"; starting 3 1/4" from the left-hand side of the page. It can "wrap" to two or even three lines with the right margin 3 1/4" from the right side of the page.

F. DIALOGUE appears one single space below either the CHARACTER'S NAME or, when used, below STAGE DIRECTIONS. Dialogue forms a "block" in the center of the page with a 2 7/8" margin from both sides of the page.

G. If a scene continues to the next page, (CONTINUED) appears in CAPITAL LETTERS with parentheses around it; two single spaces below the last portion of the uncompleted scene at the bottom of the page, flush with the right margin.

H. If a scene is continued to the next page, CONTINUED: appears in CAPITAL LETTERS followed by a colon, two single spaces below the page number on the top left side of the page.

If this seems a little confusing, just take out a ruler and measure any standard-sized screenplay (8 1/2 x 11").

In acquiring copies of screenplays from successful films, you may note that each scene, as well as specific shots, may be numbered in the margins on both sides of the page. That is not the responsibility of the screenwriter, so don't number your scenes. It is the function of the Production Manager when budgeting the film and outlining the production schedule.

SCREENPLAY TECHNIQUES

The term SCREENPLAY TECHNIQUES is applied to those counterparts of screenwriting that are most important to creating a well-structured screenplay. Each issue will be explained and, in some cases, fully illustrated. Certain screenplay components, such as the scene, are a primary and essential part of the screenplay. Therefore, it is mandatory that they be used. Other screenplay techniques, such as flashback, montage, reversal, etc., are "optional" and should only be utilized if they naturally fit into your story. Don't feel obligated to use any optional technique unless there is a definite need required by your story.

THE SCENE

After screenplay structure, the scene is the most important element in your screenplay. "Word of mouth" can make or break a film; it has more impact than the millions of dollars spent on advertising and promoting a movie. When people leave the theatre, they don't talk about the film, they talk about specific scenes. If you write a good, well-structured story and create a half dozen memorable scenes, your film has the potential to be successful.

Each and every scene should be treated with great care, so here are the most important details and guidelines relating to the treatment of scenes.

o A scene is a specific segment of dramatic action which has a beginning, middle, and end -- just like your story. Every scene must have a specific purpose such as revealing character or information about the plot. But most importantly, every scene must move the story forward towards its resolution. It is very unlikely that any scene will provide more than one function.

o "Scene Headings" note two things -- location and time of day, i.e., EXT. HOUSE - DAY or INT. HOUSE-NIGHT. Whenever location or time changes, you have a new scene. If your scene begins with INT. KITCHEN-DAY and moves to INT. DINING ROOM - DAY, you have a new scene. If your scene begins with INT. BEDROOM - NIGHT and the next one is INT. BEDROOM - DAY, it is a new scene.

- In contemporary screenplays, it is not the function of the screenwriter to write in camera angles. However, in some cases, using camera angles may be desirable in order to emphasize something important.

  Scenes are written as either MASTER SHOTS or SPECIFIC SHOTS. The master shot is what is actually described in your "scene description" -- the overall area. A specific shot is written when you want to emphasize something important within the scene. In going through THE CRIMSON MOON, you will see specific shots such as INSERT OF PHOTOGRAPH, ANGLE ON WOMAN, ANGLE ON DECKER, etc. In these cases, I felt it was important enough to warrant a specific shot.

  In some scenes, using specific camera angles may greatly enhance how the scene will work or, at least, how it is intended to look from the writer's point of view. Ultimately, it is the cinematographer's decision, in collaboration with the director, to determine camera angles.

  If at all possible, avoid using the word CAMERA in your screenplay since it is basically frowned upon. If you want to describe what the camera sees, express it like this -- we see Jack run across the street and stop next to a mailbox. That description implies what the camera sees and, subsequently, what the audience will see.

- How will you open each scene? Will it be visually dynamic, like a shot in the great outdoors? Or, will it be one expressing mood and atmosphere like the inside of a dark house or a cemetery at night?

  In THE CRIMSON MOON, the story and the very first scene open with an ESTABLISHING SHOT of Brooklyn. (An ESTABLISHING SHOT is a long or wide-angle shot revealing a particular location.)

  With the story beginning in New York and quickly moving to New Hampshire, I felt that this particular shot would make a strong impression on the audience in establishing a contrast between the two environments.

  Since every scene deals with visual elements, be creative in describing each scene. If you think of a detail which can enhance a scene, write it in, but don't be too elaborate.

- There are no rules governing how "short" or "long" a scene can be other than common sense. In THE CRIMSON MOON, look at the last scene on the bottom of page 2 or the first scene on the top of page 3. These scenes are as short as they come and while they are not significant to moving the story forward, in the sense of the plot, they do have a specific purpose in providing TRANSITORY ACTION.

  What is TRANSITORY ACTION? It is action designed to connect scenes as well as provide CONTRAST BETWEEN SCENES, another important technique. Both of these issues will be addressed shortly.

- It is strongly suggested that heavy dialogue scenes be kept under "three pages". Dialogue scenes exceeding three pages can be overwhelming and somewhat tedious; that is, with the possible exception of a high-voltage courtroom scene, etc.

- When should you enter a scene? At the last possible moment just before the "ending" of some specific action.

  If the purpose of a scene is to reveal information about a character or the plot, don't waste half a page leading to that point. Build that scene so the information can be presented immediately.

  In THE CRIMSON MOON, look at the "dialogue" scene between Matt Decker and Captain McCaffey which begins on the bottom of page 7 and ends near the top of page 10. This dialogue scene reveals things about Decker's character, his point of view, as well as it sets up the story. Everything in this dialogue scene has a specific purpose with no waste or excess fat.

- In building scenes and developing your story line, be careful of revealing too much information. That is, don't let the audience get ahead of your story and predict what will happen next.

  Learn to hold back information and gradually reveal things only as it becomes necessary. The audience should find out things at the same time as your main character, never before.

In THE CRIMSON MOON, read the scene on page 121 where Decker informs Carol Nelson that he is going to meet with the kidnaper. Carol then asks Decker, "But what about the money?" It is a valid question within the context of the story and one that cannot be ignored. However, Decker does not answer the question directly. If he did, it would take away from the final outcome.

Decker responds by saying, "No questions -- I've worked up a game plan and we need to go over it in detail." The scene deliberately and abruptly ends with that last comment. In the very next scene, Decker leaves Carol and Maggie to meet with the kidnaper. By the way those two scenes are constructed and tied together, the audience assumes, without really knowing, that Decker has "possibly" told Carol about the money or, at least, has given her instructions. Therefore, the audience knows only what they should. Everything else will be revealed as it happens.

- Don't duplicate scenes. This is another basic rule but a very easy trap to fall into without realizing it. The potential for this problem can be best illustrated on page 118 of THE CRIMSON MOON.

  Decker returns from his meeting with Judge Tyler and his run-in with Sly Rankin. When Carol tends his bruised face, she asks, "So, what happened today?" Again, it is another valid question within the context of the story and one that could not be ignored. And, of course, it would be senseless to have Decker repeat everything that happened. From Carol's question, the scene cuts to the ending of the next scene where Decker and Carol finish that conversation. Thus, the problem of repeating a scene is effectively handled.

- A very important element relating directly to the topic of scenes is the SEQUENCE. A sequence is a number of scenes tied together by one theme. During the course of your story, you will use scenes as well as sequences to tell your story.

  A sequence works like this. Two men begin a discussion on tennis. The sequence starts in one man's office, continues as they walk in the hallway, out to the parking lot, drive in a car, walk into a restaurant, have lunch together, and so on.

Remember, every time you change location or time, it is a new scene. You can combine ten scenes in one sequence; whatever works.

There are no set number of scenes or sequences in your screenplay. While you outline 15 scene descriptions as a guideline for each 30 pages of screenplay, the number you actually use may vary considerably.

You could end up with 12 or 18 scenes for Act I, the first 30 pages. In the first half of Act II, the next 30 pages, you might end up with only ten scenes or possibly 20. The scene descriptions are only an outline or a guide used for laying out your story. If you have properly prepared yourself, your story, as you write the first draft screenplay, will determine how many scenes you actually need.

As you write the first draft screenplay, you will often eliminate scenes or combine scenes, thus reducing how many you use. Or, you might see the need for adding a scene to "bridge" or "link" two others. Just trust the process.

- o Film is a visual medium so don't say what you can show. Don't talk about how breathtaking or exciting something is, show it. But, at all times, the realities of production (cost and feasibility) have to be taken into consideration. If your scenes call for things totally unrealistic or impossible to execute, your script may be unceremoniously drop-kicked across the room.

- o In some instances, you will emphasize a scene visually. At other times, dialogue will be the most effective treatment. On page 15 of THE CRIMSON MOON, there are two scenes which are presented visually. In both instances, these scenes should work well with their purpose clearly understood by the audience without relying upon one word of dialogue.

- o Story rhythm, tempo, and pacing are strongly influenced by two factors. The first is screenplay structure, the second is CONTRAST BETWEEN SCENES.

  Within every story, there are certain primary elements. In THE 12/20 CLUB, the story revolves around three primary elements: the main character's family life with a wife and two teenage children; his business career; and his music activities.

There are also two sub-categories within THE 12/20 CLUB, drama and humor. So, in reality, there were "five" elements that I could effectively rotate to establish contrast between scenes.

Awareness of what each scene is about and how long each scene will run in "film time", provides another means of controlling your story's pacing. No matter how well-structured a story may be, every film inherently has "dead space" or "slow time" from the perspective of each person viewing it. There are portions of every film, without exception, that just don't appeal to individuals. This is why consciously rotating the various elements in your story will dramatically improve the rhythm, tempo, and pacing.

In THE 12/20 CLUB, I had five distinctively different elements to work with. If the dramatic office scene does not appeal to someone, then a humorous family scene might just grab them. If not, maybe a nightclub scene where the band plays their rock 'n roll music will be appealing. In rotating the various elements within your story, never forget that each scene must move the story forward towards its resolution.

In trying to improve the pacing of your story, don't get carried away by determining the actual running time of each scene. Build your screenplay by utilizing and rotating the various elements of your story.

At the same time, maintain your awareness to potential problems like running too many pages of heavy dialogue together. Unless you are dealing with an explosive courtroom scene or something equally dramatic, heavy segments of dialogue could put your audience into a coma.

Screenplay structure, contrast between scenes, and scene length, ultimately determine the rhythm, tempo, and pacing of your story. Also, rotating interior with exterior, daytime with nighttime, and dialogue scenes with action scenes, are other considerations in providing contrast.

Don't panic or feel overwhelmed by all this; in a very short period of time it will become second nature to you.

- TRANSITORY ACTION provides the means of connecting scenes as well as "contrast between scenes". It simply means that you make every decision concerning how you tell your story. A scene ends, often abruptly, and another one begins.

  Sometimes there is no "space" between scenes. You move from a house to the beach without showing how your character gets there. That is fine. But sometimes you may want to show that transitory action in order to "visually" open up your story and to provide contrast between certain scenes.

  If one scene moved from inside a house to inside another house, you could provide nice contrast between those scenes by showing the main character tooling down the highway in a convertible with the top down. That transitory scene may only run for "five seconds" but it can visually open up your story -- especially if it separates two interior scenes which might tend to be claustrophobic.

  If you had a scene which begins in a bedroom and then moves to the kitchen, there are a number of ways of handling it. One scene can cut directly to the next without transitory action. Or, you could use transitory action to connect the two scenes just visually. As an example, the bedroom and the kitchen scenes could be tied together by having your character walk down a hallway between the two rooms.

  If you wanted to create a mini-sequence, two characters could start a discussion in the bedroom, continue the conversation in the hallway, and resolve it in the kitchen. This is another way of treating transitory action while utilizing the sequence as well. Everything in screenwriting is related.

- EXPOSITION is the technique used to convey information about your character and your story to the audience. It is an integral part of screenwriting since it provides the necessary background information to move the story forward. When exposition is required, it should be handled naturally and never impede the forward motion of your story.

It is best to weave exposition into scenes involving conflict. Look at the scene between Decker and Captain McCaffey which starts on the bottom of page 7 and ends on the top of page 10. This scene is pure exposition handled through conflict.

If at all possible, exposition should not be the function of the main character -- especially if it involves boring details that are required to set up the story. However, if the exposition is exciting and dramatic like the main character explaining how he or she will save everyone from impending danger, that is perfectly acceptable since it will enhance the image of the main character.

Exposition can be handled visually and through dialogue. In the very first page of THE CRIMSON MOON, visual exposition is used to provide background information on the main character, Matt Decker. The photographs displayed on the hutch inform the audience of his military background and his expertise with explosives. When Decker meets with his Captain in the scene running between the bottom of page 7 and the top of page 10, that is exposition handled through dialogue using conflict. It reveals facts about the character and sets up the story.

While the basic rule of film is, "don't say what you can show," there are times when you will want to use exposition to replace or eliminate other scenes. On page 11 of THE CRIMSON MOON, Decker calls the hospital to check on the condition of the two wounded officers. He also states that he will stop by the hospital in the morning. The hospital scene is not shown, but it is conveyed to the audience through exposition. This is another way that exposition functions. Instead of "showing" something happening, the action can be related through exposition.

In THE CRIMSON MOON, exposition was used to handle Alex Decker's kidnaping as opposed to creating a scene actually showing it. It would have been easy to write a brief scene showing the kidnaping without revealing the killer, but I decided it was not necessary. By having Maggie discover Alex's kidnaping, Carol then has the opportunity to read the note to Decker over the telephone. Through this use of exposition, the audience is given "all" the necessary details in a way that I feel is most effective. (See page 101 of the screenplay.)

Using and not using exposition also affects the treatment of a scene. If your main character is walking into a dangerous situation and the audience is given those facts ahead of time, again, through exposition, "suspense" can be created since the audience "knows" something is going to happen. If the audience does not know of the impending danger ahead of time, their reaction will be one of "surprise" or "shock" when the main character walks into trouble.

Exposition is constantly used throughout a screenplay every time you relate facts or information to the audience about the character or the story. Only when a writer identifies the necessity of using exposition does he or she become consciously aware of it. When the need for exposition is obvious, find a way of treating it creatively so it will flow naturally with your story. The last thing you want to do is hang a sign on it.

- BACKGROUND ACTIVITY or ACTION is another way of "texturing" a scene and creating DRAMATIC TENSION. If you created a scene with a man and woman arguing, in the background, the audience could see another man observing the confrontation. If the audience already knows that the second man is possibly an intruder, not liked by the man arguing with the woman, it creates additional tension that can greatly enhance the scene.

  If you created a scene where a man and woman were sharing an intimate moment together and had a bunch of penguins waddling behind them in the background, it would be unintentionally distracting; unless, of course, you are writing a comedy.

  On page 10 in THE CRIMSON MOON, the scene description covering the detective's squad room states: "A rare moment of solitude. No longer the center of bustling activity." The "lack of" background activity naturally complements the purpose of the scene--humor. In contrast, compare this scene to the one on page 91 at Ray's Diner. The scene description reads, "The diner is packed with tradesmen eating hearty breakfasts and engaging in boisterous conversations." This background action or activity will enhance the dialogue scene between Decker and Lt. Branford. Background activity or action is an effective tool in expanding the visual aspects and overall effect of a scene. Give careful thought to each scene and utilize this technique when it is appropriate.

- DRAMATIC TENSION can also be created and released within a scene by changing the emotional state of the characters. A harmonious family scene can erupt into a heated argument or vice versa. This is another element of dramatic writing that also provides contrast within and between scenes.

- SUBTEXT is what happens below the surface of the scene -- the emotional aspects; what the characters are actually feeling. Subtext represents the quality dimension to writing that should be an intricate part of every scene.

  In THE CRIMSON MOON, the scene on pages 13 and 14 involving the blind date is a prime example of subtext. The motive behind Decker's treatment of the blind date is, on the surface, meant to be humorous. But in subtext, it is Decker's way of telling his friends, Ron and Linda Mizak, that he does not want anyone interfering in this area of his private life.

  Another illustration on subtext, which is far more obvious, is on page 75. On the surface, Matt Decker is showing Carol Nelson how to cook. But in reality, it is the point in their relationship where they share love for the first time. That is what the scene is all about--love.

- A REVERSAL is simply "any" action or situation that turns out to be opposite to what the audience expects to happen; it is usually a surprise of some significance.

  The hero or heroine makes a fantastic escape from the villain. It could be a fast-paced sequence filled with suspense and dangerous thrills. As the tension subsides, the audience believes that the main character is now well out of danger. Then, unsuspectingly, the villain steps out of the darkness and recaptures our hero or heroine. Another example: a smiling man walks up to a woman and, without any provocation, slaps her across the face. It is something you would hardly expect to happen.

  Reversals are a very effective technique, but don't get carried away with them. Too many in one story will wear thin on your audience and turn them off.

- FLASHBACK is another effective technique which requires special consideration and very creative application. As the term implies, flashback means going backwards. Therefore, it can impede or hinder the forward motion of your story.

  If you used a flashback in opening your story, it would have to be at some critical point in the main character's life; possibly a life or death situation. As your story unfolds, the flashback would have to be strong enough to stimulate the audience and sustain their attention and interest until the final outcome is revealed.

  Don't use the flashback technique unless you can be extremely creative. Out of the three original screenplays I have written so far, I have only used the flashback technique once and very briefly. (See page 78 of THE CRIMSON MOON.) In this situation, use of flashback is both valid and very effective. In film time, these flashbacks would run only seconds -- but long enough to make an impression on the audience.

  If you decide to use a quick flashback, dialogue is not necessary. The flashback will be more effective if the treatment relies upon the visual aspects only. Think about it. When memories are recalled, we usually visualize past experiences as opposed to actually remembering the things that were said.

- MONTAGE is the technique used to combine a series of cuts to indicate a passage of time. It can be any amount of time you specify. On page 45 in THE CRIMSON MOON, a montage is used to illustrate the passing of one day as Decker conducts an investigation. The cuts are all "day" scenes. In that instance, the audience should unconsciously assume that the montage covers one day in Matt Decker's investigation.

  In THE 12/20 CLUB, a montage is used to indicate "the passing of a hectic two weeks". That is how it was written using about a dozen fast cuts interchanging day scenes with night scenes, work scenes with music scenes, family scenes with jogging scenes, etc. In using these fast cuts, the treatment relies strictly upon a visual treatment with a song playing in the background.

STAGE DIRECTIONS, as they appear in parentheses under the name of the CHARACTER speaking, have three primary applications as illustrated below.

GEORGE
(impatiently)
Bill! What the hell are you doing here?

In this use, "impatiently" relates to the character's frame of mind.

GEORGE
(yelling loudly)
Bill! What the hell are you doing here?

Here, "yelling loudly" relates to how the character delivers the dialogue.

GEORGE
(walking away)
Bill! What the hell are you doing here?

"Walking away" describes the physical action of the character while delivering the dialogue.

GEORGE
(smiling; to Bill)
I'm sorry for losing my temper.

When there are more than two people in a scene and one character is addressing another, but not by name, you may want to clarify who is being addressed.

You do so by putting the name of the person being addressed in parentheses in the stage directions under the character speaking. At the same time, as illustrated above, additional stage directions can be given to the character. In this case, George smiles as he addresses Bill.

If your stage directions are involved, meaning they cannot be expressed in two or three words, then describe them in the full margin used for scene descriptions. On the next page, there is an example of how it works.

GEORGE
Hey, Bill, I want to show you
something important...

George walks over to the desk, opens a drawer, and looks for something. Then, from under the desk blotter, he pulls out a piece of paper.

GEORGE
(continuing; handing it to
Bill but looking at Ann)
Here it is...
(smiling at Ann)
Well, Bill, what do you think?

When a character's dialogue is "continuous" but split by "stage directions" as illustrated above, "continuing" is placed in parentheses in stage directions under the character's name when the dialogue continues again.

At the same time, this illustration also shows how two additional actions are briefly stated in stage directions appearing under George's name the second time. "Handing it to Bill" refers to the paper, "but looking at Ann" designates simultaneous action.

VOICE-OVER NARRATION is a technique effectively used in those great detective mysteries of the 1940s. We would usually see the detective's car gliding down the highway while we heard him speak in voice-over narration, filling in details (exposition) about himself and/or his case.

Like flashbacks, using a narrator is very infrequent since the technique only lends itself to certain stories. One of the best illustrations of effective narration and flashback in recent films is STAND BY ME.

DIALOGUE TECHNIQUES are relatively easy to understand and use. There are two primary techniques: three dots to indicate a long pause and two hyphen marks to signify a broken tempo or slight interruption in the dialogue. Also, under stage directions in parentheses, you can use any one of three primary phrases to indicate a pause before the dialogue is delivered: (beat), (a beat; then), or (pause; and then).

Here is an example of the various dialogue techniques incorporated into one brief conversation.

GEORGE
(to Ann: a beat; then)
What do you say we throw Bill down the elevator shaft at the World Trade Center?

ANN
Gee, I don't know... Can't we find some place -- higher?

As indicated in stage directions, "to Ann: a beat; then", George pauses before he speaks to Ann. Within Ann's dialogue, she pauses after "I don't know" and hesitates between the words "place" and "higher".

TELEPHONE CALLS can be handled three different ways. Choose the technique that works best for the scene.

EXAMPLE NO. 1

INT. RESTAURANT - DAY

ANGLE ON GEORGE

He stands in the corner on the telephone. In the b.g., waitresses hustle from table to table.

GEORGE
(on phone)
... Hi, Ann. How are you doing?... That's good... What?... It's impossible for anyone to survive a fall from one hundred and seven floors!

In describing this scene, a little background (b.g.) activity was added. With this telephone technique, the person on camera (in this case, George) pauses as if he were listening to Ann speak on the other end of the telephone.

If you wanted to dramatically set up another scene without revealing exactly what is being said, you would have the character "on camera" react accordingly as he or she listens to the other party speak. It would look like this...

GEORGE
(totally shocked)
Oh, no!... Are you sure?... Okay, I'll
be right there.

In that illustration, while the audience does not hear the other character's dialogue, they know, by the character's reaction "on camera", that something significant has happened. This is a very effective way of introducing a crisis situation and building tension.

EXAMPLE NO. 2

INT. HOUSE - KITCHEN - NIGHT

George walks around the kitchen while he is on the
telephone. In the b.g., we HEAR the SOUND of a
BLENDER running at high speed.

GEORGE
(on phone)
So, what time are the visiting hours?

ANN (v.o.)
Three p.m. to nine p.m.

GEORGE
I guess we should go and visit Bill --
what do you think?

ANN (v.o.)
(a beat; then)
Maybe we could throw him down the
hospital elevator shaft!

With this telephone technique, a little b.g. diversion is created with the blender running while the two characters speak to each other. During this scene, we look at George as he speaks and as Ann speaks. While Ann's voice is heard through a voice-over (v.o.), George is constantly on camera during this scene.

In this type of telephone scene, you could have the character who is on camera doing something in addition to talking on the telephone. If you wanted to create a humorous scene, you could have the character trying to make a sandwich while talking on the telephone. Imagine someone walking around the kitchen retrieving the various ingredients. At one point, the telephone extension cord could be "too short". So, the character has to awkwardly try and reach for something that is just out of grasp while he or she is still talking. Crash, a jar of pickles hits the floor...

EXAMPLE NO. 3

INT. HOSPITAL ROOM - NIGHT

Bill is laying in bed; in traction. One of his arms and both legs are suspended by cables. He is totally wrapped up in bandages from head to toe. He looks like a mummy.

The TELEPHONE besides his bed RINGS three times before a nurse picks it up.

NURSE
(on phone)
Hello?... Just a minute, please.
(to Bill)
It's for you.

The nurse hands Bill the phone and exits.

BILL
(on phone)
Hello?

INT. HOUSE - DEN - SAME TIME

George is seated in his lounge chair with a beer in one hand and a telephone in the other. Ann stands next to him wearing a sheer nightgown.

GEORGE
(on phone)
Bill? Hey, good buddy! How are you doing?

INTERCUT GEORGE AND BILL

(CONTINUED)

CONTINUED:

BILL
(struggling to speak)
Oh, hi, George, I guess I'm doing okay... I sure hope you're taking good care of Ann while I'm recuperating.

GEORGE
(patting Ann on her behind)
Don't worry, Bill, I'm taking good care of your wife -- have no fear!
(George kisses Ann)
... Hey, Bill, how would you like to go skydiving next weekend?

As INTERCUT might indicate, the character speaking would become the subject of the shot. The camera would cut back and forth between the two characters as each one speaks.

Of course, all three telephone techniques can be combined in one scene, but there is no need to get that intricate. Just write the scene utilizing the telephone technique that works best for the situation.

SCREENPLAY TERMINOLOGY

Screenplay terminology is another facet of screenwriting that is less complicated than screenplay techniques. These are the techniques most frequently used.

- FADE IN: is the technique where an image gradually appears on a black screen. Of course, FADE OUT: would be the opposite where an image gradually fades out until the screen goes black.

Here are some basic CAMERA ANGLES and how they are used. Limit camera angles to only those circumstances where their use is needed to emphasize something important or to enhance a given scene. With camera angles, one basic rule applies -- determine the subject of the shot.

- ANGLE ON is used to indicate a SPECIFIC SHOT. Within the scene, it could be written like this...

  ANGLE ON GEORGE

  as he walks towards the window.

  ANGLE ON BOOK

  resting on top of table.

In the above illustrations, "George" and the "book" become the subject of the shot. If you wanted to maintain that emphasis within the same scene with a different shot, it would be written as shown below.

  ANOTHER ANGLE ON GEORGE

  looking out the window. He appears to be tense.

- WIDE ANGLE ON ROOM

  as George and Ann enter.

The above shot emphasizes the room as George and Ann enter. In this instance, the room might have some special significance requiring that it be revealed in a wide-angle shot. In that case, the room, as well as something of importance within it, would be briefly described in the scene description.

o CLOSE ON GEORGE looking around.

or CLOSE ON GEORGE

walking out of the motel room and cautiously looking around before he gets into his car.

If the description is brief, the shot can be written on one line as noted above. If it is more involved, you can use a shot heading for emphasis, and then describe the action two single spaces below.

CLOSE shots should be used sparingly and only when there is a need for emphasizing something dramatic.

o INSERT OF PHOTOGRAPH

revealing two young boys standing together.

BACK TO SCENE

George puts the photograph down.

Small details, such as a newspaper column, a pen, a photograph, a button, etc., are usually emphasized in INSERT SHOTS as written above.

If you use INSERT OF "SOMETHING", it is practical to use BACK TO SCENE to indicate where the scene actually continues. It is done for clarity. In THE CRIMSON MOON, scenes on pages 11, 34, 45, 48, 52, and 105 utilize this exact technique.

o GEORGE'S POV

of street from his window. He sees Bill heading towards his apartment building carrying a GUN.

POV represents George's "point of view". It is the subject of the shot; what the camera sees, the audience sees.

o REVERSE SHOT - BILL

looks up and sees George in the window.

o DISSOLVE TO:

EXT. STREET - DAY

George runs down the street while Bill follows in hot pursuit. Bill's GUN THUNDERS three times.

This example using a reverse shot sets up a "reaction" since both characters are looking at each other at the same time. Of course, the most significant reaction would be George seeing Bill with the gun.

DISSOLVE TO: indicates two images overlapping each other on the screen at the same time with one replacing the other. In this case, George looking out the window will be overlapped by the next scene of him running down the street. DISSOLVE TO: appears in the far right-hand margin. The scenes using DISSOLVE TO: are separated by two single spaces.

If you feel that a dissolve will enhance or emphasize the connection between two scenes, write it that way. In the end, it is the director and the film editor who will make all the creative decisions concerning how scenes will be connected.

o EXT. APARTMENT BUILDING - DAY

George races out the front door and runs down the street as we...

CUT TO:

EXT. STREET - DAY

Bill reloading his .357 Magnum with twenty-five grain hollow points. Then, like a flash, he chases after George.

CUT TO: is used to indicate the ending of one scene. Some writers use it between every scene. For emphasizing the connection between two scenes, I would use it as written above so the action of the scene descriptions actually connects in a continuous flow. So you read it like this: "George races out the front door and runs down the street as we CUT TO: (see) Bill reloading his .357 Magnum", etc.

o TIGHT ANGLE ON GEORGE

running on the sidewalk.

PULL BACK TO REVEAL

a big dog snapping at George's posterior.

The above scene starts off with a TIGHT ANGLE (close shot) ON GEORGE running on the sidewalk. Then, PULL BACK TO REVEAL means that the camera gradually pulls back from the subject of the tight shot to reveal a broader view --usually, some kind of surprise. The above example well illustrates the point.

o OFF CAMERA (o.c.) and OFF SCREEN (o.s.) are essentially the same thing. If a character is off camera when the shot is taken, he or she will not appear on the screen. The choice of which one you use is totally at your discretion.

I like to distinguish the difference between OFF CAMERA and VOICE-OVER in certain scenes as outlined in the next two illustrations.

INT. HOUSE - LIVING ROOM - DAY

Ann pensively stands silent with her arms folded across her chest, shaking her head in disbelief.

GEORGE (o.c.)
I ran down Hickory Street to Dover
Lane with Bill blasting away at me
with his Dirty Harry special! On top
of that, this goddamn dog is chasing
me -- and then, I tripped over a
garbage pail on the sidewalk!

ANGLE ON GEORGE

The seat of his pants has been torn out and his clothes are all soiled.

In this scene, George is in the same room as Ann but he is "off camera" or "off screen" as he speaks. While George delivers his dialogue, Ann is the subject of the shot. When George finishes speaking, he becomes the subject of the shot which reveals his condition.

INT. HOUSE - HALLWAY - DAY

Ann stands outside a closed closet door where George is hiding.

ANN
(annoyingly)
Are you coming out or what?

GEORGE (v.o.)
No way, Jose!

Since George is not in the same room as Ann, I would use a "voice-over" to indicate his dialogue.

o EXT. STREET CORNER - DAY

George nervously peeks around the corner.

SLOW PAN TO GEORGE'S RIGHT

as Bill sneaks up on him carrying a large two-by-four.

PAN TO is another technique used to indicate the direction of the camera. It moves from one direction to another in order to reveal something.

In the f.g. (foreground) or in the b.g. (background) are terms used to indicate other things happening within a scene.

EXT. STREET - DAY

George walks briskly down the sidewalk. He looks a little uneasy. In the b.g., we see Bill catching up to George. Only now, he has a BIGGER two-by-four.

o GEORGE'S REACTION

seeing Bill coming at him with the two-by-four. He looks horrified.

ANGLE ON GEORGE

tearing down the street as fast as he can move.

When you want to visually reveal someone's reaction to something, write it as shown above. This point is illustrated on page 27 of THE CRIMSON MOON.

Scenes utilizing "cars" are handled in several basic ways. Again, determine the subject of the shot when using specific camera angles. As illustrated in the first example below, a specific camera angle can be incorporated into the scene heading.

o EXT. HIGHWAY - GEORGE'S MOVING CAR - DAY

turns off Main Street onto a residential street. The brakes SCREECH as the car skids past a driveway. Quickly, the car backs up the driveway into an open garage.

INT. GARAGE - GEORGE'S PARKED CAR

George slinks down in the front seat and peers over the steering wheel. His POV of the street as Bill's car goes tearing by.

WOMAN (o.c.)
(indignantly)
What are you doing in my garage?

ANGLE ON GEORGE

Startled by the woman, he jumps up and hits his head on the roof of his car.

ANGLE ON GEORGE'S CAR

It flies out of the woman's garage leaving a huge strip of burning rubber down her driveway.

In the first illustration, the subject of the shot is both the "highway" and "George's moving car". In the second illustration, the subject of the shot is both the "garage" and "George's parked car" and then, George's "point of view" of the street as Bill's car goes tearing by.

If you wanted to emphasize just the car, the scene heading would be written as illustrated below.

o EXT. GEORGE'S MOVING CAR

turns off Main Street onto a residential street.

By reading THE CRIMSON MOON and other screenplays, you will quickly acquire a sense or feel for screenplay form and the various techniques applied to each.

CHAPTER 5: THE EMOTIONAL ASPECTS OF WRITING

THE EMOTIONAL ASPECTS OF WRITING

Before you begin writing your first draft screenplay, it is important to understand the emotional aspects of writing; those issues which have the greatest impact on a writer's emotional stability, attitude, and performance. On those days when you struggle with your work, especially the first project, this information will be extremely helpful to you and very comforting.

Writing is a lonely occupation filled with a broad spectrum of emotional experiences. Most of the time, it is very rewarding or there would not be any writers. But let's take a look at the two major extremes.

At some point in writing every project, a writer will experience despair, anxiety, apprehension, and confusion. Even when you are thoroughly prepared to write, there are moments when you cannot seem to think clearly. Your work bogs down. It becomes difficult to concentrate. You force yourself to write. After an hour or more of staring at a blank piece of paper, you finally write a few words and they are terrible.

Don't worry about it. It is a natural experience every writer contends with from time to time. Sometimes, through pure persistence, you can work your way out of this frame of mind and get back on track. If you cannot after an hour or more, take a short break. Do anything else but write. You will quickly regain your desire to write and your creative juices will once again flow.

On the other side of the coin, there are those magical moments when you rise above what you believe to be the limits of your own talent and abilities. As long as that moment lasts, the level of satisfaction you experience will be incredible. If you diligently pursue writing, you will eventually experience this phenomenon yourself.

Here are the key points and issues affecting a writer's emotional state. Being consciously aware of them makes writing much easier.

1. The more you write, the easier it gets. This applies to the development of each project and, especially, every project after your first one. Experience sharpens your writing skills and intuitive sense, as well as fortifies and strengthens your confidence. With experience, you will be able to work much faster and far more efficiently.

2. Writing is rewriting. This point cannot be emphasized too much. Don't ever make any serious judgments on your first draft screenplay or first revision. Many stories require constant refinement until the real quality of the work is evident.

3. Since you make every decision concerning the treatment of your story and characters, you will naturally make mistakes in the process. If you make a mistake, know that you have the ability to determine the solution. It may take some additional time to correct a problem, but you will do it. While mistakes are frustrating, there is a continuous benefit derived from them because they ultimately teach you new skills and new techniques.

4. Minor changes can often improve major problems and/or significantly enhance the overall quality of your screenplay. You could conceivably spend one hour fixing a problem that might dramatically improve your entire story. What might have been mediocre, quickly becomes great.

5. Towards the completion of every project, you may reach a point where you are reluctant to finish your work. You begin to stall and find reasons not to continue. You simply don't want to "give up" or "finish" your work. It is a natural experience. When it happens, accept it, but press on and complete your screenplay.

6. Is there such a thing as "writer's block"? Yes. And it happens to even the best writers. However, one distinction should be made. Inexperienced writers often put themselves into a position of "writer's block" (not being able to write) by not being properly prepared.

   If you attempt to develop your first draft screenplay without completing the necessary pre-planning steps first, you will spend a great deal of time staring at a blank piece of paper. Your story must be structured from beginning to end with all the supporting details clearly outlined, which is the function of completing all the exercises.

7. Does "creative inspiration" exist? Of course it does. But if you wait around for the mood to strike, it will never happen. Creative inspiration is a by-product of perspiration -- working hard. Without question, it is totally unpredictable and spontaneous. Working at this extraordinary level can last three minutes or possibly several hours. Being prepared and working hard following a regular schedule are the keys to sparking creative inspiration.

8. It is practical to seek advice and opinions on your work during the research stages and after the first draft screenplay is written -- but not as you write. Negative comments can be inhibiting, disruptive to your concentration, and impede your creative flow.

9. A writer's objectivity is greatly diminished because of his or her closeness to the work. The only guiding light is to follow the structure of your story in order to stay on track. And even so, it may take a year after you have finished your screenplay before you really see it objectively.

10. If you write full-time or put a lot of hours in at one time, you must learn to pace yourself. Writing is both mentally and physically exhausting. After two hours or more of constantly writing and sitting in one position, I develop what I call "dead ass". My butt actually becomes numb from sitting too long. Before that point is reached, I get up, stretch and walk around for a minute or two.

    If you reach a point where you are getting very tired but continue pushing without a pause, your work will suffer. Learn to pace yourself and take a break.

11. Being a writer and having a relationship with other people can be difficult at times. Writers tend to be introspective and somewhat moody. A writer's attitude is strongly influenced by the various stages of his or her work. When things are going well, we can be happy and delightful to be around. When things take a turn for the worse, as they do from time to time, we tend to sulk and withdraw from other people.

    Support from spouses, children, girlfriends, boyfriends, as well as tolerance from close personal friends, is a must. People who don't "write" find it impossible to understand the needs of those who must do it.

As interruptions are disruptive to a writer's train of thought and frame of mind, so are a writer's lifestyle and working habits to those close to him or her. Communicate. Talk about it. Reach agreements that come close to satisfying each other's needs. Without support and understanding, a writer cannot possibly be effective.

12. Working environment. What is it? It is a specific area of space where we write. Most importantly, each writer must create a working climate that is conducive to his or her needs. It is a personal choice and a very important consideration.

    One writer may seek the security of a comfortable setting surrounded by personal photographs and memorabilia, while another may have the need to create a "special mood" attained by effective lighting and soft background music.

    From day to day and even hour to hour, my mood shifts as well as my needs. Most of the time, the only sound I hear is the constant hum coming from my computer terminal. In that case, my primary need is total quiet and solitude. If someone interrupts me, I am likely to snap at them like a junkyard dog.

    However, there are times when I do listen to music and the decision is purely spontaneous. What do I listen to? Depending upon my mood, it could be "light FM", jazz, or thundering rock 'n roll. When the moment is right, even with my system cranked up and blasting out "Rock 'n Roll, Hootchie Koo," it is not distracting -- it is stimulating and it does not interfere with my concentration.

    Be very selective and experimental in determining the needs of your working environment because it often has a great bearing on your productivity and the quality of your work.

13. In any business, the quality of your equipment is extremely important. When my writing career first began as a hobby in the mid-1970s, I used a manual typewriter to write articles on music and fishing for national magazines. From there, I upgraded to an electric. In making the move to full-time writer, I realized the necessity and benefits of having a computer with word processing.

No doubt about it, a computer has made me 75 percent more effective and efficient in writing. If you make a decision to pursue a career as a writer, a computer is an absolute must. And today, you don't have to spend a lot of money to acquire a basic computer package with word processing capabilities.

Talk to knowledgeable personnel at a local computer store. Tell them, or even better, show them what a screenplay looks like, so they can recommend the best equipment within your budget.

If you are not in the position to buy a computer, don't fret, but find a good electric typewriter. There are companies who specialize in selling used office equipment, including typewriters. Shop around until you find one that will be dependable, within your budget.

I bought a halogen disk-type lamp which reflects light off the ceiling. Since it evenly disperses a very soft light, it is especially effective during dark hours--early morning and at night. They are not inexpensive but they can diminish "eye fatigue" caused by poor lighting conditions.

Since most writers work sitting down, fatigue can quickly set in and disrupt your concentration as well as the quality of your work. So, find a good chair. While I invested in a computer chair, which is quite expensive, my writing time is rotated between three different chairs. The different shapes of the chairs alter my sitting position and, therefore, tend to lessen my fatigue problems.

Selecting the right equipment is an important issue so consider all your options very carefully.

CHAPTER 6: THE FIRST DRAFT SCREENPLAY

WRITING THE FIRST DRAFT SCREENPLAY

If you have properly completed all the previous exercises and steps, and you are familiar with screenplay form, techniques, and terminology, you should be well-prepared and very eager to tackle your first draft screenplay. As a guideline, it is most helpful to work from your list of scene descriptions as well as the narrative treatment.

The most important rule of writing the first draft screenplay is: <u>don't begin to write your screenplay until you are thoroughly prepared; and once you start, don't stop to polish, correct, or rewrite until the first draft is completed</u>.

The first draft screenplay of THE 12/20 CLUB was absolutely horrible. And while I was tempted, I never stopped or went back to fix anything until after the first draft was completed. Stopping or going back to fix something will only impede your forward motion.

If you stop to fix one thing, you may end up in a major rewrite when your project is not even completed. You could easily become frustrated by trying to perfect what you have already written. Then, you can become discouraged and never finish the project.

It is very important not to make any judgments concerning the "quality" of your first draft screenplay as you write it. Just tell your story from beginning to end. Your screenplay will be made better in subsequent rewrites. Writing is rewriting. That is what it is all about.

THE WRITING APPROACH

From setup to resolution, tell your story scene by scene, plot point to plot point. Focus your writing on each 30-page segment, starting with Act I and the first ten pages.

There is nothing more important than the first ten pages, setting up your story, and the last "x" number of pages covering the resolution.

Within the first ten pages (ten minutes of film time), the audience will decide whether or not they like your story. If you cannot grab their attention in the first ten pages, you will have a tough time maintaining their interest unless your story dramatically improves. In that case, they might just forgive you.

More often than not, if the first ten minutes of a film are weak, the rest of the story usually does not get any better. That is almost a guarantee. From a weak opening, it is a long, dismal downhill slide into oblivion. A successful film starts with a well-structured, precisely executed screenplay that works from the very first scene to the resolution.

WRITING ACT I - THE SETUP

The purpose of Act I, the first 30 pages, is to setup your story. In the first ten pages (ten minutes), you must tell your audience who your main character is, what the story is about, and the dramatic circumstances surrounding the action.

Ten pages are more than sufficient to gradually introduce the three primary elements of your story with great care and style. It is possible to set up your story in the very first page or first couple of pages. If you can do it skillfully, without creating the impression of just "throwing" the setup at your audience, then do it.

Every story lends itself to a certain setup which is established from the opening scene. It is the writer's responsibility to determine the most effective way of opening up his or her story and introducing the three primary elements with as much clarity as possible.

If you were writing an action/adventure film, it would be appropriate to open up with a fast-paced action sequence. Thus, the premise of the story would be immediately and clearly established.

In a plot-driven mystery story, like THE CRIMSON MOON, the primary action, over and above the conflict, is the gradual revelation of facts and information by the detective. That is what sustains the audience's attention and interest.

If the story had immediately opened with an action sequence, such as the one on page 5 where Decker arrests the contract killers, it would be very misleading to the audience. From that point, the audience might expect a fast-paced, slam-bam police story. Initially, they could be disappointed when the story does not progress along that same line of action.

Even without the benefit of reading the actual first ten pages of THE 12/20 CLUB and THE FISHIN' SHACK, you can acquire a clear understanding of each story's setup by rereading their screenplay structure. From those brief descriptions, you can easily imagine the "setup" treatment that was applied to each story.

In reading other screenplays, especially from successful films, you can acquire an instant understanding of how a story is set up and why it works so well because it happens in ten pages or less. This type of analysis can be very helpful in determining the setup of your own story.

Writers spend a great deal of time conceptualizing their ideas. In the days before you begin writing your first draft screenplay, define the three primary elements of your story and determine the most effective way to introduce them. Once a smooth opening is established, your story will gradually grow stronger as you develop it.

While beginnings and endings share equal importance, there is one big difference between them. Because you have "ten pages", setting up your story is a lot easier than the resolution for one reason -- once the audience knows the ending is near, they get anxious and want a swift, conclusive ending.

That means, once the main character overcomes the last major obstacle and all issues have been resolved, the ending must be as tight as possible. Endings require much greater skill. But, for now, focus all your creative energy on opening up your story.

PAGES 11 TO 30

After you have set up your story, your focus and line of development should be aimed at the first major plot point. In the second ten pages, concentrate on the main character while moving your story forward.

With a specific objective for each scene, keep moving towards your next goal, the first major plot point. If you have the tendency to write too much, don't worry about it; and don't start counting pages. Just keep writing. Tell your story. You are far better off having too much than not enough. It is always easier to cut back scenes rather than add new ones later.

The first major plot point should be significant enough to grab your audience and propel the story forward into high gear. But a word of caution. Make sure that the first major plot point is in balance with the rest of your story. That is, it has to be strong enough to grab the audience, but at the same time, it must not be so dynamic that the rest of the story is unable to sustain itself or exceed that level. Tell your audience just what they need to know and build from that point.

WRITING ACT II - CONFLICT

The focus of Act II, from pages 31 to 90, is conflict through confrontations and obstacles with the line of development running from the first major plot point to the second major plot point.

Your story moves forward, scene to scene, plot point to plot point. Since the intervals between the plot points are relatively close together in Act II, every 15 pages or so, developing your story becomes much easier because the "goal to goal" segments are much shorter.

In Act II, through rising conflict, you progressively build your story and move towards its resolution. As your main character advances, his or her adversary delivers counterthrusts or setbacks with the action gradually increasing to the most critical point in the story.

Rising human conflict is the primary force behind drama. And, it is the most important element in every story. Conflict is also naturally indigenous to every story as well as the "internal conflicts" created by the main character in attempting to overcome or deal with his or her own personal problems.

While "rising human conflict" is the most important, collectively, all forms of conflict enhance the story and function as the adhesive force sustaining the audience's attention and interest.

Conflict varies in degrees as well as impact. Some forms of conflict are minor obstacles indigenous to the story or very dramatic confrontations involving the main character and his or her adversary. Conflict is a back and forth motion. The main character advances a step towards achieving his or her goal and then suffers a setback.

CONFLICT IN THE CRIMSON MOON

Here are examples of the various forms of conflict which are interwoven into THE CRIMSON MOON.

The story advances when Decker discovers a tie-in between his ex-wife's murder and the steamship trunk once owned by a 1930s gangster. After Decker recovers the steamship trunk, an adversary tries to run him off the road. Soon after that, he is temporarily "set back" when an adversary knocks him unconscious and takes the trunk. But the story advances because Decker removed the critical contents from the steamship trunk before it was taken away from him.

After Decker discovers a map in the binding of a book from the steamship trunk, his advance is temporarily "set back" when he learns that the map has no starting point. This "setback" is only an "obstacle" impeding his progress which is "indigenous" to the development of the story. Though very minor, it is still a form of conflict.

The story moves forward when Decker discovers the map's starting point. In checking out location number one, Northfield Cemetery, Decker discovers an empty strong box. This obstacle is another setback which is indigenous to the story. But at the same time, human conflict is created within the cemetery scene when an adversary shoots at Decker.

There is "minor human conflict" when Decker literally first "runs into" (in the sidewalk scene on page 32 in the screenplay) and later meets Carol Nelson as well as her daughter, Maggie, who will not reveal Alex's hiding place.

Decker's "internal conflict" in dealing with his alcohol-related problem, turns into a major confrontation when Carol Nelson attempts to stop him from taking a drink after Alex's kidnaping.

Rising human conflict continues to the most critical point when Decker's son is kidnaped by the killer. Since Decker's need in THE CRIMSON MOON is to find his missing son, Alex's kidnaping is the ultimate setback and the most dramatic segment of conflict within the story. It is the climax of all the rising human conflict leading to the story's resolution.

Within THE CRIMSON MOON, or any other story, all the various obstacles, confrontations, struggles, and major and minor conflicts strengthen the story and sustain the audience's attention and interest until the very end.

In writing Act II, work from plot point to plot point while maintaining awareness to rising human conflict. Have you accurately treated the conflict within your story? Is it strong enough to sustain the audience's attention and interest? Does rising human conflict gradually increase until the final climax of your story?

Take two screenplays from successful films and analyze the types of conflict, confrontations, and obstacles, as well as the intervals within each story. You will learn that the forms of conflict and how they are treated will vary greatly from story to story. Also, the intervals or space between the plot points and the different forms of conflict will differ significantly from story to story.

While every story is essentially the same in the way the rules of dramatic writing and screenwriting are applied, many exceptions are made in order to accommodate a story's needs. For each story, the writer must determine the treatment of every detail in order to make it work.

If you see problems within your screenplay as you write it, don't stop or go back, just make "notes" highlighting those obvious areas. This little procedure will greatly reduce any apprehension you might have on those days when you are tempted to stop and go back to improve something. You can always fix things later -- just move forward and tell your story.

WRITING ACT III - THE RESOLUTION

Once Act II is completed, you have hit the home stretch. Writing will become much easier as you work towards your story's resolution. Within Act III, from pages 91 to 120, there can be additional plot points connecting the action which leads to your story's ending; but that all depends upon your story.

STORY ENDINGS

The first ten pages of your screenplay, setting up your story, and the "x" number of pages ending it, share equal importance. In handling your story's resolution, there are a number of important things to keep in mind.

- o Endings require careful planning and flawless execution if they are to work properly. If the first ten pages of your screenplay, the setup, establishes the audience's interest, then the ending will determine their final judgment as to "how much" they really like your story.

- o Once it becomes obvious to your audience that your story is soon ending, it should be wrapped up as swiftly and as efficiently as possible -- after the final crisis has been overcome. The tighter the ending, the more effective it will be.

- o Every issue in your story must be clearly explained with nothing left unanswered.

- o Your story must be resolved rationally and logically without resorting to coincidence.

- o While today's movie audience wants and expects an upbeat ending, an unpredictable resolution or twist can greatly enhance the final outcome -- only if it logically explains itself. This type of treatment applies to every film genre from drama to comedy.

In my three screenplays, there is a basic logic behind the intricacies of each story's ending. Therefore, the technique involved has application to the resolution of all stories.

A quick review. THE 12/20 CLUB is a "mid-life crisis" story revolving around a businessman playing nightclubs with his old high school rock 'n roll band. THE CRIMSON MOON is a "plot-driven mystery story", while THE FISHIN' SHACK is a "slapstick comedy" using the sport of bass fishing as a backdrop.

The screenplay structures for THE 12/20 CLUB and THE FISHIN' SHACK were outlined between pages 45 and 50. Reread the structure so you can clearly understand the development of each story from beginning to resolution.

THE 12/20 CLUB RESOLUTION

In THE 12/20 CLUB, I wanted to avoid a "cliched" ending that might appear to be obvious from the outset of the story. And that was that Brian Hill, the main character, would make a change from his business career to music. If the story was about a group of musicians struggling for success in the dog-eat-dog music industry, achieving their goal, say a recording contract, would be very appropriate; but not in THE 12/20 CLUB for the following reasons.

AUTHOR'S SUBTEXT: THE STORY BENEATH THE STORY

THE 12/20 CLUB story is about mid-life crisis where a person's behavior is strongly influenced by emotional needs (the internal struggles) as opposed to decisive, rational action.

Many people, when they reach their late thirties and early forties, often wonder what their lives would have been like if they had pursued other directions -- such as a career in any "high risk" field where a person fights imaginable odds with no guarantee of success; regardless of talent and abilities.

At mid-life, after the day to day routine of a 15- to 20-year career in a less glamorous field, the uncertainties of a high-risk field become extremely attractive. People often wonder whether or not they would have "made it" as an actor, musician, writer, painter, photographer, sculptor, dancer, etc.

My guess is that maybe 80 percent or more of those people who pursue a career within the entertainment field (film, music, etc.) or the arts (writing, painting, etc.) struggle all their lives striving for success that never comes. And in the process, they make every sacrifice possible.

Also, many people who pursue creative ambitions often pass on financially rewarding careers in "stable industries" where they might have a tremendous aptitude and potential for success.

On top of that, because of the instability of a "creative" career field, many people pass on getting married and having children. They end up doing menial work just to survive the "interim" which ultimately lasts a lifetime.

In dealing with the realities of a mid-life crisis, either one or two things happen. First, you either rationalize that your chosen profession is not half bad. All things considered, it has afforded you a comfortable lifestyle, a certain amount of personal satisfaction, and, quite possibly, you have attained a very desirable level of "status" within your career field.

The second way of dealing with mid-life crisis is to be totally reckless and take the plunge into the unknown by following your "heart", not your "head". In real life, I opted for being totally reckless and following my heart after enjoying a successful business career.

In THE 12/20 CLUB, even though Brian Hill struggles with his mid-life crisis because of his driving desire to play music, he is still a practical man. He consciously recognizes the importance of his business career and realizes that he can still play music as a hobby.

Brian chooses his business career over music before he is terminated by his adversary who becomes his boss. This is an important point in establishing the resolution of the story. After Brian is terminated, he is then hired by a major competitive company for a key senior management position. The ending of THE 12/20 CLUB becomes stronger because Brian winds up with a major career advancement and, at the same time, retains his music as a hobby.

The groundwork for this job offer is carefully and subtly planted earlier in the story so when it comes at the end, it is a total surprise to the audience, and yet, logically resolved.

Most importantly, the final outcome is not revealed until the very last page or last minute of the story. Once Brian's situation is resolved, the story ends in less than half a page -- or less than 30 seconds. The ending to THE 12/20 CLUB is very effective because it is unpredictable, upbeat, and wrapped up quickly.

Let's examine the technique involved in ending THE 12/20 CLUB. The introduction of an object, character, or a situation early in a story which affects the resolution is known as PLANTING. This technique is absolutely essential to any story utilizing a twist or unpredictable ending.

It is my feeling that an unpredictable (and upbeat) ending greatly enhances a story's resolution if it is properly treated. In those instances, using the "planting" technique is an absolute necessity but it must be handled with great skill so it does not appear to be obvious.

When the plant is introduced, it should not consciously register with the audience. They should not see the significance of the plant until it is used to resolve the story's ending.

Here is how the planting technique was applied to THE 12/20 CLUB. The plant is the separate appearance of two businessmen who observe Brian Hill from a distance during the course of the story. Without revealing their identity until the very end, the two businessmen are visually and subtly introduced to the audience in several scenes.

The two men happen to be father and son, owners of a larger competitive company. Unknown to Brian, his secretary is engaged to the son. She becomes the primary catalyst in introducing them after he is unjustifiably terminated by his adversary who becomes his boss.

At the end of the story, through observing Brian firsthand and receiving favorable comments about him from major customers and his secretary, Brian is offered a key senior management position by the two executives.

THE CRIMSON MOON RESOLUTION

In a mystery story, the audience usually expects some kind of "twist" at the end. For the ending to be effective and satisfying, it must be totally unpredictable. When the villain is finally exposed, the audience must be surprised.

Until the various facts are revealed, no one in the audience should be able to pre-guess what happens next during the course of any story, and, most importantly, the final outcome.

The "twist" in THE CRIMSON MOON concerns "who" the real villain is since that person's identity is not revealed until the very end. In any mystery story like this, the villain can be anyone the writer chooses as long as it is clearly, logically, and rationally justified.

Throughout the story, the writer plants subtle facts, hints and suspicions about various characters showing their "potential" as the villain. Don't deliberately mislead the audience in setting up the various characters. If you point your finger at someone, there must be a credible element that justifies him or her as the potential villain.

In THE CRIMSON MOON, three characters were established as potential villains -- Jack Murphy, the detective from Decker's precinct; George Paxton, the antique dealer who dated Decker's ex-wife; and Judge Tyler, the wealthy and prominent figure in Willshire County. The treatment of each character was accurate and not misleading.

Since Jack Murphy remained in contact with Nora Decker over the years, his involvement and appearance in the end is logical and nicely sets up the introduction of the real villain, Gus Gilsum, the newspaper man.

In the case of George Paxton, he is a very strong-willed character who feels no obligation to explain himself to Decker concerning his involvement with Decker's ex-wife. His attitude and manner in dealing with Decker, as well as his actions outside of the barbershop (page 79) provide the audience with two logical assumptions.

In the scene where Paxton sees Decker coming out of the barbershop, he abruptly turns around and walks away. First, by being there, he could be the villain observing Decker. Or second, because the town of Clinton Hollow is small, it would not be unusual for Paxton to run into Decker. And to avoid another confrontation with him, Paxton turns and walks away.

Judge Tyler was revealed as the unknown accomplice who assisted "Cockeye" Eddie Malone in heisting three million dollars fifty years earlier. Therefore, his background certainly qualifies him for being the villain. But as you learned, the action which Judge Tyler takes against Decker is only to protect his life's work; the Northfield Nursing Home for destitute senior citizens.

Making Gus Gilsum the villain was my most logical choice for two reasons. First, he has no "active presence" in the story until the very end when he is revealed as the villain. That is, he is only seen on a "television" program (page 26) and through his "picture" appearing in his newspaper column (page 48). Second, he has no direct contact or interaction with Decker or any other active characters until he is revealed as the villain.

At the end, Gilsum's motives for killing Nora Decker are clearly explained. After ten years of looking for the buried money and writing about it in his newspaper column, he became consumed by greed; to the point where there was nothing he would not do to achieve his need.

I reasoned that Gilsum's character, as seen through other media within a film, via television and his newspaper column, would be "unconsciously" seen by the audience as a mere tool of exposition. Making Gilsum the villain is the best possible choice which greatly enhances the story's resolution.

After Matt Decker literally "blows up" Gus Gilsum, the last obstacle in his path, it takes two-and-a-half pages to resolve the story because the missing money still has to be explained. Until those final facts are revealed, the story should still hold the audience's attention and interest. Once Decker retrieves the money-filled duffel bag and explains the money issue, the story ends in less than 20 seconds.

THE FISHIN' SHACK RESOLUTION

Even with THE FISHIN' SHACK, an outrageous comedy, an unpredictable ending enhances the story's resolution. Like most film stories, THE FISHIN' SHACK'S plot develops in such a way that the resolution appears to be very predictable. Therefore, the audience would probably assume that Billy Tyler will achieve his need by winning the big fishing contest to save the family business.

But Billy loses the big bass contest by "two ounces" which sets up the final outcome of the story. In the end, Billy saves the family business by selling a manufacturer the rights to produce his custom-made lure which the national pro used to win the contest.

The planting technique was obviously applied to THE FISHIN' SHACK and here is how it was set up. Earlier in the story, a man involved in promoting the big fishing contest visits Billy Tyler at the general store. Before leaving, the man sees Billy's custom-made lure for sale in the fishing tackle section. He buys a handful of the lures telling the clerk it looks interesting and that he will try them over the weekend on his own hometown lake.

In the end, it is revealed that the man gave a few of the custom-made lures to a national bass fishing pro who uses them to win the big contest as well as another major fishing tournament a week earlier. All the facts were planted in order to support a logical ending. Once the final outcome is revealed, the story ends in less than one page or one minute of film time.

My unpredictable ending may be "less dramatic" and/or "less satisfying" to the audience for the following reason -- the glory of Billy achieving his goal is not shared in front of the huge audience (in the film story) observing the final outcome of the fishing contest which is really "the" big climax. When Billy sells the rights to manufacture his lure to this major lure company, his joy is only shared by his immediate family.

If and when THE FISHIN' SHACK is made into a film, the ending will be a point of contention. Will the unpredictable ending or the cliched ending be more effective? It would be my suggestion to film both endings and determine through "previews" which one works best.

FINAL COMMENTS ON STORY ENDINGS

While the planting technique was applied to the resolution of my three screenplays, it may only work effectively in two. Again, like any other optional screenplay technique, it should only be used when there is a definite need.

In the process of creating your screenplay story, after you establish your main character and his or her need, your next step is to determine the ending of your story. <u>Now that you have been exposed to the importance of your story's resolution at the end of the process, you should take much greater care in determining it when the process begins</u>. An effective and satisfying climax develops naturally and inevitably from the very beginning of the story. Also, the tighter you can make your story's ending, once the final climax is over and all necessary facts have been revealed, the more effective it will be.

CHAPTER 7: THE REWRITING PROCESS

AFTER WRITING THE FIRST DRAFT SCREENPLAY

After completing your first draft screenplay, take a well-earned rest and get away from your project as long as you possibly can. Don't read it, browse through it, fondle it, or talk about it. If at all possible, don't even think about it.

If you can, get involved with other activities. The more time you can put between completing your first draft and rewriting it, the better off you will be.

The biggest problem every writer has to contend with in writing and rewriting is "fragmented objectivity". Because we spend so much time with a project going through all the various exercises and writing phases, we become mesmerized and lose the ability to accurately assess our work. We are far too close to it and will be for quite a while. After a project is completed, it may take a year before you really see your work objectively.

If you could wait "two months" before approaching the rewrite of your first draft, without looking at it in the interim, your objectivity might be restored to 90 percent of full capacity. Unfortunately, it is impractical for most writers to wait that long. Nevertheless, you should be fully aware of the handicap you are forced to deal with in completing the various revisions of your first draft screenplay.

THE REWRITING PROCESS

No step in the screenwriting process is more important than rewriting. It is more important than all the previous steps combined.

Many screenplays require constant refinement before the real quality of the work is evident. A screenplay which might be mediocre is made great through successive rewrites and polishing. You may spend considerably more time completing your rewrite than you did in handling all the previous steps up to that point.

You may "rewrite" or "revise" your first draft screenplay two, three, or even four times until you are really satisfied. So don't feel compelled to complete the revision as quickly as possible. Give it as much time as it takes.

The rewriting process looks something like this after you have taken a break from writing the first draft screenplay.

Step One:

Analyze your first draft screenplay, rewrite it, register* it with either The Writers Guild of America or copyright it through the Library of Congress, and then take a break.

Step Two:

Analyze your revised first draft, rewrite it, and then take another break.

Step Three:

Analyze your second draft and rewrite it.

Step Four:

Take a break while two trusted readers** evaluate your second draft screenplay.

Step Five:

Evaluate the feedback from the trusted readers, make those changes which you feel are necessary, and then polish the screenplay, down to the last detail.

Step Six:

Have someone "proofread" your screenplay for spelling, punctuation, and grammatical errors.

Step Seven:

Fine-tune your final draft until you are totally confident in the way it "looks" and "reads". A professional-looking screenplay enhances the reader's initial impression and often influences a more positive response. Or, at least, it insures that it will be read.

*The details of registering your work are explained on page 130.

**"Trusted readers" refers to two people who are qualified to assess creative writing and provide you with accurate, constructive feedback.

Unfortunately, some writers adopt the half-baked attitude of, "why bother correcting my work now, it will only have to be rewritten later." Anything less than a full commitment to rewriting is a total waste of time.

If you follow all the procedures outlined for rewriting the first draft, you will more than likely see any critical flaws in your story or in the treatment of your characters; they are too obvious to miss. Initially, some problems may be difficult to identify, but through the rewriting process, they will eventually surface. Often other issues within your screenplay may bring those problems to your attention. You will quickly realize that a minor change will often improve a major problem and/or significantly enhance your entire screenplay story.

If you happen to miss some small errors (such as a misspelled word, a mistake in punctuation, a few words of dialogue that could be better phrased, etc.) when you have a final polished first draft screenplay, it should not detract from the overall quality of your work.

However, handing out a sloppy piece of work riddled with errors is a different situation. A sloppy screenplay can distract a reader's attention and create an impression that the writer is unprofessional. Too many errors may prompt a negative response from the reader, even though the story may be basically very good.

After my screenplays are "polished first drafts" and I am confidently satisfied with the results, I no longer desire to read them for one good reason: it might prompt unwarranted second thoughts about certain aspects of the story or inconsequential details. (Making changes at a later date may be necessary and very practical, but this issue will be covered later.)

Screenwriting is an imperfect art form in that most writers never reach a point of total satisfaction with their work. At any later date, when a fresh perspective is acquired, rereading your screenplay always prompts the desire to change the treatment of some issues.

Also, there is a natural tendency for writers to "second-guess" their work. That is why it is important to follow the rewriting procedures and make every effort to properly fine-tune your work through the initial phase of rewriting. You don't want to be dealing with major problems after you have circulated your work.

Before the details of the rewriting process are covered, a few other issues should be addressed.

CONSTRUCTIVE FEEDBACK

Because of our inability to see our work objectively, it is next to impossible for a writer to "fine-tune" his or her work without the assistance of at least two qualified readers. We really need other opinions on our work and someone to assist with final proofing which is a completely different function.

While it is extremely difficult to find two qualified readers, talk to your friends first. If they cannot do it, it is quite possible they might know someone who is qualified to evaluate creative writing and willing to help you. Or, you may be able to get the name of a "free-lance" reader through a film studio's story department.

Over and above ability, the value of any reader is totally dependent upon "how honest" that person is in revealing his or her findings. If the reader is a sensitive person, he or she might be reluctant to tell you the truth rather than hurt your feelings -- no matter how insistent you may be in stressing your need to know.

To reiterate an earlier point -- you should only seek advice on your project during the research stages and after the first draft is completed. Discussing your work while writing can be inhibiting and disruptive.

The only time your work should be turned over to two trusted readers is when it is fine-tuned to the point where you have "initially" exhausted your rewriting capabilities. If you turn over your project before that stage, there may be too many errors which might distract the readers from properly seeing the critical elements of your screenplay--structure, plot, character treatment, dialogue, and story pacing.

In dealing with trusted readers, you have two choices. First, you can turn over your screenplay to them without saying a word about the project and what they should be looking for. This way, they would approach your work totally unbiased and respond instinctively. If they are qualified readers, they will see things clearly. Second, you can give your readers an outline of the "review procedures" as presented in this chapter. Then they will know exactly what to look for.

I prefer the first method. If the readers are qualified, they will see all the important issues. Also, when you discuss the reader's findings later, you can ask all the questions you want which prompt spontaneous replies. In the end, you should acquire more helpful feedback.

HOW TO EVALUATE CRITICISM

A writer must be totally open-minded and receptive to input -- even if you know that the person expressing an opinion on your work is totally unqualified.

It is quite possible that someone who knows absolutely nothing about creative writing or screenwriting might bring something to your attention that may be a very accurate judgment.

At the same time, the person whom you feel is qualified and are dependent upon, may not provide accurate feedback. In some cases, the "trusted reader" might have very strong personal feelings about the subject matter that clearly influences unrealistic criticism.

How do you evaluate criticism, constructive and otherwise, from anyone who reads your material? The answer is quite simple. A writer must instinctively know if the criticism is valid or not.

If a person makes a comment about something in one of my screenplays, I know instantly if he or she is correct. And if that is the case, I will probably act upon that person's input and make the necessary changes.

If another person offers me criticism which is obviously ludicrous, his or her remarks will be ignored. A word of advice. It is a complete waste of time defending your work to any "unqualified source" because that person often has as much tenacity, conviction and stamina in defending his or her point of view as you do. Listen, thank the individual for his or her opinion, and quickly move on.

When it comes to your screenplay, there is only one rule: heed good advice, ignore frivolous comments, and trust your own instincts. Ultimately, you must decide what is best for your screenplay.

THE VALUE OF CONSTRUCTIVE FEEDBACK

In the early stages of THE 12/20 CLUB, I was very fortunate to make contact with Rita Ulrich, who had just left Warner Brothers in California as a reader. At the time we met, Rita was on the east coast visiting family and I had just "revised" the first 13 pages of the first draft screenplay.

After reading those 13 pages, Rita came back with the most insightful analysis of my work. She pointed out seven particular issues, some major and others minor. Her comments covered everything from the treatment of the story's setup, to the characters, to the dialogue, etc. Every point she made was valid as well as the solutions she proposed.

Through Rita's input, I was able to complete Act I, the first thirty pages, before she returned to California. In reviewing this work, she acknowledged my improvements and, at the same time, pointed out very subtle ways of improving other issues by making slight alterations.

It was not a question of finding someone who shared my point of view, it was simply a situation of Rita having the talent, the knowledge of screenwriting, and ability to see my work objectively. Everything she proposed was rational and logical. After that last session with Rita, I was able to approach the revision and complete THE 12/20 CLUB far more effectively.

If you can find someone like Rita, who is a qualified reader and willing to help, you will be in a position to refine your work and hone it to the point where you are totally secure with the final results.

Here is another situation involving feedback that was significantly helpful. In writing THE FISHIN' SHACK, I knowingly worked around a major element of dramatic writing in the way I treated the story's conflict. Remember, only rising human conflict is strong enough to sustain an audience's attention and interest.

Part of the conflict in THE FISHIN' SHACK is "inanimate opposition" -- a second mortgage which threatens the hero's family business. I also created human conflict, but to a lesser degree, which focused on Billy Tyler, the hero, and his relationship with two girlfriends.

By combining the conflict from inanimate opposition and Billy's conflicts with his two girlfriends, I thought the story would be strong enough. Boy, was I wrong.

I sent my screenplay off to an old fishing buddy, Steve Gass, who now lives in Indiana. After he read it, we had a telephone conversation and his remarks hit me like a brick. Steve's exact words were these, "I really enjoyed your story -- but it needs a villain." As soon as he said those words, I knew he was right. As one dairy product commercial advertised years ago, "don't fool with Mother Nature!" And the same holds true for conflict in your story.

With very little effort, I was able to write in a villain without making a major structural change to the story. I simply plugged in 12 short scenes and trimmed out a few excess comments from some of the scene descriptions. The story ended up with two additional pages after only six hours of work. Also, adding the villain improved the story's resolution. (Remember, minor changes can often improve major problems or significantly enhance your screenplay story. In this case, it accomplished both.)

Here is another example of a minor change making a major improvement. The resolution of THE CRIMSON MOON was enhanced by one change. George Paxton's character was initially written as somewhat of a "wimp" who acted nervously around Decker. Therefore, the audience would have probably ruled him out as the villain, leaving just Jack Murphy and Judge Tyler as the potential villains.

Paxton's wimpy character could have been exposed in the end as a cold-blooded killer revealing his true nature. But without somehow revealing Paxton's "potential" for being a killer, that kind of a character treatment is unfair to the audience. You might as well introduce a Girl Scout as the villain in the end.

In two scenes, Paxton's character was rewritten to make him aggressive in dealing with Decker. Then, that little scene was added when Paxton observes Decker walking out of the barbershop on page 79. The work did not take more than 10 minutes to complete but it significantly improved the story's resolution by creating three logical suspects instead of two.

SHARING YOUR WORK WITH FAMILY AND FRIENDS

You should be very selective in whom you show your finished work to. Unfortunately, it is inevitable that family members and friends may ask to read your work if, in fact, you have made them aware of your writing activities.

When you turn over your work to family and friends, you are often setting yourself up for disappointment.

Don't be surprised if...

a) They actually don't read it.
b) They read it but never tell you what they think of it unless you prompt them for an opinion.
c) They don't like it. And if they don't, they will probably say something like, "it was interesting," so as not to hurt your feelings.
d) They come back with all kinds of worthless criticism such as, "I think that Matt Decker should be a hairdresser instead of a detective." Don't laugh too soon; you will see what I mean.

REWRITING AND POLISHING

Before the actual approach to rewriting your first draft screenplay is covered, a distinction should be made between a rewrite (or revision) and a polishing.

A screenplay is rewritten when changes are made affecting more than 25 percent of what you have initially written. That applies to structural changes, eliminating or adding scenes, moving scenes, altering the treatment of characters, and so on. (For the first screenwriting experience, it is not unusual for a writer to change 50 to 80 percent of the first draft screenplay. So if that is the case, don't be alarmed.)

Polishing is best described as a "clean-up" step where your activities are confined to tightening up scene descriptions and improving dialogue.

For most writers, once the story's structure and character treatment are sound, the greatest amount of time will be spent improving dialogue. You will always find a better way of treating dialogue no matter how many times you rewrite it.

THE REWRITING APPROACH

The most effective way to approach the rewrite of your first draft screenplay is to evaluate the various elements separately.

By isolating them, you are able to focus and see things much more clearly. It is much easier to identify problems and the subsequent solutions.

If you are using a computer, it is best to work from a "hard copy" since you can write comments and notes in the margin. Later, all the revisions will be completed at your terminal.

In addition to using a pen or pencil to make notes in the margin, you can use a yellow-colored "highlighting pen" to mark sections which require special attention.

There is one basic rule which applies to rewriting: don't feel locked in to anything. If something does not work, make it better or create something that does. Flexible thinking is a key function of good writing. Sometimes, you may write a brilliant scene but it does not work within the context of your story. Be ruthless and cut it out. Save discarded scenes in a file for later use. Who knows, you may be able to work a discarded scene into another story.

Here are the steps involved in reviewing your first draft screenplay.

1. Concentrate on your story. Does it work? Is your story interesting and exciting? Will it evoke an emotional response from the audience? (Remember, the audience reacts emotionally, not intellectually, to film stories.)

   How is the rhythm, tempo, and pacing of your story? Does it drag anywhere? If so, where, why, and how can you fix it? Do the plot points work? Are they positioned at the proper intervals? Is there "contrast between scenes"? Have you properly rotated the primary elements in your story?

2. How strong are your first ten pages? And how about your ending -- does it really work? Do you see a more effective way of treating your story's setup and/or resolution?

3. Review each scene. If a scene does not have a purpose, throw it out. If a scene needs to be improved, how will you do it? Is there a need for any additional scenes? If so, why, and where will the new scene be inserted?

4. Have you fully developed your main character? Have you fully explained his or her motives and goals? Does your main character go through a progressive character change in your story? If so, what is that change and does it happen gradually over the course of the story? Is your main character likeable -- someone the audience will root for?

5. How well does your dialogue read? Does your dialogue have a purpose? Does it reveal information about your main character, his or her emotional state, or the plot? Does it move the story forward? Is your dialogue smooth? Does it flow? Is it believable?

6. Have all the spelling, punctuation, and grammatical errors been corrected?

Screenplay form is very difficult to proofread because it lacks the uniformity of all other forms of writing. Everything is separated -- scene headings, scene descriptions, camera angles, and dialogue. You have to work slowly, carefully, and look closely at the various details. If you don't, later on you will realize a multitude of minor and possibly major mistakes.

<u>We become so conditioned to reading our own work we actually read "right over" mistakes time after time.</u>

As an example. A scene heading might be written INT. when you intended it to be EXT. Or, you may have used an incorrect location in your scene heading. Sometimes, you will designate the wrong character speaking or possibly leave out a word or two in a section of dialogue. If you are not extremely careful, no matter how many times you reread that first draft and the various rewrites, you will not see every mistake.

Proofreading requires total concentration when you do it and help from other people. Take your time when evaluating and rewriting your first draft screenplay. And after that phase is completed, wait another week or so and reread your revised first draft. More than likely, you will find other mistakes and be grateful for taking the extra precautions.

If you evaluate your first draft screenplay in sections as outlined, your rewriting phase will be far more productive. Take as much time as you need. Don't rush.

Every writer must contend with agents, studios, independent producers, etc., when you circulate your work into the "system". The last thing you want to do is give someone an excuse not to read your work. You want to turn over a professional-looking script that is so well-written it is given serious consideration.

THE PROFESSIONAL READER

In one of the books I read on the film industry, a producer was quoted as saying something like, "studio readers are all egomaniacs who are nothing more than frustrated writers predisposed to trashing other writers' work." That may not be the exact quote, but the meaning is quite clear.

In every career field, there is a small nucleus (five percent) of top performers -- people who clearly exceed all others in ability, performance, and achievements. That means, out of all the doctors, lawyers, athletes, studio readers, or whatever, only "five percent" of the total are true professionals performing at the highest possible standards. From that point down, everyone else functions at different levels, in lesser degrees of efficiency.

Some major talent agencies and studios are well aware of this problem and, therefore, don't rely upon one reader's judgment. They might have three or four readers review the same material and respond according to the majority consensus.

If a writer's work is being reviewed by one reader, which is probably what happens most of the time, the writer is at the mercy of the reader. It becomes a game of roulette. Regardless of how "objective" people try to be, subjective reactions strongly influence and often dominate our opinions. Studio readers are no exception.

Look at comedy, for instance. Humor is totally subjective and reactionary; you either like something or you don't. How could a reader recommend a comedy that does not appeal to him or her? The reader cannot. That is why AIRPLANE was turned down by every studio until "someone" identified with the humor and recognized its potential. And AIRPLANE was a box-office hit.

A writer has no way of knowing how fairly and accurately his or her work is being appraised by a reader or a group of readers. Therefore, you must be totally confident in knowing that you have turned over your best possible work.

Sloppy work may distract a reader's attention and ultimately influence a negative review even if the story is basically very good. In my former career as a sales manager, I was constantly involved in hiring district sales managers. It was an ongoing activity where my skill in this area was very high to begin with and continued to improve with experience.

Careless mistakes in introductory letters or resumes tended to turn me off to people who were potentially qualified candidates. Knowing how those things influenced my judgment, I have to believe that talented readers may render those same opinions on writers. So, it may be safe to assume that a studio reader might not read or pass on what is potentially a good film story if the work contains some sloppy errors.

Another problem writers face is little or no feedback on our work from people in the industry. In most cases, the work is returned or rejected without any comments. A story could be well-written but turned down because the subject matter is simply unappealing. But not knowing that can create doubts. Next thing you know, you start second-guessing your work.

Also, a studio reader might be hesitant to recommend a screenplay if a minor flaw detracts from what may be basically a great story. Unfortunately, the reader might not realize how easily these problems could be corrected -- if only the writer was made aware of them. In any case, a writer may never know for sure why his or her work was rejected. And it is a shame, because everyone could benefit.

Some writers, after their polished first draft screenplay has circulated a while and has been constantly rejected, may believe that "punching it up" or changing certain things might stimulate a more positive response. If you really feel confident that your screenplay is strong, then leave it alone. It may be just a question of poor timing. For whatever reason, a screenplay that is turned down today may become a hot property tomorrow.

Don't make yourself crazy by trying to second-guess the market and the quality of your work. If, at a later date, someone suggests a way of improving your story, and it makes sense, then making changes might be worthwhile.

SCREENPLAY TITLE

In the literary world, the average best-selling book title is 1.8 words -- so it is not a bad guideline for determining your own screenplay title.

Creating a title that sounds appealing and is significant to your story is a practical consideration. It becomes a process of kicking around ideas until you find a title that feels good and sounds right.

The significance of THE 12/20 CLUB title ties into the story theme. Brian Hill's first professional gig as a musician was at THE 12/20 CLUB. Subsequently, 20 years later, he plays his last gig there.

THE CRIMSON MOON title hit me one day after I had determined the eerie graveyard scene at Northfield Cemetery during the full moon period. According to The American Heritage Dictionary, crimson is described as "a deep to vivid purplish red to vivid red." Somewhere else, and I don't recall where, crimson was also described as a "bloodish-red color".

In the screenplay, I created the significance of the title in the scene on page 87. Since the cemetery scene would be shot at night during the full-moon period, I assume the cinematographer, using a special filter, could capture the eerie mood described in that scene.

The title for THE FISHIN' SHACK came to me almost immediately and seemed very appropriate since fishing is the backdrop for the story.

As soon as people hear the title, they will most likely assume it is the fishing version of CADDYSHACK. In one respect, they would be right. And because of the similarities between the titles, THE FISHIN' SHACK could possibly attract a big portion of the CADDYSHACK audience. That would be a nice plus.

REGISTERING YOUR WORK

Before you turn over your screenplay to even two trusted readers, it would not be a bad idea to register it first in case the material is accidentally lost.

You can register your work with The Writers Guild of America or copyright it through the Library of Congress. This evidentiary procedure helps to establish you as the author of the work.

If a writer ended up taking someone to court over plagiarizing his or her work, a decision is not automatically rendered in favor of the person with the earliest registration or copyright date; authorship, as well as ownership, must be proven. Therefore, it would be advisable to keep your work under wraps until it is properly registered. And then, circulate it to those friends and people you trust.

In any plagiarism case, the person making the claim must prove that the other party had "access" to his or her material. As a precaution, maintain a record of "who" your screenplay copies have been distributed to. While most people in the film industry are honest, you never know when you are likely to come in contact with someone who is unscrupulous.

Since the registration procedures might change with either the Library of Congress or The Writers Guild of America, it would be best to write them ahead of time and ask for those instructions.

To "copyright" your screenplay, write or call the Library of Congress for instructions. They will provide you with the "PA" (Performing Arts) Form.

Register of Copyright
Library of Congress
Washington, DC 20540

(202) 287-9100

If you prefer, many writers utilize The Writers Guild Of America to register their work. The details can be acquired by writing or calling either one of these locations:

The Writers Guild of America, East, Inc.
22 West 48th Street
New York, NY 10036

(212) 575-5060

The Writers Guild of America, West, Inc.
8955 Beverly Boulevard
Los Angeles, CA 90048-2456

(213) 550-1000

You can send your material via "certified mail" with a "return receipt" to insure its arrival. Several weeks later, you will receive a receipt from The Writers Guild with a registration number establishing your date of registration. Attach the registration receipt with the "return receipt" from the certified mail and file it in a safe place.

CHAPTER 8: THE SCREENWRITER

THE SCREENWRITER

Writing a screenplay is something one does not approach casually, even if it is a part-time interest or hobby-related activity. It requires a tremendous commitment and a lot of work. A person must first learn the basic rules of dramatic writing, screenwriting, read and analyze screenplays from successful films; and then, go through the various steps and exercises involved in creating a finished screenplay from a basic story idea.

It is my guess that it takes anywhere from four to eight months, as a rough average, to complete a screenplay. The amount of time involved is influenced by many factors that will vary from writer to writer and project to project. Much depends upon whether or not the writer is experienced with screenwriting, or has the basic talent, or works full-time or part-time on the project, the level of commitment, how much research is involved, and so on.

If you approach screenwriting as an interest and really dig into your first project, you will quickly acquire a sense of what is involved. You will either press on and finish your project or give up early out of frustration and lack of commitment.

If you feel strongly motivated and want to make a career out of screenwriting, then the balance of this chapter will be extremely important to you.

There are eight basic qualities or attributes you must have if you are going to be a successful screenwriter. They are: IMAGINATION, DESIRE, DISCIPLINE, CONFIDENCE, PERSEVERANCE, THE ABILITY TO PITCH (TELL STORIES), A POSITIVE ATTITUDE, and PUNCTUALITY AND FOLLOW-THROUGH.

IMAGINATION

Imagination is the most important element in writing and a God-given gift that provides a person with the ability to create something from nothing.

When you write an original screenplay, you are doing exactly that -- creating something from nothing. We all write from experience but the process of conceiving and conceptualizing all the basic elements of a story, such as plot, characters, and action, is a direct function of imagination.

Does everyone have imagination? Of course. But it does vary from person to person and that is what determines the edge in screenwriting. A writer's potential is only limited by imagination. You can be exceptionally bright, have excellent writing skills, an extensive vocabulary, and total command of the English language -- but without imagination, you will not succeed in screenwriting or any form of creative writing.

If you possess this important attribute, everything else will take care of itself. Writing skills and techniques, vocabulary, etc., can all be acquired and developed through training and experience.

Imagination is also stimulated by the process of creating something. Even people who feel and say they don't have a good imagination learn that it is a hidden attribute. When a person gets involved with a creative project, the thinking process becomes heightened to the point where ideas are forced to the conscious level. Sometimes, you even end up surprising yourself. Part of stimulating imagination has to do with understanding the "mechanics" and "techniques" of the creative process itself.

DESIRE

Desire to create by writing is a strong need in every serious writer. The urge to write can come early or even late in life. So don't prejudge or dismiss any wavering feelings you have concerning your desire to write. If you really want to do it, you will -- regardless of any outside influence, whether it is supportive or not.

DISCIPLINE

To insure progress, writing requires discipline which is established and controlled by setting realistic writing goals and maintaining a firm writing schedule. It is the only way to insure that progress is made -- even if your writing is a part-time hobby.

You need to work at least three or four days a week on your screenplay project if you are going to generate any creative energy. You may only be able to write two hours a day, but that is fine.

Plan to write at the same time every day. Select those writing periods when interruptions are least likely and when your productivity is the highest. You could be an early bird and work between five and seven a.m., or a nighthawk working between eleven p.m. and one a.m.

What is a realistic writing goal? Two pages a day? Three? Ten? You decide. Productivity varies from writer to writer and from project to project. My first screenplay project, THE 12/20 CLUB, was a killer that almost buried me. I wrote six pages in four or five hours and burned myself out for the rest of the day. I can remember almost crawling out of my office wondering why I ever started with this madness.

With THE CRIMSON MOON, I averaged ten pages in three hours throughout the entire project. And even after concluding that hectic "three hour" pace each day, I was certainly capable of writing more, but I did not. Would the quality of the additional pages be as good as the first ten? No... but they would have been worth doing.

I had a good reason for not exceeding ten pages a day. Not too long after I stopped writing and refreshed myself, I was eager to continue writing. But, by waiting for the next day, I was so anxious to write I was literally bursting with creative energy, drive, and motivation. Creative inspiration soared so high during that project that if my house ever caught on fire while I was writing, they would have found my charred body slumped over the remains of my computer terminal. To date, it has been the most satisfying writing experience of my life.

Between each writing session, I think about the story's development and the new scenes to come. Through this constant conceptualization, the writing comes much easier.

In THE FISHIN' SHACK, productivity was not as high as THE CRIMSON MOON, but the overall quality of my work was considerably better. That is the value and benefit of experience.

When it comes to measuring progress as a writer, proper preparation, realistic writing goals, and a firm writing schedule are the most important factors.

CONFIDENCE

If you had to find another element of writing that would balance imagination on a seesaw, it is confidence -- in yourself and your work. Without confidence, your "hash" will be quickly settled by all those unqualified people who will tell you your work stinks and what is wrong with it without really knowing.

Keep reminding yourself that very few people are qualified to accurately and objectively assess any form of creative writing and provide the writer with effective, constructive criticism. And you are also dealing with a reader's subjective judgment as opposed to an objective evaluation.

Most people are incapable of recognizing writing talent until after it has been proven... by someone else. It requires a great deal of self-confidence and commitment on the part of an agent or producer to take a chance on an "unknown and unproven talent".

What ultimately happens to every successful writer is this. Over whatever period of time, many people will reject a writer's work until finally one day, someone recognizes the writer's talent. Therefore, you must strive to maintain a high level of unwavering confidence in yourself and your work.

PERSEVERANCE

For the writer, perseverance is a critical element that determines opportunities and influences success. It is the staying power that sustains your efforts over a long period of time. Most screenwriters don't sell their first screenplay. As a matter of fact, many, who are now famous screenwriters, have written five, ten, or more screenplays before "one" of their projects has seen production. How long does it take to break in? One year? Five years? It is next to impossible to guess because there is no formula for success.

Regardless of talent, a few writers are very lucky and sell their first screenplay for big money, no less, while more talented writers struggle for years without success. Over and above confidence, it takes perseverance on the writer's part to find that person (logically, an agent first, then, maybe, a producer) who will recognize his or her talent and see the potential of his or her work.

The writer's career cycle is one of writing and selling, writing and selling, etc., because you never know what project will be desirable at any given time. You cannot sit back with one, two, or more screenplays and assume that one of them might be saleable. You must continue to develop new projects while you sell your material and/or attempt to acquire writing assignments.

All during this process, you will be subjected to rejection, senseless insults, and frivolous criticism; they are all part of writing. These comments are not made to discourage, but enlighten you to the realities of the profession. Understand it, but embrace those elements that will ultimately bring you success. Confidence and perseverance are a must for a writer.

THE ABILITY TO PITCH

Pitching is an art, skill, and tool of selling. In the film industry, the strength of a writer's presentation can often have more influence over a producer's decision than the quality of the project itself. It may be very difficult to believe, but it is true. In reality, this premise applies to every industry. How many times have you bought something you really did not need because the person selling was persuasive or very enthusiastic?

If you are given the opportunity to pitch your story, here is the approach you should take. Starting with the title, but using no esoteric details, tell the listener what your story is about. Keep your presentation under "one minute" -- no more than three or four sentences.

You must pitch your story with confidence and enthusiasm and grab the listener with those elements of the story that are most appealing. You must motivate the listener and put him or her in a position of saying, "This is a great story, I want to do it."

Most people who are inexperienced with selling or public speaking may be totally intimidated and apprehensive at the thought of pitching their story. But, there are a number of things you can do to reduce your anxiety and bolster your confidence at the same time. First of all and most importantly, be totally prepared. Know exactly what you are going to say because that will fortify your confidence. In making your presentation, learn to pace yourself because your pitch should be no more than "one minute". Try to relax and take a deep breath before you begin. Don't feel forced to blurt out your story and race for the doorway.

Practice the delivery of your story pitch to friends and "out loud" as you drive to your meeting. You want your pitch to flow naturally and not come across as a "canned speech".

My description of THE CRIMSON MOON as outlined in the sample agent letter on page 158, concisely encapsulates the essence of the story and can be told in less than one minute. Very enthusiastically, my pitch would start, "I've got a great mystery story. It's called THE CRIMSON MOON. It's about a New York City homicide detective who is told that his ex-wife..."

No doubt about it, writers with dynamic personalities who exude charm and project self-confidence have a major advantage over those writers who don't. If you feel that you do not match that image exactly, you need not worry about it. Your awareness to what is important in being prepared, pitching, the quality of your work, and persevering with confidence will ultimately compensate for any shortcomings in the "dynamic personality" department.

POSITIVE ATTITUDE

The art of being diplomatic, tactful, displaying a positive attitude in dealing with people, and a willingness to cooperate and be supportive, is an important part of survival in every industry. But in the movie business, it is absolutely essential. The close collaborative climate of film is often volatile where, unfortunately, egos often stand in the way of good judgment.

It is certainly no secret, the greatest complaint every screenwriter has is that scripts are unnecessarily rewritten over and above the vast foray of legitimate reasons. And, in many cases, the quality aspects of a screenplay are literally and totally obliterated.

Contributing to unnecessary script rewrites are two factors. First, "everyone" thinks he or she is a writer and qualified to make changes. Second, people in power, the director and/or stars, can most easily flex their muscles by insisting on script changes whether they are warranted or not.

It is impossible for writers to protect the integrity of their work unless they produce or direct the project themselves.

If a writer's project is sold outright, other writers may automatically be brought in to fine-tune the work or punch up the dialogue -- even if changes are unnecessary. If you, as the original author of a screenplay, are given the opportunity to handle the rewrite, there is still no guarantee you can preserve the integrity of your work. But, at least, you are in a position to try.

If you are involved in rewriting before or during production, you should take pride in your work but not deal with it on an emotional level. There are a number of temperamental writers who feel their work is "sacred" and that nothing should be touched. This is a totally unrealistic and unreasonable attitude to maintain since script changes are always required.

In preparing a shooting script, there are many legitimate reasons why adjustments are needed such as: the budget may necessitate cutting scenes, a certain location may not be available so the scene has to be rewritten, awkward dialogue needs improving, etc.

Also, while a writer is usually the most qualified person concerning his or her work, the writer is not always right. On occasion, we don't see certain issues objectively because we are far too close to our work. It is a reality of writing and every writer is affected.

From a standpoint of posture, you must be receptive and flexible in dealing with other people who have direct input into your work. A writer must display good judgment by knowing when to compromise on less important issues but stand firm when proposed changes would obviously cause severe damage to the screenplay.

Sometimes, dialogue is written or phrased in such a way that it is difficult for an actor to deliver. Or, quite possibly, the dialogue looked good and read well on paper but simply does not work when played. In any case, if an actor or actress wanted certain segments of dialogue rewritten so he or she would be more comfortable in delivering the lines, I would do it without argument. My goal would be to rephrase the dialogue without changing its purpose within the context of the scene.

If a writer makes an issue out of every small detail, he or she will lose credibility and be quickly replaced. If a writer earns a reputation of being very difficult to deal with, people might not be inclined to work with him or her.

When meetings get hot, as they sometimes do, try to keep your emotions intact and logically reason with the other party or parties involved. It is easier said than done but this type of posture, in most instances, can have a far more positive impact than loud bellowing.

Don't be too quick to defend your point of view until you have thoroughly listened to the other person. This is a practical consideration as well as a courteous gesture. If you "really" listen to someone else's ideas you may ultimately agree with his or her input and possibly find a way of improving your story or, at least, fix a potential problem.

A writer should protect the integrity of his or her work and, at the same time, place equal importance on what is best for the project. That means listening to other people and compromising on less important issues.

The way you carry yourself and the attitude you project, often influences how receptive other people will be in dealing with you. These points may seem unimportant and unrelated to writing, but they are ultimately more critical in determining opportunities and success.

PUNCTUALITY AND FOLLOW-THROUGH

In the business world, the ultimate measure of professionalism is how punctual people are in showing up for appointments and following through on commitments on a timely basis. Since "time" is our most precious commodity, there is nothing more important in this world than using it wisely.

Unfortunately, a majority of people fail to recognize the value and importance of punctuality and follow-through since they most frequently deal with people who share the same attitude. However, when your business brings you in contact with "professionals" who understand and expect punctuality and follow-through, you will either succeed or fail based upon your performance in these areas. The basic rules of punctuality and follow-through are: allow for extra time in arriving for appointments and if you know you are going to be more than ten minutes late, call and advise. And when you arrive for the appointment, apologize for any inconvenience you might have caused. In regard to follow-through, don't make commitments you cannot keep; and if you are running late on meeting a commitment, advise the party involved of the delay and when you most likely can fulfill the obligation made.

CHAPTER 9: THE QUALITIES OF SUCCESSFUL FILMS

THE QUALITIES OF SUCCESSFUL FILMS

With all the demographic studies Hollywood undertakes to determine "market trends" and what the next potential blockbuster will be, the public continues to make decisions for the industry. Most frequently, the public passes on films that the studios feel are contenders for the all-time box office receipts and makes blockbusters out of the most unlikely films.

It is truly impossible for anyone to predict the success of a film. However, when you analyze successful films, there are a few common denominators that can provide the writer with some sense of security in creating and developing an original screenplay story.

As a general rule, successful movies have always been well-written, well-acted, well-directed, well-made films dealing with a subject matter that the majority of people can relate to. A film must be entertaining, have a likeable main character for the audience to root for, and an upbeat ending.

Since the industry duplicates successful films, many writers feel compelled to take the same approach. But remember this: every successful film which has been made into a sequel started as a fresh, original idea. Look at DEATH WISH, ROCKY, POLICE ACADEMY, and so on; the list is endless.

It is far more practical for a writer to create and develop new ideas by following and relying upon his or her own instinct, judgment, intuition, and taste.

What appears to be "offbeat" subject matter, at least on the surface, might become very appealing through the proper treatment. Any subject matter can be made interesting by the writer who finds the right approach.

Another point, stressed earlier, which ties directly into creating original stories is that the audience reacts emotionally, not intellectually, to film stories. So if a writer can satisfy the audience's emotional needs and, at the same time, stimulate them intellectually, it is a unique accomplishment worthy of special recognition. Many of the successful film stories listed on the next page have nicely achieved both.

Film stories centering on "human relationships" such as ORDINARY PEOPLE, ON GOLDEN POND, STAND BY ME, TERMS OF ENDEARMENT, BODY HEAT, KRAMER VS. KRAMER, TENDER MERCIES, and BLOOD SIMPLE are appealing and very practical because they deal with a handful of characters with a limited number of production difficulties attached to them.

A story focusing on human relationships, emotions, and values is a very positive area to pursue and, as proven, next to impossible to duplicate or develop into a sequel.

While every actor and actress complains about how bad today's scripts are in terms of "quality stories" with "challenging character roles", the choices for actresses are far more dismal.

Even though things are changing, we are still living in a predominantly male-oriented society where the focus, emphasis, and importance of everything is geared towards the male gender. Create an interesting story with a strong female lead character and the top actresses will kill for the part.

Writers should also give consideration to which film genres are currently popular when developing an original screenplay project. The choices are very broad when you consider the various categories and sub-categories of film: drama, melodrama, action, action/adventure, war, mystery, horror, thriller, comedy, fantasy, sci-fi, western, sprawling epic, etc.

At a time when the interest in westerns is at an all-time low, it may be very impractical to focus on this film genre. SILVERADO is a recent exception but it also had a proven talent behind the film, writer/director Lawrence Kasden.

PRODUCTION CONSIDERATIONS

In creating a story, it is important to maintain an awareness of "production issues" such as cost and feasibility. Exotic locations, elaborate sets, the number of characters in your story, the use of special effects, the degree of difficulty involved in executing action sequences and stunts, all affect production costs.

A screenplay's saleability will be greatly diminished if it is burdened by unrealistic and unreasonable production demands -- even if the story is very good.

CHAPTER 10: COLLABORATION/ADAPTATIONS

COLLABORATION

Filmmaking is a collaborative art form where the final results are influenced by the combined talents and skills of all the artists and technicians involved.

From the standpoint of writing, the choice of working with another person should not be taken lightly. If two people can be more effective working together than alone, a collaborative relationship is worth investigating.

What does it take? It takes two people who can complement each other, talent-wise, and, at the same time, develop a strong relationship based upon trust and mutual respect. Collaboration calls for a clear line of communication and compromise where egos have to be parked at the door -- whether you actually work together or handle various duties separately.

The biggest problem with most "partnerships" is that one person usually emerges as the dominant force. If you or your partner have no objection to who leads the way, then the relationship might work. However, if one person believes that the other is contributing less than what was agreed upon; or that the quality of his or her partner's work is not up to par, the relationship can quickly deteriorate. If one person constantly "keeps score" on who is contributing what to the partnership, the results will be disastrous.

If two people considered working together, it would be wise to sit down and talk about it at great length. Each person has different motives for collaborating and they should be known. One writer may find it difficult writing alone while the other has a need to find someone who may be strong in an area where he or she may be weak -- such as dialogue, etc. Or, one person may enjoy doing research while the other is great at developing story lines and characters.

In the field of comedy, many writers collaborate and effectively develop material through interaction. One writer has an idea, the other becomes a sounding board or embellishes it.

Each person must be aware of his or her potential partner's weaknesses as well as strengths. This way, each knows what to expect from the other so there are no surprises later on. We all have idiosyncracies, so bringing those facts to light can only be helpful.

One person may get "hyper" or "aggressive" if things don't develop smoothly while the other may tend to withdraw. All these things must be known ahead of time, so this means communicating.

There is no formula or standard agreement between collaborators except the ones you create. If there is potential compatibility and you are willing to try working together, establish goals and working responsibilities that are mutually agreeable.

The agreement you reach with your partner should function as a guideline with built-in flexibility. If something does not work out as intended, make the necessary adjustments without pointing fingers at each other.

If your partner does something that really irritates you, you must discuss it "only" with that person before it reaches a stage where you have an outburst. You must approach these problems rationally and tactfully, without any element of rising emotion or anger. It is a lot easier than it sounds, but a necessity if you are to maintain a strong working relationship.

Think of this possibility for a moment. Two important issues were stated before. First, minor changes can often improve major problems within a screenplay. Second, a writer needs constructive feedback from a trusted reader. Therefore, you may elect to have a collaborator work with you after the first draft is completed. If that other person can fine-tune your work into a masterpiece, it might be well worth sharing writer's credits and determining an agreeable split of the financial rewards. With the bulk of the work done by you, the other writer may be willing to put his or her magic touch to your project for 10 or 20 percent of your fees and profits.

What if you wrote a comedy and needed to have some dialogue "fine-tuned" or "punched up"? It would certainly make sense to find a comedy writer who could enhance your material.

Collaboration can be a very productive arrangement when the right people get together and work things out. If you are not sure that collaboration appeals to you, talk to some experienced writers for their advice. Most collaborations probably come out of spontaneous situations. If that opportunity knocks on your door, check it out.

ADAPTATIONS

Even if you are not immediately involved with this segment of screenwriting, it is important to understand the basic facts about adaptation. The term "adaptation" means to "adapt", not copy, from one medium to another.

If you are adapting a novel, play, short story, or magazine article into a screenplay, the treatment will be the same as writing an original screenplay.

The material you are adapting from becomes a "source". Sometimes the source material is so well-structured, you can develop it into a screenplay without a lot of modification.

At other times, adapting a novel into a screenplay can be an extremely difficult task if the story does not lend itself to dramatization. You may have to add new characters, additional scenes, and elaborate on the story line in order to make it work. It is not a matter of copying or transferring the source material into screenplay form.

When you adapt a novel, you are not required to remain true to the original material. However, if the novel is very popular and well-known, you would be well-advised to remain faithful to the original work.

If you were given the assignment of adapting a 650-page novel covering the lifespan of a woman, your approach may be to highlight the most significant and interesting segment or segments of the woman's life. In many cases, an adaptation can be more difficult than an original screenplay since the treatment requires a higher level of creative skills to make it work.

Most of the adaptation work in the film industry is controlled by the studios who acquire the rights to the source material. In that case, a screenwriter is hired by a producer who usually has very definite ideas as to how the material should be developed. Of course, the screenwriter's viewpoint and input on the source material can be extremely helpful to the producer in determining the actual treatment.

More than ten years ago, a friend, John Mastrobuono, lent me a book and told me that it would make a great film; it was long before I had any interest in screenwriting. The book was FIRST BLOOD (RAMBO). Shortly after the book came out in 1972, I would guess that the rights could have been acquired for a very modest price. It was finally optioned by Columbia Pictures in 1979 for $90,000.

While all the prime source material -- best sellers, plays, magazine articles, etc., is usually scooped up by the studios and major independent producers, there is still a glut of potential winners out there for the writer who is willing to make a careful search.

Remember, every decision concerning what is potentially a commercial property is "subjective". A producer might pass on a particular source material if he or she cannot envision a treatment that would work as a film. But a creative writer may find a way of approaching the source material and turning it into cinematic gold.

More than likely, there are many books out there that would make great films even though they never made the best seller's list. They might have been published this year or twenty years ago. Look at how many years FIRST BLOOD was around before someone recognized its potential as a film.

Maybe a friend can give you or recommend a book that he or she feels would make a great film story; something that everyone else has overlooked. People who work in bookstores are usually voracious readers so they could be another great source. Someone might be able to recommend an obscure novel that would adapt well to film; possibly, a personal favorite that the critics panned.

Rummage sales, garage sales, stores specializing in used books, are but a few of the potential sources for finding older novels that might adapt well to film. Just keep searching.

If you find an interesting book or magazine article that would make a good film story, you may want to engage an entertainment attorney to secure, check, and clear the rights for you. Ahead of time, the attorney can advise you as to the cost involved so you would know exactly what your investment might be.

Look hard enough, you just might find a real opportunity out there.

CHAPTER 11: AGENTS

AGENTS

While it is next to impossible for an unknown writer to secure an agent, it is absolutely imperative since film studios, producers, and independent production companies generally don't accept unsolicited material directly from writers. It is a step taken to avoid potential lawsuits from people who claim their work has been plagiarized.

Remember, proving "access" to the material is a key element in this type of legal action. So rather than run any unnecessary risks, most industry people deal directly with agents. In an agreement with licensed agents, studios are protected from lawsuits and have access to an endless supply of material. Agents also know which studios would be most interested in certain projects and can contact the decision maker without delay.

If you are an "unknown writer", the only time you make contact with anyone in the industry is when you have a completed and polished screenplay you are confident and proud of showing. Never submit an outline, narrative treatment, or synopsis. A finished screenplay is the only way a writer's talent can be assessed as well as the quality and potential of his or her work evaluated. In some cases, you might not sell your screenplay but land a writing assignment based upon the quality of your work.

How does an unknown writer go about getting an agent? There are two basic steps. Talent aside, who you know often determines opportunities. While this statement applies to every industry, it is significantly more important within the movie business since the nucleus of active players is relatively small in comparison to those desiring entry and work.

The first step in seeking out an agent is to make a list of all the people you know within the film industry. Make contact with them, tell them you are a writer with one or two completed original screenplays and you need an agent. You are looking for any form of assistance; most preferably, an introduction to an agent or to someone who may know an agent.

In many instances, a "firsthand" referral to an agent or someone who knows an agent can be very effective. The mere mention of a name often magically opens doors. The person making the referral does not have to be famous or even in the industry, just known by the other party.

You may have a friend, an old college roommate, a distant cousin, know of a friend's friend who may be in the industry, or be aware of someone in a peripheral business who can open a door for you.

If you are approaching somecne you have remained in contact with over the years, he or she will probably be willing to help you. If you are approaching someone you have not seen or had contact with in "many" years, it is another story. In these circumstances, don't "hem" and "haw" and say that you have been meaning to call sooner; especially when it is obvious that you are calling for a favor. Be honest and straightforward. Explain to that person what you are trying to do while expressing your gratitude for any assistance he or she may be able to provide.

<u>The practice of reaching out and contacting people and utilizing their contacts is known as "networking"</u>.

Networking is an important function of every business but especially valuable for the unknown writer. This means using the telephone, written correspondence, socializing, following up on contacts, and creating visibility for yourself.

As you develop contacts, make up an industry telephone directory so you can keep track of everyone you meet. It is also important to inform people who attempted to help you of your progress; even if their lead turned out to be a dead end. Let them know what you are doing and thank them for their help anyway. Your gesture will be well-received and greatly appreciated.

The second step in pursuing an agent is to contact The Writers Guild of America for an approved list of agents which, to the best of my knowledge, is updated on a monthly basis. It is available to non-members for a nominal fee of one dollar and it is the most effective source of finding reputable agents. The list not only provides the agencies' name, address, and telephone number, but it also indicates whether or not the agent will accept unsolicited material.

<u>Don't forward your material to anyone without first contacting them and receiving a positive response</u>.

In most cases, the agent, studio, producer, or independent production company will only return unsolicited material to the sender unopened and "unread".

It has always been my opinion that initial contacts should be handled by written communications and followed up by telephone calls. For the most part, I would be very surprised if you can, as an unknown writer, reach an agent who has the time or who is willing to talk to you; unless, of course, you are being referred by someone they know. A well-written letter often establishes a positive impression, a tangible identity, and some indication of your writing talent in the way you express yourself.

Writing an effective letter of introduction is a key to attracting someone's attention and interest. Make it short and to the point; no more than one page. The purpose of your letter is to introduce yourself and briefly describe the material you are offering. Never send a "form letter" addressed to just the agency. Get the name of an agent, properly spelled.

In describing your material in the introductory letter, tell the agent just enough to grab his or her attention. To be effective, your story description must be precisely written if it is to stimulate the agent's interest. If it works, the agent will want to know more.

A big part of the battle is getting an agent to read your material because it requires two hours that they just don't have.

While having an agent like your work is something totally out of your hands, at the very least, you want an agent to read your work. Hopefully, one out of all those who does becomes enthusiastic and wants to represent you.

Agents, as well as other people in the industry, are deluged by correspondence and handicapped by long working hours under extreme pressure. It may take three weeks or longer before an agent has an opportunity to respond, so don't be impatient.

If there is no response after three weeks, call to verify the arrival of your letter. Ask to speak with the person to whom you addressed the correspondence. At the same time, learn the name of the agent's secretary.

Being friendly with the secretary can often be very helpful. If the secretary "screens" the agent's calls and takes a liking to you, you might be passed through. Also, today's secretary might be tomorrow's agent. If a telephone call is unsuccessful, follow up with another letter restating the points of your first one.

Sample of introductory letter.

Date

Mr. Able Agent
Big Time Agency
Sunset Blvd.
Hollywood, CA

Dear Mr. Agent:

I am a screenwriter seeking representation. Having completed THE CRIMSON MOON, an original screenplay, I am confident it will make an excellent feature film.

THE CRIMSON MOON is a mystery story about a New York City homicide detective who is told that his ex-wife, whom he has not seen in 19 years, was killed in an automobile accident.

When the detective arrives in New Hampshire to settle his ex-wife's affairs, he is informed that she was murdered. He also learns, for the first time, that he has an 18-year-old son who has since disappeared.

In searching for his son, the detective solves his ex-wife's murder as well as a 50-year-old mystery involving three million dollars buried in New Hampshire by a 1930s gangster.

It would be appreciated if you would read my screenplay. I look forward to hearing from you at your earliest convenience.

Sincerely,

Robert A. Berman

If you are struggling to find an agent, there is an additional approach you can take. Contact those studios, producers, and independent production companies who are willing to read unsolicited material if the writer signs a release form. (Signing this agreement precludes the writer from taking any kind of legal action. If you are dealing with established industry people, you should have no hesitancy to sign a release form.)

In the chapter on RECOMMENDED READING, see page 177. There is a "WHO'S WHO" directory available that includes information on the major studios as well as the major production companies with an executive roster. If a producer expressed interest in your work, you could contact an agent and explain that there is a potential deal in the works. Even if it does not come to fruition, the agent still might be willing to represent you.

If you are lucky enough to sell your work to a producer or, at least, have it optioned before you were able to engage an agent, you would not be dealing with an agent problem for very long. The word would be out and agents would be contacting you. At that point, you would have to beat the agents away with a club.

A contract with an agency usually runs for two years. Within a specified period, the agent must find the writer work or the writer has the option of withdrawing from the agreement. Since everything in this world is subject to timing, it would be advisable to maintain close contact with your agent -- once or twice a week, to determine the status of his or her efforts in your behalf. If you know your agent is hustling for you but has not sold your work or acquired employment, don't be too capricious and jump ship right away. It could be just the timing so another agent or agency might not do any better.

In seeking out an agent, don't get discouraged or count on any single line of action; utilize every avenue possible and, most importantly, be creative. While every unknown writer faces a lot of rejection, keep one thing in mind -- the industry always has a need for a good screenplay. If you know you have the talent, then it is just a question of persevering until success is achieved.

One last important comment. Having an agent is a step towards establishing your career, it is not a cure-all. Many, many writers ultimately acquire the work themselves and only expect their agents to negotiate the deal. Each writer must define his or her own path to success.

AGENT POST SCRIPT

Now for the realities of dealing with agents. At the last possible moment, just before turning over this manuscript to my publisher, I wanted to relate to you my experiences in dealing with agents. But first, some background on my approach.

Using the WHO'S WHO IN THE MOTION PICTURE INDUSTRY directory, I completely broke down how many agents were listed there and how many writers each one represented. I came up with 28 agencies representing 216 of the top screenwriters. The three big agencies, CAA, ICM, and William Morris, represented 60 percent of the writers.

In calling the agencies to find out "who" to address correspondence to, I was flatly told and, in some cases, rudely told, "Don't bother." Even when I was given a minute to explain that I have completed three original screenplays in one year, I have a book on screenwriting coming out this fall, and a background in writing for national magazines, they still said, "Thanks, but no thanks. We're too busy and besides, we don't accept unsolicited material."

I then sent a brief one-page letter to all 28 agencies highlighting the three points of my telephone pitch and included a copy of the mechanics of my screenwriting book cover. Here are the results to date:

Two agencies agreed to read one of my projects. The first agent replied with a very ambiguous letter criticizing my treatment of the main character without elaborating. There were no comments as to whether or not the story was any good, or, if there would be any interest if the character treatment was improved. I wrote the agent a letter expressing my gratitude for reading my screenplay and stated that I did not clearly understand the remarks about my character treatment. I told the agent that I am very receptive to constructive criticism and eager to know more. The agent did not reply.

The second agent returned my material saying no more than, "Thanks, but it's not for me."

Like a homing pigeon, four letters found their way back to the home roost. Two agents had gone out of business or moved without a forwarding address.

The third letter came back bearing a label "RETURN TO SENDER - NO FORWARDING ORDER ON FILE - UNABLE TO FORWARD." The fourth letter had written over the entire front of the envelope in bold magic marker (in two colors, no less): "RETURN TO SENDER - UNOPENED."

Three other agencies responded with "personalized" letters stating that they could not read my material at this time, but wished me good luck. One other agency sent me a one-line form letter addressed, "To whom it may concern," stating their policy not to accept unsolicited material.

Out of the 28 agencies contacted, 18 lacked the courtesy to even respond with a form letter -- which I would have considered acceptable, since it is better than no reply at all.

Today, the power in the film industry lies with the agents because they control the talent. And for that reason, I believe that many agencies feel no compunction to reply to the hordes of people contacting them. No doubt, agencies are swamped with telephone calls and correspondence from many people, most of whom probably don't have any talent whatsoever. But, anyone who makes an effort to contact someone in business is entitled to respect and, at least, the courtesy of a reply; even if it is only a form letter. While 95 percent or more of the people contacting agencies may have no talent, there are still some very creative artists drifting with the tide; and, unfortunately, there is no selective screening so everyone, talented and untalented, is treated alike.

The agents who don't respond at all are very shortsighted because some day, the writer who is not even given the courtesy of at least a reply, will still have choices with other agencies. In my case, six agencies (the two who read and the four who at least replied) will be given consideration by me on the day I get my foot in the door. So, it will not be a question of me cutting off my nose to spite my face. When a deal is in the works, one or more of those six agencies will be more than willing to represent me at that point.

While the situation is frustrating, it does not discourage me. To the contrary, it has stimulated my creative forces to determine new ways of being recognized. It is also forcing me to work much harder at contacting directors and producers. Like all those writers before me, I will find a way to break in.

SCREENPLAY SUBMISSIONS

In reproducing your screenplay, use a high quality copier on 8 1/2 X 11 inch white paper only. At this time, the cost of reproducing screenplays on a quality copier runs a little over $10.00 a copy in lots of ten. Single copies are more than twice that amount so it is far more practical to print at least ten copies at one time. Use a standard three-hole punch and secure your screenplay with No. 5 paper fasteners; never submit it loose.

Don't use any fancy covers or binders, just a clean and simple title page as illustrated for THE CRIMSON MOON--as it appears before the screenplay.

In the center of the title page, position the screenplay title in bold CAPS; two single spaces below, Original Screenplay By; and two spaces below that, your name. In the far left-hand margin halfway between the center of the page and the bottom, designate "First Draft". One single space directly below that, the date of completion. In the far-right margin on the bottom of the page, your complete address and telephone number.

Regardless of how many times you have rewritten your screenplay, only use a "first draft" declaration on the title page. It has nothing to do with being dishonest, it is only a practical consideration.

If you were to submit a screenplay bearing the legend third draft, some people might assume that you have reached the limits of your writing abilities or have written yourself out. Therefore, if your project is optioned or bought outright, there might be a concern over your ability to complete any rewrite work. Not for one minute will anyone within the film industry believe that a writer is turning over an actual first draft copy. So, maximize your position at all times.

When you have the opportunity to submit your screenplay to an agent or production company, don't include a "self-addressed stamped envelope" unless requested. While it may be practical in one sense, it is unprofessional in another. You are investing in your career and your future. In most cases, the screenplay will be returned to you. And it may be so "dog-eared" that it should not be submitted to another agent because it will create an impression that it has been passed around a lot, and rejected. To insure a positive response, only a clean-looking copy should be submitted.

CHAPTER 12: THE CREATIVE PROCESS ILLUSTRATED

THE CREATIVE STEPS BEHIND THE CRIMSON MOON

So you can understand exactly how the creative process works, I will outline some of the basic details and steps as to how THE CRIMSON MOON story was created from its inception.

As stated earlier, most screenplay ideas come to writers spontaneously and they are either developed or discarded. Having always been intrigued by CHINATOWN, by Robert Towne, I made a conscious decision one day to write a contemporary mystery story.

From the standpoint of reading a screenplay and seeing the film, the experiences are quite different. In some cases, one can be considerably better than the other. In quite a few instances, the screenplay, as a reading experience, can be far more enjoyable than the actual film. I saw CHINATOWN when it first came out in 1974. My first exposure to the script was only 18 months ago when reading screenplays was part of my learning process. I enjoyed the film, but feel that the screenplay is even better. It is simply a great read.

After making a decision to write a mystery story, did I start with subject matter or character? Subject matter, of course. I wanted to write a "contemporary" mystery.

Before I created the main character, which is normally the next step in the process, I needed to create a "backdrop" for my story. Based upon a factual incident, Robert Towne used a water scandal that occurred in Los Angeles at the turn of the century as the "backdrop" for CHINATOWN. From that point, he developed his story.

In thinking about a backdrop for over a month, an idea finally came to mind. And at that point, my first screenplay was almost completed so I was getting anxious to line up another project. My idea was this. One of the most interesting and colorful periods in American history was the 1930s. But, as I already stated, it was my intention to write a contemporary mystery story.

Two weeks later, while I was out on the golf course "working", another thought surfaced. It just came to me that "buried treasure" is another appealing element that could be tied into my story and possibly linked to the 1930s.

I finally said to myself, "what if" a 1930s gangster buried millions of dollars in New Hampshire and it had not been found all these years? I was then dealing with a mystery that survived "50" years -- another interesting point linking the other two elements.

In trying to find a story to set up the backdrop, I researched the 1930s by reading two books on bootleggers and gangsters. I did not know what I was looking for but "knew" that if something was strong enough, it would stand out. When I was well into the second book, I read a few innocuous remarks about an incident involving Louie Lepke, a notorious gangster, and things started to click.

What I used out of those two books to set up the story's backdrop was just this -- Louie Lepke had bribed U.S. Customs Inspectors at the New York Port. They provided him with "customs stamps" which he affixed to incoming luggage containing drugs. The scam worked for about six months until other Customs officials discovered it. Everything else that I used to create the story backdrop, from the characters to the amount of money involved, was purely fictional.

My next step was to actually create a newspaper article detailing and embellishing the incident using a fictional staff writer for a fictional newspaper in New Hampshire. Why New Hampshire? I have been very fortunate to spend summer vacations there for many years which is in bold contrast to my home area in metro New York.

I developed the article going as far as setting up a "two-and-a-half-inch" standard newspaper column in order to establish a realistic look. When it was completed, I knew that I had a strong backdrop for my story. But what story? I did not even have a main character yet.

Two weeks later, back on the golf course, it came to me. A New York City homicide detective would make an interesting main character. Think of the contrast between the hero's lifestyle in gritty New York City and the tranquil serenity of scenic New Hampshire. It sure sounded good.

I was then faced with the next problem; how do I get the detective to New Hampshire? He would have to have a good reason for going there. Possibly a vacation? Not good enough; I needed something stronger.

How about the death of his ex-wife whom he has not seen in many years? She has no other immediate family, so the detective has to go to New Hampshire in order to settle her affairs. The idea appealed to me and immediately it became the "setup" for my story.

Next, I had to determine the detective's need which ultimately became the first major plot point. Several days later, the first major plot point started taking shape. I said, "what if" the ex-wife's death was first declared an accident, but when the detective arrives in New Hampshire, he is informed that she was murdered.

I knew the hook was good but wanted something stronger and it came to me right away. Again, "what if" the detective learns, for the very first time, that he has an 18-year-old son who has since disappeared. Right then and there, my story was on wheels and it started moving forward. I had immediately reasoned the son's age at 18 so he would be old enough to be independent, after the murder of his mother, and yet, young enough to be immature. The son's age obviously influenced the age of the detective. One detail influences another.

After the first major plot point was nailed down, I realized the importance of determining the ending next. For almost three weeks, I racked my brain trying to come up with a resolution that would be both visually (in a sense of physical action) and emotionally dynamic. It was a very frustrating period for me because I kept drawing a blank.

Finally, I ended up in New Hampshire on vacation and decided to do some "location scouting" to see if that would help. When I explained the project to my friend, Jerry Bernier, and asked if he knew of any "unique" or "exotic" locations in the immediate area, we spent a day driving around. As a Lieutenant for the New Hampshire Fish & Game Department, Jerry is intimately familiar with several counties, including all of the out-of-the-way places that his work would bring him in contact with.

Jerry finally took me to an old "mica quarry" surrounded by a dense woods. It is a beautiful and very impressive setting and a fantastic shooting location that is very accessible from the road. Next to the quarry's rim, as described in the screenplay, there is an open precipice that is more than fifty feet deep. Seeing the quarry and the precipice, I knew my story would end here.

I then determined who the villain would be, and why, as well as all the intricate details of the story's resolution.

Regardless of when the writing process actually begins, you will spend a great deal of time conceptualizing the key elements of your story. Something that started as a basic idea soon develops into a story. The more you do, the easier it gets. One thought prompts another and soon things fall into place.

It is impossible to predict "how much" time is involved with any step of screenwriting. So don't be concerned or become overly anxious if it takes you longer to complete a certain exercise.

Ideas come from all kinds of bizarre sources such as reading something or listening to the radio, a TV news program, or overhearing two strangers speaking, etc. Sometimes, what you read or what you hear may not necessarily be important, but it happens to trigger a new idea or possibly the solution to an issue you have been struggling to resolve.

For THE CRIMSON MOON, "book research" and "location scouting" were significant factors in expanding my story line. You may only use a small percentage of your research material, but it can make all the difference in the world.

FADE OUT: FINAL COMMENTS

One of the most exciting moments for every writer is discovering an idea for a story. The point of inception has often been preceded by weeks or, possibly, many months of futility and agony.

Step by step, the writer then begins to fill in the details until all the key elements have been defined; but, at this point, not developed, nor fully explored. Once the basic concept of the story takes shape, the unique creative process moves into high gear -- constantly building momentum.

Writing and rewriting, the process continues. Without realizing it, many weeks or months of "your life" pass by. On any given day you will stop and reflect upon what you are doing. It could be at a high point in the writing or at some moment as you struggle with a problem. Like conflict in your story, this is what writing is all about. You make advances. Then, you suffer a setback. But you keep moving forward towards your ultimate goal -- a completed screenplay you will be very proud of.

As you follow each procedure in screenwriting, keep in mind that you now have a solid understanding of the entire process so you can work from a position of confidence. Through sheer determination, you can and will overcome every obstacle in your path until your goal is achieved.

Completing an original screenplay is a wondrous experience and a tremendous accomplishment. You may be capable of writing an Academy Award-winning screenplay that everyone will enjoy and remember for a long, long time. So, what are you waiting for?

APPENDIX

RECOMMENDED READING

When you are not writing, you should read as much as you possibly can. This comment applies to reading "anything" from novels, to screenplays, to magazine articles; whatever you get your hands on.

It has always been my opinion that reading just one "how-to book" is not enough for someone learning a new skill. I strongly recommend that you read some of the following screenwriting books and film industry books listed in this chapter.

DRAMATIC WRITING

1. THE ART OF DRAMATIC WRITING
   Lajos Egri
   Touchstone Books

   Simon & Schuster, Inc.
   Rockefeller Center
   1230 Avenue Of The Americas
   New York, NY 10020

   For anyone seriously interested in screenwriting and unfamiliar with dramatic writing, this book is an absolute must. It thoroughly illustrates the treatment of character, creating conflict within your story, as well as many intricate details concerning dramatic writing in easy-to-understand language.

SCREENWRITING BOOKS

1. SCREENPLAY
   Syd Field
   Dell 58225

2. SCREENWRITER'S WORKBOOK
   Syd Field
   Dell 57647

   Dell Publishing Co., Inc
   1 Dag Hammarskjold Plaza
   New York, NY 10017

   Syd Field is one of the leading screenwriting teachers. Field's approach to teaching the screenwriting process is very well-defined. His books cover everything from the technical aspects of screenwriting to detailed analysis of screenplays of successful films. Excellent reading.

3. FILM SCRIPTWRITING
Dwight V. Swain
Focal Press ISBN 0 240 511980

Butterworth Publishers
80 Montvale Avenue
Stoneham, MA 02180

This is a well-structured manual which addresses both the documentary/factual film and the feature film. It effectively utilizes sample scripts as well as illustrates everything from dramatic writing techniques to the intricacies of creating scenes.

4. THE TV SCRIPTWRITER'S HANDBOOK
Alfred Brenner
Writer's Digest Books ISBN 0-89879-178-2

Writer's Digest Books
9933 Alliance Road
Cincinnati, Ohio 45242

An Emmy-winning screenwriter and scriptwriting teacher at UCLA, Brenner's book provides much insight beyond "TV" scriptwriting. There is tremendous depth in this book covering many diversified areas. He takes you through the progressive steps covering both the business functions as well as the writing aspects of a writer in developing a project. His book contains many helpful details.

5. WRITING TELEVISION & MOTION PICTURE SCRIPTS THAT SELL
Evelyn Goodman
Westbourne Enterprises

Westbourne Enterprises
P. O. Box 3263
Hollywood, CA 90028

Evelyn Goodman is a professional writer with many produced scripts to her credit. Her experience also includes teaching television and motion picture writing classes at UCLA. Her book provides excellent focus and depth on dramatic writing from the treatment of characters to developing a strong line of rising conflict within a story. Her book also uses a complete television script to illustrate the various points.

INDUSTRY BOOKS

If you are seriously interested in a career within the film industry, regardless of the area, you would be well-advised to read all of the following books. It is extremely important to understand how the industry functions, especially the influence and effect that politics has on one's career. Political posture may be far more important than talent, ability, commitment, and hard work. Sad, but true.

If you are a sensitive, timid soul, you may prefer a more passive career field such as full-contact karate with no protective gear. If you are a talented person of great determination and perseverance, or a sly, sneaky back-stabbing S.O.B., you will probably succeed in film.

While no one pursuing a career in film is immune to the competitive and ruthless climate, and the vicissitudes of the industry, knowing what the potential problems are is far more practical than walking into them stone cold and totally unprepared.

1. REEL POWER
   Mark Litwak
   Plume Books/New American Library 25990

   Nal Penguin
   1633 Broadway
   New York, NY 10019

   This book presents the most intelligent and perceptive overview of the entire film industry. If you want to understand how the political machinery of Hollywood really functions, read this book. Litwak addresses the various areas of film in separate chapters (on agents, writers, directors, producers, actors, etc.) relating well-known incidents as well as quoting those people brave enough to step forward and speak out.

2. THE MOVIE BUSINESS
Edited by Jason E. Squire
Touchstone Books 0586995

Simon & Schuster, Inc.
Rockefeller Center
1230 Avenue of the Americas
New York, NY 10020

This book is not an expose' on Hollywood but a microscopic view of the industry's segmented areas through the eyes of 42 professionals from the various fields of expertise. Since every subject is treated separately in a brief chapter addressed by one expert, it is easy to read and comprehend.

3. ADVENTURES IN THE SCREEN TRADE
William Goldman
Warner Books 38-385

Warner Books
666 Fifth Avenue
New York, NY 10103

A two-time Academy Award-winning screenwriter, Goldman relates his experiences in the industry over a long and successful career starting back in 1965. This book is very helpful to someone considering or pursuing a career as a screenwriter. Even writers with his talent and stature in the industry suffer indignities and abuse as his experience has proven. Goldman approaches this book with bold honesty and a strong sense of humor. Like his screenplays and his novels, this book is a great read. (The expanded edition contains the complete screenplay, BUTCH CASSIDY AND THE SUNDANCE KID.)

4. THE CRAFT OF THE SCREENWRITER
John Brady
Touchstone Books 0482-1095

Simon & Schuster, Inc.
Rockefeller Center
New York, NY 10020

Brady, author of "The Craft of Interviewing", applies his expertise to six famous screenwriters including Paddy Chayesfsky, William Goldman, Ernest Lehman, Paul Schrader, Neil Simon, and Robert Towne. A great read filled with insightful information.

5. THE MOVIE PRODUCER
   Paul N. Lazarus III
   Barnes & Noble EH 724

   Harper & Row, Publishers, Inc.
   10 East 53rd Street
   New York, NY 10022

   Lazarus, producer of WESTWORLD and CAPRICORN ONE, clearly defines the responsibilities and function of a producer. THE MOVIE PRODUCER is well-written, logically organized, and covers the subject matter with the right amount of depth and details. For the aspiring writer, this book is extremely practical since the producer is ultimately the screenwriter's boss.

INDUSTRY SOURCE BOOK

1. WHO'S WHO IN THE MOTION PICTURE INDUSTRY
   Edited by Rodman Gregg
   Packard Publishing Co.

   Packard Publishing Co.
   P. O. Box 10372
   Beverly Hills, CA 90213

   This is a directory of the key producers, directors, writers, and cinematographers within the industry. It not only lists each person's film credits, but indicates which agency represents them. "WHO'S WHO" also includes a list of major studios and production companies with an executive roster.

SCREENPLAY AND FILMBOOK SOURCES

- Coliseum Books
  1751 Broadway
  New York, NY 10019 — (212) 757-8381

  Carries screenplays and filmbooks

- Larry Edmunds
  Cinema Bookshop, Inc.
  6658 Hollywood Blvd.
  Hollywood, CA 90028 — (213) 463-3273

  Carries screenplays, filmbooks, and movie posters

- Samuel French's Theatre & Film Bookshop
  7623 Sunset Blvd.
  Hollywood, CA 90028 — (213) 876-0570

  Carries filmbooks

- Gotham Books
  41 West 47th Street
  New York, NY 10036 — (212) 719-4448

  Carries screenplays and filmbooks

- Hollywood Book & Poster
  1706 N. Las Palmas Avenue
  Hollywood, CA 90028 — (213) 465-8764

  Carries screenplays, filmbooks, and movie posters

- Script City
  1765 N. Highland Avenue, #760
  Hollywood, CA 90028 — (213) 871-0707

  Carries screenplays, filmbooks, and movie posters

COMPUTER PROGRAMS FOR WRITERS

- STORYBOARDER
  Desktop publishing for film, advertising, and television applications
  $495 retail

  SCRIPTWRITER
  Screenplay and dual column writing with intelligent page breaking; script formatting; teleprompting
  $495 retail

  American Intelliware Corp.
  P.O. Box 6980
  Torrance, CA 90504 — 213 533-4040

- MAC MOVIE FORMS;
  MAC MOVIE FORMS II - BUDGETS
  Motion picture production; budget forms
  $39.95 each retail

  ABC Software
  2050 Stanley Hills Place
  Los Angeles, CA 90046 — 213 654-2239

- WRITER'S WORKSHOP
  Organizer for writers and researchers
  $99 retail

  Futuresoft System Designs, Inc.
  160 Bleecker St.
  New York, NY 10012 — 212 674-5195

- MOVIE MAGIC
  Film and television budgeting program
  $595 retail

  SCRIPTOR
  Motion picture screenplay formatting program
  $295 retail

  Screenplay Systems, Inc.
  150 E. Olive Avenue, Ste. 305
  Burbank, CA 91502 — 818 843-6557

<u>THE CRIMSON MOON</u>

Original Screenplay By

Robert A. Berman

First Draft
September 1, 1988

Street Address
Town, State, Zip Code
Telephone Number

FADE IN:

ESTABLISHING SHOT - BROOKLYN - AT DAWN

The jagged skyline of Brooklyn casts ethereal shadows on the streets below as another hot day in mid-July begins.

INT. APARTMENT - LIVING ROOM - DAY

The apartment is comfortably furnished and, for a man who lives alone, surprisingly neat. In the corner of the room, a small table is covered with electronic components, complex wiring diagrams, soldering gun, and small, delicate-looking tools.

Near the kitchen entrance, a HUTCH displays various personal items including three framed PHOTOGRAPHS. The first picture shows a bunch of Marines posing during an R & R session. The b.g. topography, Vietnam. Another photo reveals two young marines standing next to a crate of MILITARY EXPLOSIVES. One of them is wearing a tee-shirt with bold printing across the chest, DEMOLITION DERBY. The last picture shows two rookie cops in uniform standing next to a patrol car -- their smiles not yet hardened by experience in the field. A sealed bottle of SCOTCH occupies a recessed position on another shelf. It is the only item COVERED with a thick layer of DUST.

INT. KITCHEN - DAY

Suspended from a crossbeam, pots, pans, and cooking utensils sparkle in the early morning sunlight filtering through the kitchen window. On the kitchen table, a .38 SPECIAL rests in a clip-on holster. Next to it, a BADGE and I.D. CARD. It identifies the owner as DETECTIVE LIEUTENANT, NYPD, ROBBERY/HOMICIDE.

The RADIO plays easy-listening music. MATT DECKER enters the kitchen. About forty, he is rugged-looking with a quiet air of confidence about him. He is somewhat cynical and someone who delicately walks an emotional tightrope.

Decker stands over the stove preparing a Spanish omelet with the flair and style of a gourmet chef. At the kitchen table, he slowly eats his breakfast while glancing over a street map of lower Manhattan. With a pencil, he makes notes on the map.

INT. LIVING ROOM - DAY

Decker stands over the table covered with electronics and picks up a palm-sized unit and holds it in his hand.

(CONTINUED)

CONTINUED:

It has a VU meter on the front. He places it inside the breast pocket of his suit jacket. He also picks up a small tin marked DETONATING CAPS. It goes into a side pocket. Decker clips on his service revolver. He momentarily stares at the badge and I.D. before picking it up.

INT. APARTMENT HALLWAY - DAY

Descending the stairs, Decker is greeted by ANNIE McDOUGAL -- a portly woman about seventy with a slight Irish brogue who has maternal feelings for him.

McDOUGAL
(warm, friendly)
Good morning, Matthew. I'd like to thank you for talking to CHICO. I haven't had any problems with him or his friends since.

DECKER
(stops; smiles)
Think nothing of it, young lady. It was just a question of speaking his language... You have a nice day.

EXT. APARTMENT BUILDING - DAY

A Spanish youth sits on the steps looking up at Decker coming out the door. The youth's head is wrapped in a bandage and his arm is in a cast. The once belligerent look is now somewhat passive.

DECKER
(passing him)
Mornin', Chico.

An unmarked police car sits at the curb. Decker gets into the front seat.

INT. MOVING CAR - DAY

T.J. TYNER sits behind the wheel -- a black rookie detective who is extremely competent and very serious about his work. In the back seat, JOHNNY PELLARONI, another rookie and another story. A nice-looking kid but a little immature, he tends to annoy a lot of people in the department -- especially Decker.

EXT. HIGHWAY - MOVING UNMARKED POLICE CAR

crosses over the Brooklyn Bridge and heads downtown.

EXT. STREET - LOWER MANHATTAN - DAY

Decker, Tyner, and Pellaroni get out of their car and walk briskly to the entrance of an apartment building.

INT. EMPTY APARTMENT - DAY

Across the street on the third floor of an empty apartment is unit two commanded by ROCCO MATELLI. He is a street-wise detective in his late forties with a face chiseled from stone and a body designed by "pasta fagioli." His fledgling partner is DAN KAMANSKI -- a tall, thin, wisecracking kid whose mouth often functions before his brain.

In the kitchen, Matelli sits on a crate where the refrigerator once stood -- a danish in one hand, cup of coffee in the other, a newspaper across his lap, and a cigarette dangling from his lips. Matelli looks up to see Kamanski leaning out of the open window with his elbows resting on the sill.

MATELLI
Kamanski! We're on stake-out --
we're not here to watch a parade.

Kamanski pulls back from the window.

EXT. APARTMENT ROOFTOP - DAY

Across the street, Decker leads Tyner and Pellaroni over rooftops in single file. They pass a CLOTHESLINE with laundry hanging out to dry. Pellaroni stops and holds up a HUGE BRA hanging on the line. Decker and Tyner turn and look at him.

PELLARONI
(big grin)
Hey, Lieutenant, look at this --
an artillery jacket for the Guns
Of Navarone!

Decker shakes his head and gestures for Pellaroni to follow.

INT. EMPTY APARTMENT - DAY

Kamanski sits glued to the window and eagle-eyes the street below. Matelli looks up from his newspaper...

MATELLI
Any sign of our boy yet?

(CONTINUED)

CONTINUED:

KAMANSKI
Nope... but look, Rocco, an Italian catering wagon is coming down the street.

Matelli moves his big hulk to the window and looks down to the street. A BIG GARBAGE TRUCK is making pickups.

MATELLI
(exploding)
Kamanski -- if that's an Italian catering wagon then what it serves would be a gourmet meal for a dumb Polack like you.

KAMANSKI
(laughing)
Take it easy, Rocco. I'm only kidding.

Matelli walks back to his seat muttering...

MATELLI
Why do I always get stuck with these idiots.

A few moments later, Kamanski comes to attention. A long-haired freak walks down the street carrying what looks like a guitar case. Kamanski motions to Matelli and picks up his TWO-WAY RADIO.

KAMANSKI
(clutching the radio)
Unit two to unit one.

A sharp CRACKLING SOUND.

DECKER (v.o.)
Go ahead, unit two.

KAMANSKI
CRUISER just entered the building.

EXT. ROOFTOP ENTRANCE - DAY

DECKER
(on two-way radio)
This is unit one to all units. Give our boy five minutes to settle in. Then, unit three, you handle the evacuation of the second floor tenants.
(MORE)

(CONTINUED)

CONTINUED:

DECKER (Contd.)
It must be done quietly so we don't tip our hand. All other units hold your positions until further orders.

INT. APARTMENT BUILDING - DAY

Decker, Tyner, and Pellaroni make their way to the second floor. From the stairwell, Decker looks towards the suspect's apartment at the end of the hall.

Quietly, uniformed policemen knock on second floor doors and escort puzzled tenants out of the building. Decker gestures for Tyner and Pellaroni to follow behind him.

Soon, the SOUND of a CONTEMPORARY SONG with an infectious beat filters through the walls of the suspect's apartment. Decker and Tyner turn to see Pellaroni strutting behind in animated dance steps. Decker's eyes turn ice cold. He grabs Pellaroni by the arm and drags him back to the stairwell.

DECKER
(firmly with authority)
Look, Pellaroni, we're here to arrest two contract killers -- so if you want to go home in a body bag, just keep it up.

Pellaroni stands frozen. Decker releases his grip on him and moves quietly towards the suspect's door.

INT. HALLWAY - DAY

Decker looks at the door. It is covered with HEAVY STEEL PLATES. He rubs the back of his neck with his right hand. He looks tense. He waves his arm and a policeman delivers a box marked EXPLOSIVES to his feet.

Decker efficiently applies the putty-like explosives to the door frame. He then takes the DETONATING CAPS from the small container and presses them into the charges. Cautiously, he backs away from the door.

The back-up team stands near the stairwell, poised and ready for action -- helmets, flack vests, and riot shotguns. Decker reveals the small detonating device. He flicks the sliding lever and the VU needle jumps to red. In a THUNDEROUS EXPLOSION, the door is blown off the hinges.

INT. HALLWAY - THE BACK-UP TEAM

rushes into the suspect's apartment through clouds of billowing SMOKE. From INSIDE the apartment, automatic weapons open up. In a hail of automatic gunfire, the police squad retreats to the hallway dragging two wounded officers.

INT. HALLWAY - DAY

A uniformed sergeant stands at the side of the suspect's doorway and calls into their apartment.

SERGEANT
Give up -- you don't stand a chance.

One of the killers, with a demonic face and piercing eyes, appears from inside the apartment with an automatic weapon. He FIRES four long bursts towards the police flanking the front door. The bullets chew up the walls with a LOUD STRAFING SOUND. At the same time...

KILLER
(yelling insanely)
F*#% you, a*#hole -- take us if you can!

The sergeant and the back-up team hug the hallway wall. Decker gestures for Tyner, Pellaroni, the cop handling the explosives, and two back-up cops to follow him.

INT. STAIRWELL - DAY

Decker and his crew descend one flight of stairs.

INT. HALLWAY - DAY

Decker and his crew proceed to the apartment directly below the suspect's. A uniformed cop escorts the young woman living there out of the building. She is eager to go.

INT. APARTMENT - LIVING ROOM - DAY

Decker quietly leads his team into the living room and motions for everyone to be quiet. He patiently listens to the MUFFLED VOICES and SCUFFLING FEET from above. Strategically, Decker applies the plastic explosives to the ceiling and inserts the small detonating caps.

From behind the kitchen wall, Decker and the back-up team wait. Decker sets off the charges using the small detonating device.

INT. APARTMENT - LIVING ROOM - DAY

The ceiling collapses in a DEAFENING ROAR. Along with portions of the ceiling and furniture from the apartment above, the two killers drop to the floor like sacks of potatoes. Clouds of dust rise from the floor as the back-up team moves in.

Crawling on his knees in a daze, one killer tries to raise his weapon. He is not fast enough. Decker's foot delivers a smashing blow to the side of his face.

A uniformed cop looks at the gaping hole in the ceiling and the amount of devastation to the apartments.

COP
(to Decker)
Hey, Lieutenant, I don't think they're gonna be happy with you on this one.

Decker ignores the remark and walks out of the apartment with Tyner and Pollaroni following.

INT. 23RD PRECINCT - DETECTIVES' SQUAD ROOM - DAY

Matelli sits at his desk. When Decker passes...

MATELLI
Lieutenant, I just checked with the hospital. SAVINO and JACKSON will be all right.

DECKER
Thanks, Rocco.
(walking away)
Keep me posted on their condition.

At the door to his office, a secretary stops Decker.

SECRETARY
Lieutenant, the Captain would like to see you now.

Decker walks across the squad room to a door marked, CAPTAIN JACK McCAFFEY, Chief of Detectives. He knocks and enters.

INT. McCAFFEY'S OFFICE - DAY

McCaffey, a twenty-eight year veteran of the police department, is a strong figure with a distinguished face. He is a man who maintains tight control over his men. That is, with the exception of Decker.

(CONTINUED)

CONTINUED:

Decker stands in front of the Captain's desk while McCaffey reads Decker's report. Every so often, McCaffey looks up at Decker and finally closes the folder.

McCAFFEY
Lieutenant, this fiasco today will probably cost the city over sixty thousand dollars -- and we were very fortunate in not having any serious civilian or police fatalities.

DECKER
Considering the fortifications of their apartment, Captain, I did what I had to.

McCAFFEY
(pause; and then)
I'll accept this report. But I've got a real problem with your methods of questioning suspects -- I'm referring to SAL BRAVARO. His partner found him unconscious on the floor of their pizza parlor moments after he saw you leave.

DECKER
So, what's the problem?

McCAFFEY
(angrily)
What's the problem? The man was unconscious. His face was covered with pizza dough. There was tomato sauce in his hair. Two black olives were protruding from his nostrils. And, slices of pepperoni were hanging out of his ears!... You made a pizza out of his face!

DECKER
(firing back)
Look Captain, I'm tired of our liberal judicial system that provides loopholes for criminals. I'm just trying to get the job done and balance out some of the inequities.

(CONTINUED)

CONTINUED:

McCAFFEY
(with rising anger)
Damn it, Decker,.. you can't go around administering your own brand of justice. How many times have we had this conversation?...

Decker stands silent and, finally...

DECKER
... Is there anything else, Captain?

McCaffey shakes his head in frustration. Then, in a more normal tone...

McCAFFEY
Matt, please take a seat... I need to talk to you about something personal.

Reluctantly, Decker sits down. The obvious change in the Captain's posture and tone of voice convinces Decker that unpleasant news is forthcoming.

McCAFFEY
(continuing)
I received a telephone call from the New Hampshire State Police an hour ago... They informed me that NORA was killed in an automobile accident yesterday... I'm sorry.

Decker looks directly at the Captain showing no sign of emotion. It registers with McCaffey.

McCAFFEY
(continuing)
Matt -- did you understand what I said?

Decker nods his head ever so slightly.

DECKER
... Captain, Nora and I were divorced nineteen years ago -- I haven't seen or heard from her since.

McCaffey walks around his desk and stands near Decker.

(CONTINUED)

CONTINUED:

McCAFFEY
According to this LIEUTENANT BRANFORD from the New Hampshire State Police, it's quite possible that you may be Nora's closest surviving relative. If you'd like, I can arrange for you to take some personal time off... Again, I'm sorry.

Without saying another word, Decker gets up and leaves the Captain's office. McCaffey shakes his head.

INT. DETECTIVES' SQUAD ROOM - DAY

A rare moment of solitude. No longer the center of bustling activity. The detectives finish up reports and make calls home as their shift draws to an end. Sitting at a desk across from Matelli, Kamanski starts in...

KAMANSKI
Hey, Rocco, did I ever tell you about that Italian girl I used to date?

Skeptically, Matelli looks up from his desk at Kamanski but does not reply.

KAMANSKI
This girl was something else!

PELLARONI
(butting in)
Yeah! And I bet her name was MARIA?

KAMANSKI
(looking at Pellaroni)
Wrong, Pepperoni -- she was a vision from Venice -- long, black hair, soft olive skin, and dark eyes. Her name was... BRUNO.

Like a bolt of lightning, Matelli jumps to his feet.

MATELLI
Keep it up, a*#hole, and you'll be assigned to scraping up dog s*#t from the sidewalk.

KAMANSKI
(laughing)
I'm only kidding, Rocco. No need to get your a*# all jacked up.

INT. DECKER'S APARTMENT - LIVING ROOM - NIGHT

Decker sits in his comfortable armchair listening to the RADIO and reading the newspaper. The TELEPHONE RINGS but he ignores it.

He walks towards the kitchen. At the hutch, he pauses. From the bottom drawer, he pulls out an envelope filled with photographs and takes one out.

INSERT OF PHOTOGRAPH

showing Decker and Nora many years ago. She looks beautiful -- almost radiant with her dark hair, dazzling eyes, and warm smile.

BACK TO SCENE

The more Decker studies the picture, the tighter his face becomes. He puts the envelope back. His eyes lock on the dust-covered bottle of Scotch. He stares at it for quite a while. He rubs the back of his neck with his right hand and then, slowly turns away.

Decker picks up the telephone.

DECKER
(on phone)
... This is Lieutenant Decker from the 23rd Precinct. I'd like to know the condition of officers Savino and Jackson?... Thanks, I'll be by early tomorrow morning.

INT. 23RD PRECINCT - DETECTIVES' SQUAD ROOM - DAY

Matelli, Tyner, Pellaroni, and a few other detectives are busy interviewing assorted riffraff.

Seated across from Tyner is JIMMY SLICKS, a wide-eyed bundle of nervous energy twitching anxiously.

TYNER
Okay, Jimmy Slicks -- what can you tell me about FRASER'S murder?

SLICKS
(rubbing his hands together rapidly)
Nothin', man.

TYNER
Come on, Jimmy, you were near the alley when somebody aired him out.

(CONTINUED)

CONTINUED:

SLICKS
(rubbing the back of
his hand across his chin)
Honest, man, I dunno a thing.

Decker walks by Tyner's desk. DETECTIVE LIEUTENANT RON MIZAK enters the squad room. In his early forties, Mizak is tall, trim, and the outgoing organizer for the department's social events -- as well as Decker's.

MIZAK
(calling out)
Hey, Matt!

Decker turns to see Mizak's smiling face. In the b.g...

TYNER (o.s.)
Stop jiving my a*#, Jimmy, and
give me some news.

DECKER
Hi, Ron. How's the vice division
doing today?

MIZAK
(smiling)
Just great. We busted a Park
Avenue hooker last night. And
guess who was wearing a leather
saddle strapped to his back?...
COUNCILMAN SAYERS! Some of the
guys wanted to enter him in the
third race at Belmont but...
(putting his arm
around Decker)
We'll see you at seven-thirty
tonight for dinner -- right?

DECKER
Right. I'll see you then.

Mizak walks out of the squad room...

MATELLI
(to Decker; lighting
up a cigarette)
Hey, Lieutenant, I overheard Lt.
Mizak talking to his wife this
morning...
(smiling)
It looks like they're fixing you
up with another blind date.

(CONTINUED)

CONTINUED:

DECKER
(exasperated)
It looks like I'll have to put a stop to this business.

MATELLI
(shaking his head)
Poor girl...

INT. APARTMENT HALLWAY - NIGHT

Decker knocks on the door. Ron Mizak's smiling face appears on the other side, "Come on in, Matt."

INT. MIZAK'S APARTMENT - LIVING ROOM - NIGHT

Ron leads Decker into the living room. Ron's wife, LINDA, gives him a big hug and kiss. Like her husband, Linda is bright, trim, and energetic.

LINDA
It's so good to see you, Matt. You look terrific. I'd like you to meet SARAH STRATON.

Sarah Straton is attractive but obviously very prim. Decker extends his hand to her and smiles.

LINDA
(continuing)
Sarah teaches classical literature at Kinley-Adams. It is Brooklyn's most elite private school. Now if you'll excuse me, I need to tend to our dinner.

MIZAK
(ushering them to a love seat)
You two get acquainted, I'll be right back with the drinks.

Decker waits until Ron is out of the room and then...

DECKER
Is it true that the teachers at Kinley-Adams are promiscuous?

Sarah is mortified. She cannot believe what she just heard. Ron re-enters the living room. He gives Sarah a glass of white wine and Decker his usual, a club soda with a lime twist.

(CONTINUED)

CONTINUED:

MIZAK
I'll be right back with the hors d'oeuvres.

DECKER
(leaning towards Sarah)
You look like the muscatel type to me -- someone who takes a hit on a pint bottle between classes.

Shocked, Sarah pulls back from Decker. Ron re-enters the living room with the hors d'oeuvres and realizes, from Sarah's expression, what Decker is up to.

MIZAK
You know, Sarah, Matt has a great sense of humor.

SARAH
(to Ron but looking coldly at Decker)
Oh? You think so?

A LITTLE LATER, Linda enters the living room...

LINDA
Dinner is ready everyone.

Decker follows Sarah into the dining room. On the way in he whispers quietly into her ear...

DECKER
Why don't we take a ride into the Bronx later and strip a few cars.

Sarah moves quickly away from Decker and takes a seat across from him at the dining room table.

INT. DINING ROOM - NIGHT

Sarah keeps her nervous eyes glued on Decker. Ron gestures to Decker to "cut it out." Linda enters the dining room with a large oven-stuffer.

DECKER
(standing up; to Linda)
If you don't mind, I'll carve.

LINDA
Matt is an accomplished chef, Sarah. He could easily open up his own restaurant.

(CONTINUED)

CONTINUED:

Sarah smiles but not for long. Standing over the bird, Decker produces a GIANT SWITCHBLADE KNIFE that literally jumps in his hands when he snaps it open. He proceeds to carve. Mortified beyond belief, Sarah rises from her seat and...

SARAH
That's it! I'm leaving.

Sarah exits the dining room with Linda following and calling after her. Ron sits at the table shaking his head in exasperation.

MIZAK
You had to do it, didn't you?

DECKER
(a big smile)
How 'bout a nice breast?

EXT. STREET - LOWER MANHATTAN - DAY

From a distance, we see Decker and Tyner talking to street people hanging out on corners and outside of bars. All of them appear reluctant to talk. They shake their heads "no" to the questions they are being asked.

INT. UPPER EAST-SIDE RESTAURANT - MANHATTAN - DAY

In a private dining room, Decker and Tyner enjoy a sumptuous luncheon with ARMAND RIVEAU, the owner/chef of the posh east-side restaurant. Attentive waiters in tuxedos efficiently respond to Riveau's subtle gestures. Tyner is both impressed and amused as Decker and Riveau discuss the culinary arts and exchange recipes.

EXT. APARTMENT BUILDING - NIGHT

Decker's car pulls into the parking lot of an apartment building. He walks briskly towards the front entrance.

INT. APARTMENT - BEDROOM - NIGHT

Decker is lying on his back in bed with his hands clasped behind his head. He looks relaxed. In the b.g., the SOUND of RUNNING WATER.

FEMALE VOICE (o.s.)
Matt, why don't we go out tonight? There's a bunch of people from my office who'll be at Harry's Bar.

(CONTINUED)

CONTINUED:

When Decker does not respond, NANCY TODD enters the bedroom wearing a terrycloth bathrobe drying her hair with a towel. In her thirties, she is an attractive, bright, and sensuous woman of the world.

NANCY
Matt?... Did you hear me?

DECKER
... Not tonight, Nancy.

Before speaking again, Nancy pauses.

NANCY
(congenial)
Come on, honey, let's go out for a change?

DECKER
Not tonight.

Nancy's soft tone radically changes.

NANCY
(very deliberate)
Not tonight? Matt, we haven't been out together in four months... All you do is come here...
(forcing the words)
for sex. You show no emotion and no interest in anything else!

DECKER
(sitting up in bed)
Nancy, when we first started going out, I told you that there would be no commitments from me -- you understood that.

NANCY
(emotions rising)
That's fine, Matt. I'm not looking for a commitment, but I feel like I'm being used just to satisfy your sexual desires... There's got to be more to a relationship than just sex -- at least for me...

Decker remains silent as he gets out of bed and begins to dress. Nancy walks to the window and looks outside.

(CONTINUED)

CONTINUED:

She softly addresses Decker with her back towards him.

NANCY
(calmly but
emotionally drained)
Matt... I can't handle this dead-
end relationship any more...
please leave.

Nancy weeps quietly as Decker stands behind her. She thinks he is going to say something but he does not. She HEARS his RETREATING FOOTSTEPS and the FRONT DOOR SHUT. Knowing the relationship is over, she drops to the bed and weeps.

INT. 23RD PRECINCT - DETECTIVES' SQUAD ROOM - DAY

Kamanski and Pellaroni enter the squad room together. Matelli, Tyner, and the other detectives are already busy writing reports, making telephone calls, and interviewing people.

Matelli looks up from his desk at Kamanski and smiles to Tyner. As usual, Kamanski drops into his chair and reaches into the top right drawer of his desk. There is a LOUD SNAPPING SOUND. Kamanski SCREAMS in pain as he pulls his hand from the desk drawer with a MOUSE TRAP clamped to his fingers. Everyone in the squad room breaks into laughter.

Kamanski looks at Matelli who just smiles back at him. When he attempts to get up from his chair, Kamanski's pants are stuck to the seat with SUPER GLUE. More laughter. Kamanski gets up in a hunched-over position and tries to walk with the chair glued to his seat. The detectives go berserk with laughter.

KAMANSKI
(very annoyed)
Goddamn wise guys.

INT. DECKER'S OFFICE - DAY

Decker meets with Tyner.

DECKER
(to Tyner)
Why don't you look into that bar
on Second Avenue, Mateland's.
Frazer used to hang out there.

(CONTINUED)

CONTINUED:

TYNER
(taking notes)
Okay. I'll also check out that massage parlor he used to frequent on the west side.

Decker's intercom BUZZES. He flips the switch. It is the Captain's secretary, ANGIE. Her mellifluous voice brings a smile to Decker.

ANGIE (v.o.)
Lieutenant, Captain McCaffey is ready to see you now.

DECKER
(flipping the switch)
Thanks, Angie, I'll be right there.

INT. McCAFFEY'S OFFICE - DAY

McCaffey is on the telephone when Decker enters.

McCAFFEY
(on phone)
Yes, MR. BLAUSTEIN, I'll consider your proposal and get back to you later...
(hanging up; to Decker)
That was Bravaro's attorney, he's willing to drop police brutality charges against you if we reduce the charges against JACK SLINEY.

Decker shakes his head. As usual, he does not take a seat. He stands over the Captain's desk.

McCAFFEY
(pause; and then)
I see you requested some personal time off starting tomorrow.

DECKER
That's right, Captain. I need to go to New Hampshire to settle Nora's affairs.

McCAFFEY
All right... But you have an appointment with MS. RHOADES today at five o'clock. Make sure you keep it.

Decker turns and leaves the Captain's office.

EXT. MIDTOWN MANHATTAN - DAY

Decker crosses Third Avenue and enters an office building. On the way in, a uniformed cop standing in front recognizes Decker and throws him a salute.

INT. OFFICE BUILDING LOBBY - DAY

Decker looks a little tense as he waits for the elevator. He rubs the back of his neck with his right hand. The elevator door opens and a large group of anxious-looking office workers spills into the lobby. Decker enters the elevator. The doors close.

INT. HALLWAY - DAY

The name on the door reads, BARBARA RHOADES, PSYCHOLOGIST. Decker draws a deep breath and enters.

INT. PSYCHOLOGIST'S OFFICE - DAY

Decker sits in a chair. Barbara Rhoades sits behind her desk and looks at Decker. In her early forties, she radiates sensuality with fiery red hair and a sleek physique. It is obvious that Decker is very reluctant to be here as he shifts around in his seat.

RHOADES
(casually)
So, Matt, how are things going this week?

DECKER
About the same -- I guess.

RHOADES
Oh?... I understand that your ex-wife was just killed in an automobile accident -- that's quite significant?

DECKER
... As you know, my marriage went down the toilet nineteen years ago. I haven't had contact with my ex-wife since...

RHOADES
(pause; and then)
How do you feel about her death?

DECKER
... I feel saddened by it -- but that's all...

CONTINUED:

RHOADES
... How is your relationship with
Nancy Todd doing?

DECKER
... It ended this week.

RHOADES
(pause; and then)
Let's talk about it.

DECKER
There's nothing to talk about.

RHOADES
... Matt, why don't you let me be
the judge of that...

Decker sits impassively.

RHOADES
(continuing)
By holding back in these sessions,
I can't help you. More
importantly, you can't help
yourself... What about your
drinking problem?

DECKER
It has been six months, two weeks,
eight days, and --
(looking at his watch)
twelve hours since my last drink.

Rhoades is alarmed by Decker's detailed response.

RHOADES
... Are you still -- "sitting on
the edge" as you so aptly put it?

DECKER
The urge is always there.

DISSOLVE TO:

LATER THAT HOUR

RHOADES
Matt, there's one subject I want
you to discuss -- it has been
fifteen years since the death of
your ex-partner, JACK DRYER.

(CONTINUED)

CONTINUED:

Decker quickly stands up.

DECKER
(emphasizing each word)
The subject is closed for discussion.

RHOADES
(firmly)
Matt, you can hide everything from me -- but not yourself. If you continue to suppress these problems, things will only get worse for you.

DECKER
(looking at his watch)
Ms. Rhoades, my hour is up.

Decker turns and leaves Rhoades standing alone. She is both disappointed in not being able to help Decker and concerned for him as well.

INT. DECKER'S APARTMENT - BEDROOM - DAY

Decker enters his bedroom and places his shaving kit in the suitcase on the bed. He closes the suitcase and turns off the lights.

EXT. HIGHWAY - DECKER'S MOVING CAR

glides swiftly with the early morning traffic. The Manhattan skyline gradually fades in the b.g.

TIME CUT TO:

EXT. HIGHWAY - DECKER'S MOVING CAR

crosses over the Connecticut River and passes a large sign: WELCOME TO NEW HAMPSHIRE - THE GRANITE STATE.

INT. DECKER'S MOVING CAR - DECKER'S POV

looking at the scenic countryside and rolling hills of New Hampshire.

INT. DECKER'S MOVING CAR - DAY

CLOSE ON DECKER

He sits casually behind the wheel. There are no signs of tension in his face. He actually looks relaxed. The RADIO plays softly in the b.g.

EXT. HIGHWAY - DECKER'S MOVING CAR

passes a sign, CLINTON HOLLOW - 8 MILES. Around the next bend in the road, he pulls his car into the NEW HAMPSHIRE STATE POLICE - TROOP B BARRACKS. Decker parks next to a state police cruiser and gets out.

EXT. NH STATE POLICE BARRACKS - DAY

On the walkway to the front entrance, Decker passes two big state troopers in their mid-twenties. They are all spit and polish. Decker looks at them with amusement.

INT. NH STATE POLICE BARRACKS - FRONT DESK - DAY

A burly-looking sergeant stands behind the front desk.

SERGEANT
Can I help you, sir?

DECKER
The name is Matt Decker. I'd like to see Lt. Branford concerning the death of my ex-wife.

SERGEANT
(on telephone)
... Lieutenant, there's a Mr. Decker here to see you... Okay, sir.
(hanging up receiver)
Mr. Decker, third door on the right down the corridor.

Decker thanks the sergeant and walks down the corridor. He stands in front of a door marked, LIEUTENANT GERALD BRANFORD. He knocks and enters.

INT. BRANFORD'S OFFICE - DAY

Branford stands behind his desk. In his late forties, he is tall with close-cropped hair. He looks ex-marine and all business.

BRANFORD
(extending his hand)
Mr. Decker, Lt. Branford. I'd like to offer my condolences over the death of your ex-wife.

DECKER
(taking a seat)
Thank you, Lieutenant... I'm here to settle her affairs.

(CONTINUED)

CONTINUED:

BRANFORD
Mr. Decker, the report on your ex-wife is being changed from an accidental death to homicide...

DECKER
(genuinely surprised)
What?

BRANFORD
Late yesterday afternoon, a witness came forward and testified that your ex-wife's vehicle was forced off the road causing it to strike a tree head-on. She died from severe internal injuries before the paramedics arrived.

DECKER
Was it a drunk driver?

BRANFORD
Given the extensive details from the witness, I'd have to say no.

DECKER
Can I see the witness' statement?

Branford hands Decker the report. Decker reads it thoroughly, looks up at Branford, and...

DECKER
I see what you mean... All you have is a description of a black, sporty, late-model, two-door coupe with tinted glass. From this description, it could be a Firebird, a Trans Am, a Camaro, or possibly a Chevy Z-28...
(shaking his head)
No license plate!

BRANFORD
... One other thing, Mr. Decker, we've been unable to locate your son, ALEX.

DECKER
(taken back)
What are you talking about, Lieutenant, I don't have a son.

CONTINUED:

BRANFORD
You have an eighteen-year-old son named Alex.

DECKER
That's impossible.

BRANFORD
The county D.A. obtained the records from your wife's safe deposit box. In there with other documents was a birth certificate naming you as the father.

Decker is stunned. He cannot believe it.

DECKER
... How is it possible? I haven't seen or heard from my ex-wife in nineteen years?

BRANFORD
It's obvious, when you and your wife broke up, she was pregnant.

DECKER
(confused)
... But why the hell wouldn't she have told me?

BRANFORD
... I'm sorry -- but I can't answer that question.

DECKER
If I do have a son -- what are the circumstances concerning his disappearance?

BRANFORD
So far, all we know is that he disappeared the day of his mother's death and he hasn't been seen since... We've filed a missing person report with all the state and local law enforcement agencies throughout New England.

DECKER
Can you provide me with some information on my ex-wife and son? I'd like to look for him myself.

(CONTINUED)

INT. NH STATE POLICE BARRACKS - FRONT DESK - DAY

Decker stands near the front desk. Lt. Branford hands him a set of keys and several pieces of paper.

BRANFORD
(firmly with authority)
Mr. Decker, I am providing you with this information under one condition. And that is, you confine your activities to searching for your son. If you interfere in your ex-wife's homicide investigation, no professional courtesy will be extended to you -- do I make myself clear?

DECKER
I understand your position, Lieutenant, thanks.

Decker shakes Branford's hand and exits the barracks.

INT. DECKER'S MOVING CAR - DAY

Decker drives as if he were in a trance.

INT. DECKER'S MOVING CAR - DECKER'S POV

passing a sign, CLINTON HOLLOW, TOWN LINE. He pulls his car into THE CLINTON HOLLOW MOTEL.

INT. DECKER'S MOTEL ROOM - NIGHT

Decker walks around his motel room -- knotty-pine walls, black and white television set, and two small, single beds separated by a night table with a telephone on top.

Decker turns on the television, lays on the bed, and watches the evening news report. Soon, he drifts into a deep sleep.

EXT. CLINTON HOLLOW MOTEL ROOM - DAY

Decker gets into his car as tractor trailer trucks ROAR by the motel. Decker's car heads north into Clinton Hollow.

EXT. RAY'S DINER - DAY

Decker's car pulls into the diner's parking lot. It is filled with pickup trucks and tradesmen's vehicles advertising their services on the side in bold print.

INT. RAY'S DINER - DAY

Decker enters the diner. It is packed with a colorful crowd of rugged-looking workers from nearby factories, mills, and construction companies. Decker takes a seat at the counter and orders breakfast. Behind the counter a sign advertises THE WILLSHIRE COUNTY FAIR.

Above the counter, a TELEVISION SET is tuned to a local program, THE NEW HAMPSHIRE SCENE. It is hosted by CLAYTON HOWARD, a loquacious character in his early fifties dressed in a tacky sport jacket.

His guest today is GUS GILSUM, a staff writer for THE CONCORD CHRONICLE. In his late thirties, Gilsum is a tall, slender man with only traces of dark hair above his ears. A narrow-cut mustache covers his upper lip.

Half of the diner crowd watches the tube while the other half CHATTERS in the b.g.

TV SCREEN
(GILSUM; talking on CAMERA)
As outlined in my column last week, the incident happened in New York City more than fifty years ago. Louie Lepke, the underworld king-pin, had bribed U.S. Customs Inspectors in New York. They provided Lepke with customs stamps which he affixed to incoming baggage containing heroin. The three million dollars used to finance this operation was stolen by "Cockeye" Eddie Malone and an unknown accomplice.
(MORE)

DECKER

looks at the TV screen. The waitress refills his coffee cup.

VOICE OVER
(HOWARD interrupting)
Excuse me, Gus. We'll continue with your story after a few brief messages from our sponsors.

Decker scans the diner crowd. In the b.g. we HEAR various commercials on the TELEVISION. Soon a NEWS BULLETIN interrupts the broadcast. Decker looks back to the television screen.

(CONTINUED)

CONTINUED:

TV SCREEN
(NEWS ANNOUNCER; standing in front of a liquor store)
We have just received a report from the state police confirming another hold-up by two armed gunmen at this state liquor store near Bedford. They got away with three thousand dollars in cash.
(MORE)

DECKER'S REACTION

to the rest of the bulletin. He comes to attention.

NEWS ANNOUNCER (v.o.)
(continuing)
According to eyewitnesses, they were driving a black, late-model Trans Am with Massachusetts license plates. It is now believed that the gunmen have headed back to Willshire County where their hold-up spree began two weeks ago. This is MARK TANNER for KNED TV. Now, back to our regular programming.

Decker gets up from the counter and walks to the cash register. We faintly HEAR the TELEVISION in the b.g.

CASHIER
(friendly)
Was everything all right?

DECKER
(handing her money)
Fine... Can you tell me how to get to Pine Hill Road?

From behind...

WORKMAN (o.s.)
Who are you looking for?

Decker turns and sees a rugged-looking workman in his late twenties standing there.

DECKER
I'm looking for EMMA WADSWORTH on Pine Hill Road -- but there's no number.

(CONTINUED)

CONTINUED:

WORKMAN
I know where Ms. Wadsworth lives.
Your best bet is to--

DISSOLVE TO:

EXT. RAY'S DINER - DAY

Decker walks out of the diner, gets into his car, and drives away. The rugged-looking workman and three younger men walk out behind him. They watch Decker drive off. All of a sudden, they burst out laughing.

EXT. HIGHWAY - DECKER'S MOVING CAR

turns off the highway onto PINE HILL ROAD. Near the top of the hill, his car stops in front of a house which is in dire need of refurbishing.

EXT. HOUSE - DAY

Decker gets out of his car and walks to the front door. He knocks. A moment later, he HEARS SHUFFLING FEET from behind the door. The door opens slowly. A woman gazes out at him suspiciously.

DECKER
Emma Wadsworth?

The door opens all the way, the woman bids him to enter. In her late fifties, her hair is frizzy and her eyes flicker like a candle's flame in the wind.

INT. HOUSE - DAY

The house is a mess. Newspapers, dirty dishes, and clothes are strewn all over the living room floor. The woman gives Decker a strange look and...

WOMAN
Do you like chickens?

DECKER
(puzzled)
... Sure -- I guess so.

Immediately, the woman begins to flap her arms, and move her head like a chicken pecking the parched earth. At the same time, she makes a CLUCKING SOUND and moves around on her spindly legs.

Decker realizes that he has been set up. Like a flash, he heads for the door and exits the house.

EXT. HOUSE - DAY

Decker walks back to his car muttering under his breath, "That son-of-a-b*#%h." A U.S. Mail truck passes Decker.

MAILMAN
It looks like you're lost?

DECKER
I was looking for Emma Wadsworth but some local joker sent me here.

MAILMAN
You just paid a visit to CLARA DODD -- she's a harmless eccentric. Emma's house is the next one over the top of the hill.

DECKER
(getting into car)
Thanks.

EXT. HOUSE - DAY

Decker gets out of his car. The house and yard look well-tended. He walks to the front door and knocks. The door opens to an elderly man with a cane.

DECKER
Good morning. Mr. Wadsworth?

WADSWORTH
Yes?

DECKER
My name is Matt Decker. I was told by the state police that your wife witnessed--

WADSWORTH
(interrupting excitedly)
Oh yes, Mr. Decker, please come in.
(looking o.s.)
Emma, Mr. Decker is here.

INT. LIVING ROOM - DAY

The room is comfortably decorated and immaculate. Decker sits in a comfortable armchair drinking an iced tea and listening to Emma Wadsworth. In her early seventies, Emma is bright, alert, and speaks softly. Her husband sits on the edge of his chair like a little kid listening to a ghost story.

(CONTINUED)

CONTINUED:

EMMA
Please understand that I was afraid to come forward right away. But I realized that it was my responsibility to do so when I learned that the police were calling Mrs. Decker's death an accident.

DECKER
I understand, Mrs. Wadsworth. Now, please tell me what you saw.

EMMA
On the day of the incident, I was picking wild flowers just off the state highway. I heard this commotion -- you know, horns honking and tires screeching. Anyway, I saw this black car force Mrs. Decker's vehicle off the ro--

WADSWORTH
(interrupting excitedly)
It was a Chevy Blazer, Emma.

EMMA
(politely)
Thank you, William... Now, where was I?

DECKER
You saw this black car force Nora's Chevy Blazer off the road.

EMMA
Oh yes. Thank you, Mr. Decker. Anyway, after the Blazer struck the tree, the black car stopped. The passenger door opened as if someone were getting out. But oncoming traffic, I believe, frightened them off. The black car pulled out--

WADSWORTH
(interrupting excitedly)
Just like in Smokey and the Bandit -- tires screeching and the stench of burning rubber in the air.

Emma gives William a look of reprimand.

CONTINUED:

WADSWORTH
(continuing)
... I'm sorry, dear. Please continue.

EMMA
Anyway, it happened so fast that I didn't notice the license plate. And the car had tinted glass all the way around so I couldn't see anyone inside.

DECKER
Is there anything you might have recalled after giving your statement to the police?

EMMA
(holding her index finger to her lip)
... I'm sorry, Mr. Decker, that's all I can remember.

DECKER
(standing up)
Thank you, Mrs. Wadsworth.

Emma walks Decker to the front door.

EXT. HOUSE - DAY

As Decker gets into his car, Emma runs out of the house.

EMMA
Mr. Decker, please wait.

Decker walks back to her.

EMMA
(continuing)
Since the accident, something has been bothering me. I'm not sure but I think there might have been a passenger riding with Mrs. Decker. After her vehicle struck the tree and the black car took off, I thought I heard a door slam shut. From where I was standing, I could only see the driver's side of her Blazer. Someone could have gotten out of the passenger's side without me seeing them.

CONTINUED:

DECKER
Thanks again, Mrs. Wadsworth, you've been very helpful. If you recall anything else, I'm staying at the Clinton Hollow Motel.

EXT. MAIN STREET - CLINTON HOLLOW - DAY

Decker is walking on the sidewalk when a woman, looking the other way, CRASHES into him. She is very attractive and obviously aggravated.

WOMAN
(very hostile)
Why don't you look where you're going!

DECKER
(annoyed)
Hey, lady, what part of Staten Island are you from?

The woman walks away, turns to Decker, and slaps her left hand on her right forearm -- the traditional gesture for "up yours." Nearby, two young men observe the incident and laugh loudly. Decker turns to them...

DECKER
(sarcastically)
Imagine going home to that?

INT. RESTAURANT - CLINTON HOLLOW - DAY

Decker sits at a small table. In front of him, a hamburger and a cup of coffee. He takes a bite out of the hamburger. It is terrible. He lifts the roll, looks at a dried-out hamburger patty, and pushes it away in disgust.

DECKER

stands in the corner on the telephone.

INT. 23RD PRECINCT - DETECTIVES' SQUAD ROOM - SAME TIME

T.J. Tyner walks past his desk when the TELEPHONE RINGS.

TYNER
(on phone)
Homicide, Detective Tyner.

INTERCUT DECKER WITH TYNER

CONTINUED:

DECKER
(on phone)
T.J., it's Matt Decker.

TYNER
Hi, Lieutenant. Are you still in New Hampshire?

DECKER
Yeah. How are Savino and Jackson doing?

TYNER
They're both doing well. Savino may be going home today; Jackson, in a week or so.

DECKER
Good. Any progress on the Frazer case?

TYNER
So far -- nothing!

DECKER
Keep after it, something will break. Why don't you transfer me over to the Captain's office.

TYNER
Okay, Lieutenant.

INT. 23RD PRECINCT - DETECTIVES' SQUAD ROOM - SAME TIME

Tyner transfers Decker's call and hangs up his phone.

MATELLI
Hey, T.J., did I hear you say that Matt is in New Hampshire?

TYNER
Yeah.

Matelli turns to Detective JACK MURPHY -- a big, even-tempered man in his late forties who keeps to himself.

MATELLI
Hey, Murph, didn't you just get back from New Hampshire?

Murphy sits at his desk writing a report. He answers Matelli without even looking up.

(CONTINUED)

CONTINUED:

MURPHY
I was traveling all over New England, Rocco.

Matelli shrugs and goes back to work.

EXT. NORA DECKER'S HOUSE - DAY

Decker's car pulls into a driveway past a mailbox marked, DECKER. The house is nice-looking with a manicured lawn and flower gardens. He gets out of his car and is obviously impressed by what he sees. Decker walks to the front door and takes a key out of his pocket. It is unlocked. He steps inside.

INT. NORA DECKER'S HOUSE - LIVING ROOM - DAY

The house has been sacked -- furniture turned over, drawers spilled onto the floor, etc. Decker looks on the floor. Among a bunch of papers, a PICTURE FRAME lies face down. He bends over and picks it up.

DECKER

stares at the photograph. His face tightens.

INSERT OF PHOTOGRAPH

shows Nora and Alex hugging each other affectionately. Nora looks beautiful with dark hair and those dazzling eyes. Alex looks like a clean-cut kid with a wide, infectious grin.

BACK TO SCENE

Decker takes the picture out of the frame. He carefully folds it so there is no crease in either of their faces. He looks at it again and then puts it into his wallet.

INT. STUDIO ROOM - DAY

A room filled with original oil paintings signed by Nora Decker. An easel with an unfinished painting stands near the window. Decker takes the photo out of his wallet. He sits in a chair near the window and stares at it in a trance-like fixation. After a moment, he gets up and walks out of the room.

INT. DINING ROOM - DAY

Decker stands up a knocked-over chair. He opens a cabinet and finds a sparse liquor selection.

(CONTINUED)

CONTINUED:

He reaches for a bottle of Scotch. Gripping the bottle, his face tightens. He stares at the bottle for quite a while. Then, he takes a deep breath, pushes the bottle to the back of the cabinet, and closes the door.

EXT. NORA DECKER'S HOUSE - DAY

Decker walks from the house to the garage. He opens the doors and gives the garage a cursory glance. Then, he gets into his car and leaves.

EXT. HIGHWAY - DECKER'S MOVING CAR - HIS POV

looking at a state police car parked behind a late-model station wagon on the side of the highway. He pulls in behind it. The tall trooper looks at Decker as he gets out of his car. The trooper's name tag identifies him as GEORGE GATES -- he looks ex-marine.

GATES
(as he writes a summons)
Can I help you, sir?

DECKER
Would you know if Lt. Branford is at the barracks now?

GATES
(looking at Decker)
He'll be there by three-thirty. He starts the four to twelve shift today.

The driver of the car looks out the window at Decker. It is the woman who ran into him in town. She gives Decker a look of annoyance.

DECKER
Thanks, officer.

Decker walks back to his car and notices a BUSTED TAIL LIGHT on the woman's station wagon.

DECKER
(continuing)
Officer, did you see this?

The big trooper walks to the back of the station wagon. Decker points to the busted tail light.

GATES
How could I have missed that?

(CONTINUED)

CONTINUED:

The trooper flips over his citation pad and starts writing another summons. The woman sticks her head out of the window, looks at Decker with burning eyes, and...

WOMAN
(to Decker)
You son-of-a-

GATES
(as he writes)
Friend of yours?

DECKER
I don't think so.

Decker gets into his car. He drives slowly by the woman, flashes a big smile, and waves "bye, bye." She is infuriated and livid to the point that she wants to grab the trooper's .357 Magnum and blow Decker away.

EXT. BROWN'S HARDWARE STORE - DAY

Decker gets out of his car and walks into the store.

INT. BROWN'S HARDWARE STORE - DAY

Decker walks around the well-stocked store. He spots a man wearing a light cotton jacket with a name tag which reads, DEXTER BROWN. In his mid-thirties, he is stocky but does not give the impression of being flabby. Brown is an eager-beaver type of guy who moves swiftly through the store straightening out the merchandise.

DECKER
Excuse me, Mr. Brown, I'm Matt Decker -- Alex's father.

BROWN
(surprised)
Alex's father?
(extending his hand)
I'm glad to meet you. We were all shocked by Nora's murder. It's so hard to believe that it happened. I sure hope the police catch the person responsible.

DECKER
So do I... I'm trying to find Alex, Mr. Brown, any idea where he might be?

CONTINUED:

BROWN
No -- and I'm very concerned. It's so unlike Alex not to call if he couldn't come to work. He's reliable, hard-working, and a person with initiative -- a rare commodity in today's youth.

DECKER
I'm pleased that you feel that way about him... Can you tell me about his friends?

BROWN
Well, JIMMY BANKS is probably his best friend. Jimmy works for Briggs Construction. They're working at the Kendall's home on Mayfair Avenue and he's probably there right now... Of course, there's Alex's girlfriend, MAGGIE NELSON. She lives on Norwood Street. I'll write down the directions for you.

Decker follows Brown to his office.

EXT. STREET - DECKER'S MOVING CAR

turns right in the center of town and crosses over a steel-structured bridge past several old factory buildings. His car turns left on Mayfair Avenue and comes to rest behind a truck advertising BRIGGS CONSTRUCTION.

EXT. HOUSE - DAY

Six young men sit under a tree in front of a house chugging beers and discussing the recent Red Sox game. The young men go silent as Decker approaches.

DECKER
I'm looking for Jimmy Banks?

A scrawny-looking kid with red hair and freckles cautiously raises his hand. Decker leads him away from the other young men.

DECKER
Jimmy, I'm Matt Decker, Alex's father. Can you tell me where he is?

CONTINUED:

JIMMY
(skeptically)
... Alex told me his father died before he was born?

DECKER
I assure you, Jimmy, I'm his father. He's disappeared and I'm trying to find him.

JIMMY
(still uncertain)
... I don't know where he is.

DECKER
Have you spoken to him since his mother's -- murder?

JIMMY
Yeah -- but he didn't tell me where he was.

DECKER
Jimmy, I'm trying to help him. If he gets in touch with you or you learn something later, I'm staying at the Clinton Hollow Motel.

Jimmy does not say anything else. He rejoins the work crew as they go back on the job.

EXT. HIGHWAY - DECKER'S MOVING CAR

heads north out of town and turns left on Norwood Street. His car stops next to a mailbox marked NELSON.

EXT. CAROL NELSON'S HOUSE - DAY

Decker gets out of his car and walks to the front door. He knocks and waits. No answer. He knocks again.

ANGLE ON WOMAN

standing behind Decker. It is the same woman who ran into him on the sidewalk in town. It is also the same woman who got an extra summons because of him. She looks thrilled to see him.

DECKER'S REACTION

when he turns around and sees the woman standing there. His face drops as in, "Oh s*#t!"

(CONTINUED)

CONTINUED:

WOMAN
(harshly)
What the hell do you want?

DECKER
The name is Matt Decker. I'm looking for Maggie Nelson -- she knows my son, Alex.

NELSON
I'm CAROL NELSON, Maggie's mother. ... From what I understood, Alex's father died before he was born.

DECKER
(pause; and then)
That seems to be a very popular story around here.

Carol gives Decker a critical inspection and...

CAROL
If you're Alex's father -- he could have done a whole lot better than you.

DECKER
(very annoyed)
You know, lady, you've got some attitude!

CAROL
(firing back)
The name is Carol or do you suffer from lapses of memory?
(sarcastically)
You're some father -- is this the first chance you've had to see your son?

DECKER
(trying to maintain a civil tone)
Look... I just found out today that I have a son. Okay?

CAROL
You're kidding?

Decker shakes his head "no."

(CONTINUED)

CONTINUED:

DECKER
... Carol, Alex disappeared the day of his mother's murder and I'm very concerned for his safety. Does Maggie know where he is?

CAROL
(cordially)
When the newspaper ran an article and picture covering Alex's disappearance, I asked Maggie if she knew where he was. She wouldn't say, but I'm sure she does.

DECKER
Why wouldn't she tell you?

CAROL
My daughter is very independent ... and we don't exactly see things eye to eye.

DECKER
I'd like to talk to her.

CAROL
If you return after six-thirty tonight, she's usually home by then.

DECKER
I'll be back later.

Carol watches Decker as he leaves.

INT. DECKER'S MOTEL ROOM - DAY

Decker sits on the bed holding the telephone.

BAKER (v.o.)
State Police, Troop B, SERGEANT BAKER.

DECKER
(on phone)
Sergeant, this is Matt Decker, is Lt. Branford there?

BAKER (v.o.)
I'm sorry, Mr. Decker, the Lieutenant is out.

CONTINUED:

DECKER
Would you please advise him that my ex-wife's house has been ransacked. It didn't appear to be the work of vandals -- someone turned the place upside down looking for something.

BAKER (v.o.)
I'll give him the message, Mr. Decker. Where can he reach you?

DECKER
I'm staying at the Clinton Hollow Motel... Thanks, Sergeant.

Decker hangs up the receiver, walks over to the television and turns it on. He lays on the bed and listens to the local news program.

INT. CAROL NELSON'S HOUSE - LIVING ROOM - NIGHT

Carol answers a KNOCK on the door. It is Decker.

CAROL
(cordially)
Please, come in...
(walking towards the kitchen)
Maggie is late but the dinner is ready. Care to join me?

DECKER
Sure.

INT. KITCHEN - NIGHT

Carol pulls a roasting pan out of the oven. Decker grimaces at the meat, it is charred beyond recognition.

CAROL
There's beer in the refrigerator or liquor in the cabinet if you'd like to make yourself a drink.

DECKER
Thanks, I don't drink.

INT. DINING ROOM - NIGHT

Decker looks at the meat on his plate. It looks like a LAVA specimen. The vegetables are also overcooked.

(CONTINUED)

CONTINUED:

Carol notices Decker struggling to eat.

CAROL
(embarrassed)
It's not very good -- is it?

DECKER
(being polite)
I'm not really that hungry -- I had a big lunch this afternoon.

INT. LIVING ROOM - LATER THAT NIGHT

Decker and Carol sit in the living room waiting for Maggie to arrive home. After a long awkward silence...

DECKER
Are you divorced?

CAROL
(sarcastically)
No, my husband was killed in a hunting accident two years ago -- some idiot from New York had mistaken him for a deer.

DECKER
I'm sorry.
(pause; and then)
What do you do for a living?

CAROL
You sure are inquisitive!

DECKER
It comes with my line of work -- I'm a homicide detective in New York City.

CAROL
It figures.
(pause; and then)
I manage the Willshire County office for North Country Realty -- we handle both residential and commercial properties.

DECKER
That sounds interesting. When we collided earlier today, what set you off?

(CONTINUED)

CONTINUED:

CAROL
I was trying to collect the rent from a tenant who is always late and always makes flimsy excuses.
(smiling)
... My temper tends to get the best of me sometimes.

DECKER
No kidding... You'd fit right in with most of the passengers on the Eighth Avenue subway.

CAROL
Somehow -- I don't think that was meant to be a compliment...

Decker smiles.

CAROL
(continuing)
You know, Maggie and Alex are very much in love.

DECKER
You approve?

CAROL
Yes, I do. Alex is a fine young man. You'll be very proud of him.

DECKER
... I assume you knew Nora -- what was she like?

CAROL
Nora was a wonderful mother and a very talented artist. She had a number of suitors but no one could get close to her -- she was a very private person.

In the b.g., the SOUND of a DOOR opening and closing. Maggie enters. Like her mother, she is very attractive and projects an air of confidence and independence.

MAGGIE
Hi, Mom.

CAROL
Hi, Honey. This is Matt Decker, Alex's father.

CONTINUED:

MAGGIE
(very surprised)
What? Alex doesn't have a father.

Decker looks at Carol.

CAROL
Honey, believe me. This is Alex's father. Please tell him where Alex is.

Maggie pauses and then shakes her head "no."

DECKER
Maggie, I'm very concerned for Alex considering his mother's murder. If you know where he is, please tell me?

MAGGIE
(adamantly)
I don't know where he is and if I did -- I wouldn't tell you anyway.

With that remark, Maggie leaves the living room and goes to her bedroom. Carol quickly follows her.

From the living room, the SOUND of MUFFLED VOICES can be heard arguing from behind a closed door. Decker stands silently waiting. Soon, Carol returns.

CAROL
I'm sorry. Maggie knows where Alex is but she won't even tell me. I'm sure he's all right. Let me talk to her later...

Decker heads for the front door.

CAROL
(continuing)
Why don't you call me tomorrow at my office during the day or here in the evening.

DECKER
(walking out the door)
I'll get in touch with you tomorrow. Thanks.

EXT. NORA DECKER'S HOUSE - DAY

Decker gets out of his car at Nora's house, walks to the front door, and enters.

INT. NORA DECKER'S HOUSE - LIVING ROOM - DAY

Very carefully, Decker sifts through the disheveled living room. Between the wall and an antique roll-top desk, he picks up a CHECKBOOK and REGISTER.

INSERT OF CHECK REGISTER

showing several entries: One to GEORGE PAXTON ANTIQUES for two hundred and twenty-five dollars; another to WILKINS CARPENTRY for seventy-five dollars, etc.

BACK TO SCENE

Decker picks up the telephone directory from the floor and begins to thumb through the pages.

MONTAGE - THE INVESTIGATION BEGINS...

A series of cuts showing Decker interviewing the people listed in his ex-wife's checkbook register.

EXT. STREET - DAY

Decker stands behind a truck talking to a young, lanky man with curly blond hair. JASPER WILKINS CARPENTRY is boldly displayed on the side.

EXT. SHOEMAKER'S STORE - DAY

From outside, we LOOK INTO the store and see Decker talking to an elderly man behind the counter. The man shakes his head "no" to Decker's various questions.

INT. GAS STATION - DAY

Decker and a mechanic stand together in an open bay. The mechanic listens to Decker while he wipes his dirty hands on a rag. The mechanic shakes his head "no."

EXT. BIG BARN - DAY

Decker and two young men stand under a sign, BELLETEAU TREE SERVICE. One man looks at the other and shrugs his shoulders. The other shakes his head "no."

EXT. PAXTON'S ANTIQUE SHOP - DAY

Decker's car stops near a sign, GEORGE PAXTON ANTIQUES.

INT. PAXTON'S ANTIQUE SHOP - DAY

Decker enters the house to see a room filled with antique furniture, lamps, and knickknacks.

(CONTINUED)

CONTINUED:

Dressed like a preppie, a good-looking man in his late thirties with wavy blond hair appears.

PAXTON
(friendly)
Good morning, I'm George Paxton, can I help you?

DECKER
I'm Matt Decker -- Nora Decker's ex-husband.

Paxton's friendly smile quickly fades. Decker notices.

DECKER
Mr. Paxton, two days before my ex-wife's murder, she bought something from you for two hundred and twenty-five dollars. Can you tell me what it was?

Paxton walks over to a desk in the corner and searches through stacks of paper. He produces a small book and thumbs through it.

PAXTON
She bought a coffee table. It needed to be refinished so I gave it to her for a special price.

DECKER
Is there anything else you might be able to tell me?

PAXTON
No, not really.

In the b.g., the TELEPHONE RINGS.

PAXTON
(continuing)
You'll have to excuse me, Mr. Decker. I am expecting this call and I should be quite a while.

DECKER
All right. If something should come to mind -- I'm staying at the Clinton Hollow Motel.

EXT. PAXTON'S ANTIQUE SHOP - DAY

Decker gets into his car and happens to look back at the house. He sees Paxton looking at him from the window.

EXT. PRICE'S BOARDING HOUSE - DAY

Decker knocks on the door. A wispy-looking woman in her seventies opens the door.

DECKER
Martha Price?

PRICE
I'm Martha Price.

DECKER
I'm Matt Decker. I believe my ex-wife, Nora, bought something from you.

She smiles, opens the door, and invites Decker inside.

INT. PRICE'S BOARDING HOUSE - DAY

PRICE
Oh, yes. She bought an old steamship trunk from me when I had my garage sale.

Ms. Price walks over to a bookcase and pulls out one page from a newspaper.

PRICE
The Concord Chronicle did an article on garage sales and featured me in their story.

She hands Decker the newspaper page.

INSERT OF NEWSPAPER PAGE

with column heading: "GARAGE SALES -- THE TRADITION CONTINUES." A picture accompanying the article shows Martha Price standing in front of her boarding house among a collage of items: old furniture, lamps, books, and clothing. In the picture's b.g., a large STEAMSHIP TRUNK can be seen with the initials E.M. clearly stenciled on the side.

PRICE (o.s.)
(her finger points)
That's the trunk she bought from me -- the one with the initials E.M. on the side.

BACK TO SCENE

Martha Price relates her story to Decker.

(CONTINUED)

CONTINUED:

PRICE
My parents owned this boarding house since the early twenties. Many of the items I sold were left here by summer residents. Some of these items, the trunk included, have been in this house for fifty years or more.

DECKER
Was there anything in the trunk?

PRICE
Mostly old clothes -- I guess.

DECKER
Thank you, Ms. Price, can I keep this newspaper page?

PRICE
Sure, I have an extra copy.

INT. DECKER'S MOTEL ROOM - DAY

Decker sits on the bed talking on the telephone.

DECKER (on phone)
Would you tell Carol Nelson I called and that I'll call her at home tonight... Thanks.

He looks at the newspaper page he got from Martha Price. An article in the bottom corner grabs his attention.

INSERT OF NEWSPAPER ARTICLE

favoring GUS GILSUM'S picture prominently displayed with his column. He was previously seen on HOWARD CLAYTON'S television show. The column heading reads, "THE SEARCH CONTINUES FOR GANGSTER'S LOST LOOT."

CLOSE ON OPENING PARAGRAPH

which reads, "It has been fifty years since a small-time New York City hoodlum, "Cockeye" Eddie Malone, supposedly buried $3,000,000 in cash somewhere in Willshire County."

BACK TO SCENE - DECKER'S REACTION

He stands up with the newspaper page in hand. His eyes go wide.

(CONTINUED)

CONTINUED:

Decker drops the newspaper and heads for the door.

EXT. HIGHWAY - DECKER'S MOVING CAR

glides swiftly up the highway.

INT. DECKER'S MOVING CAR - DECKER

looks very anxious.

EXT. NORA DECKER'S HOUSE - DAY

Decker's car SCREECHES to a halt in the driveway. He walks briskly to the front door and lets himself in with the key. From OUTSIDE the house, we see Decker THROUGH VARIOUS WINDOWS as he moves from room to room.

EXT. NORA DECKER'S HOUSE - DAY

Decker exits the house and heads for the garage.

INT. GARAGE - DAY

Decker inspects the garage loft. After rummaging around, he climbs down the ladder. Halfway down, he stops and sees something on the floor.

On the garage floor, Decker picks up an unusual-looking KEY with the number C-32 on it. He puts the key into his pocket and walks back to the house.

INT. NORA DECKER'S HOUSE - THE KITCHEN - DAY

Decker enters the KITCHEN. He takes a glass from a cabinet and fills it with water. He turns from the sink and takes a drink. In the GLASS CABINET DOOR across the room, Decker sees a REFLECTION. From OUTSIDE the KITCHEN WINDOW, someone is SIGHTING DOWN on him with a HANDGUN. He dives for the floor as the gun THUNDERS TWICE shattering the cabinet across the room. Decker looks pale. He bolts out the back door.

EXT. NORA DECKER'S HOUSE - BACKYARD - DAY

Decker runs into the backyard. From deep in the woods behind the house, he HEARS the SOUND of someone RUNNING away. He looks for a path, but none is visible.

DECKER
(calling out)
Alex! I'm your father. Alex, come back.

(CONTINUED)

CONTINUED:

Decker stands there for a while. Convinced that Alex is long gone, he gets into his car and drives off.

INT. CAROL NELSON'S HOUSE - LIVING ROOM - NIGHT

When Carol opens the front door, Decker does not wait for an invitation to enter -- he barges right in.

DECKER
(demanding)
Where's Maggie?

CAROL
(defensively)
Where the hell do you get off barging in here and demanding to see my daughter?

DECKER
I was at Nora's house looking around -- Alex just tried to kill me.

CAROL
(shocked)
What are you talking about?

DECKER
I was in the kitchen and he was outside. He fired through the window at me with a handgun. I clearly saw his face.

CAROL
Good God... Maybe he thought you were someone breaking into the house.

DECKER
(stressing)
Carol, I've got to find him before he kills someone or ends up like his mother. Now, where's Maggie?

CAROL
She's not home and I don't know where she is... But if you want to wait for her, you can.

INT. LIVING ROOM - LATER THAT NIGHT

Decker paces anxiously while Carol sits and watches him.

(CONTINUED)

CONTINUED:

CAROL
... So you believe there's a connection between Nora's murder and the steamship trunk she bought at this garage sale?

DECKER
So far, it's the only tie-in.

CAROL
Do you really think there's three million dollars buried somewhere in Willshire County?

DECKER
It sounds preposterous to me -- but someone may believe it... In looking around Nora's house, I couldn't find the trunk or this antique coffee table she bought days before her death... Do you know George Paxton?

CAROL
Sure. He's an antique dealer, but why do you ask?

DECKER
Nora bought a coffee table from him, so I paid him a visit today. What can you tell me about him?

CAROL
(hesitating)
... I believe that Paxton had taken Nora out a few times and...

DECKER
And what, Carol?

CAROL
Like I said before, Nora was a very private person. But, she once told me a man she had dated got pretty rough with her -- but she wouldn't say who.
(pause; and then)
I know he's divorced and never lonely for female companionship. ... I once heard a rumor that he sometimes gets rough with the ladies if he drinks too much.

INT. DINING ROOM - LATER THAT NIGHT

CLOSE ON CLOCK FACE - It is 1:32 a.m.

BACK TO SCENE

Decker and Carol sit across from each other at the dining room table with empty coffee cups in front of them. They both look tired.

CAROL
If Maggie isn't home by now, I don't think she'll be home tonight.

Decker gets up and heads for the front door.

EXT. CAROL NELSON'S HOUSE - NIGHT

Outside the front door...

CAROL
As soon as she shows up, I'll give you a call.

DECKER
Thanks.

CAROL
(as he turns to leave)
Matt, don't worry -- we'll find Alex.

Decker forces a smile and walks to his car.

INT. DECKER'S MOVING CAR - DECKER'S POV

passing a BAR with FLASHING NEON LIGHTS.

DECKER

is stretched like a rubber band to the breaking point.

EXT. DECKER'S MOVING CAR

makes a u-turn, heads back to the bar, and parks in front.

INT. DECKER'S PARKED CAR - NIGHT

Decker stares into oblivion. The bar's NEON LIGHTS FLASH INTERMITTENTLY on his anguished face. After a long moment, he reaches for the car door handle. But instead, he rams his car into reverse and backs out of the parking lot.

INT. DECKER'S MOTEL ROOM - DAY

Decker wakes to the SOUND of POUNDING on his DOOR. Still groggy, he walks to the door, opens it a crack and sees Carol. He slips on his trousers and lets her in.

CAROL
I tried calling a little earlier but there was no answer.

DECKER
(still groggy)
I must have been out because I didn't hear it ring.

CAROL
Maggie never came home last night.

DECKER
Is that unusual?

CAROL
No. But she usually calls if she won't be home.

DECKER
Could she have spent the night with Alex?

CAROL
She could have... I know that she was at Northfield Farm late yesterday afternoon -- I asked her to drop off some papers for JUDGE TYLER. That was the last I saw or heard from her.

DECKER
I'll run up to Northfield Farm and see what I can find out.

CAROL
Okay. The farm is three miles north of town off Spring Hollow Road. If you learn anything, would you call me at the office?

DECKER
Sure.

EXT. CLINTON HOLLOW MOTEL - DAY

As Decker gets into his car, a state police cruiser pulls in next to him. Lt. Branford gets out.

(CONTINUED)

CONTINUED:

BRANFORD
Good morning, Mr. Decker.

DECKER
Lieutenant.

BRANFORD
Can you tell me what happened at your ex-wife's house yesterday?

DECKER
I called your office and reported that the house was turned inside/out.

BRANFORD
I'm not talking about that. I'm talking about gun shots and the shattered kitchen cabinets?

DECKER
I don't know what you are talking about.

BRANFORD
Are you going to deny that you were up there late yesterday afternoon?

DECKER
I was there. But I don't know anything about gun shots being fired.

Branford looks at Decker with disbelief.

BRANFORD
... Why do I have a tough time believing you?

Decker stands silent. Branford gets into the state police cruiser and drives off.

EXT. HIGHWAY - DECKER'S MOVING CAR

passes through two columns supporting a big overhead sign: NORTHFIELD FARM.

On an elevated ridge, Northfield Farm is one of the most scenic spots in Willshire County. Decker's car passes acres of well-tended farm land and stops in front of the magnificent main house. He gets out of his car. The beautiful house and manicured grounds are impressive.

EXT. NORTHFIELD FARM - MAIN HOUSE - DAY

Decker stands next to his car and sees a sign:

NORTHFIELD FARM - JUDGE WILLIAM J. TYLER

He heads for the front door when from behind...

HOLLIS (o.s.)
I'm BRAD HOLLIS, the foreman, can
I help you?

Decker turns around and sees a powerful-looking man in his mid-forties with thick, wavy hair walking towards him. The man is wearing a tan-colored work shirt with Northfield Farm embroidered over the left pocket.

DECKER
I'm looking for Maggie Nelson, she
was here yesterday afternoon.

HOLLIS
I don't know any Maggie Nelson so
she couldn't have been here
yesterday...
(firmly)
This is private property so I have
to ask you to leave -- now.

DECKER
... Maybe I should talk to the
Judge?

HOLLIS
(aggressively)
I asked you nicely once. If you
don't leave now, the only person
you'll be talking to is a doctor.

Decker stands firm and glances up at a second story window. Out of the corner of his eye, he notices the curtains move in one window as if someone pulled away as he looked up.

He looks at Hollis, gets into his car, and slowly drives off the grounds.

INT. PAXTON'S ANTIQUE SHOP - DAY

Decker walks inside and sees a young couple looking at antiques. Actually, the wife is looking at antiques while her bored husband plays grab a*#. Without taking her eyes off a unique flower vase, the young woman slaps her husband's hand as he grabs her shapely posterior.

(CONTINUED)

CONTINUED:

George Paxton enters the room and addresses the young couple. At the same time, he notices Decker standing across the room.

PAXTON
(to young couple)
Can I help you with anything?

YOUNG WOMAN
Not right now, thanks.

Paxton approaches Decker.

PAXTON
Mr. Decker, what can I do for you?

DECKER
When I was here the other day and asked you questions about my ex-wife, you never mentioned the fact that you went out with her.

PAXTON
I really didn't think it was important -- we only saw each other twice.

DECKER
Mind telling me where you were the day Nora was murdered?

PAXTON
(defensively)
Look, I took the day off and went fishing up at Lake Sunapee. I went alone and saw no one who would remember seeing me.

DECKER
Do you often just take a day off?

PAXTON
(aggressively)
Mr. Decker, I told you where I was and that's all I've got to say.

YOUNG WOMAN (o.s.)
(addressing Paxton)
Excuse me, can you tell me about this piece over here?

CONTINUED:

Without saying another word to Decker, Paxton turns and walks over to the young couple. Decker looks at Paxton for a moment and decides to leave.

INT. BROWN'S HARDWARE STORE - DAY

The store is busy with both tradesmen and local residents talking to clerks and making purchases.

Decker stands next to the KEY MAKING MACHINE and compares the key he found at Nora's house with those on the rack. Dexter Brown approaches Decker from behind.

BROWN
Can I help you, sir?
(as Decker turns)
Oh! It's you, Mr. Decker. How are you doing? Have the police found Alex yet?

DECKER
No, not yet.

BROWN
Were Jimmy Banks or Maggie Nelson of any help?

DECKER
Not really.

BROWN
(noticing the key in Decker's hand)
That's an unusual-looking key -- where did you get it?

Billy, a passing clerk, sees the key and overhears them.

BILLY
Excuse me, Mr. Brown, that is the type of key used at the Mid-Valley Storage Facility -- it's just south of town.

BROWN
Thank you, Billy. Did you find that seal for Doby's tractor?

BILLY
Yes, sir. He picked it up early this morning.

(CONTINUED)

CONTINUED:

Decker walks towards the front door with Dexter Brown.

DECKER
Thanks for the help.

Brown watches Decker walk to his car. Brown goes to his office, picks up the TELEPHONE, and closes the door.

EXT. MID-VALLEY STORAGE FACILITY - DAY

INT. DECKER'S MOVING CAR - HIS POV

looking at the Mid-Valley Storage Facility surrounded by a heavy-duty cyclone fence. Rows of concrete and steel compartments rest in the center of a dirt compound. The facility is a stark blemish in comparison to the rest of the scenic landscape of New Hampshire.

Decker's car enters between the front gates. With the exception of one young couple unloading furniture from a pickup truck in front of an open locker door, the storage facility is quiet.

EXT. STORAGE LOCKER - DAY

Decker's car stops in front of the locker marked C-32. He gets out of his car and looks around.

He opens the locker with the key and swings the door open. The room is tightly packed with furniture, lamps, rolled-up carpets, and sealed boxes.

INT. STORAGE LOCKER - DAY

Decker walks through a narrow passageway inspecting the items he passes. In the back of the locker, a HUGE ITEM is COVERED with a DROP CLOTH. Decker pulls the cover off and finds a LARGE STEAMSHIP TRUNK with the initials, "E.M.," boldly stenciled on the side. He drags the trunk outside of the locker to the rear of his car.

EXT. STORAGE LOCKER - DAY

Decker lifts the steamship trunk and angles it into his open car trunk. With a rope, he begins to tie it down.

EXT. STORAGE LOCKER - DAY

From Decker's car, we see a CAR parked OUTSIDE of the storage facility just off the highway. Even from this distance, the BLACK, LATE-MODEL TRANS AM with TINTED GLASS is recognizable. From the passenger's open window, a PAIR OF BINOCULARS reflect in the afternoon sun. They are clearly trained directly on DECKER.

EXT. HIGHWAY - DAY

POV FROM TRANS AM - LOOKING THROUGH BINOCULARS

at Decker securing the STEAMSHIP TRUNK with a rope.

EXT. STORAGE LOCKER - DAY

From Decker's car, we see the passenger's window in the black Trans Am close and the car slowly drive away.

EXT. HIGHWAY - DECKER'S MOVING CAR

heads south out of the storage facility with the steamship trunk protruding from his car's trunk.

INT. DECKER'S MOVING CAR - HIS POV

looking into the OUTSIDE REAR-VIEW MIRROR. He sees the black Trans Am closing in at a high rate of speed.

INT. DECKER'S MOVING CAR - DECKER

pulls his .38 special from underneath the front seat of his car and places it next to him.

EXT. HIGHWAY - DAY

The Trans Am attempts to overtake Decker's car but he swerves his car across the dividing line blocking the coupe's path. The Trans Am drops back in line.

The Trans Am makes another move. But this time, a SHOTGUN barrel emerges from the passenger's window. Pulling alongside Decker's car, Decker pulls across the dividing line again. This time, the Trans Am swerves and the SHOTGUN EXPLODES. DOUBLE OO BUCK tears into the corner of the steamship trunk.

INT. DECKER'S MOVING CAR - HIS POV

looking at the Trans Am in the OUTSIDE REAR-VIEW MIRROR anxiously weaving back and forth waiting to make another move.

EXT. HIGHWAY - DAY

An intermittent line of TRACTOR TRAILERS moving fast in the NORTHBOUND LANE block any chance of the Trans Am pulling alongside Decker.

INT. DECKER'S MOVING CAR - HIS POV

looking at a CROSSROAD INTERSECTION ahead. He grips the steering wheel tightly and takes a deep breath.

EXT. HIGHWAY - AT THE CROSSROADS - DECKER'S CAR

cuts across the intersection in front of a tractor trailer truck with only seconds to spare.

EXT. HIGHWAY - THE TRANS AM

sails by the intersection with a TRACTOR TRAILER TRUCK bearing down on its rear. The truck's HORN bellows LOUDLY. The Trans Am comes to a SCREECHING stop on the highway's shoulder. But it is too late, Decker is gone.

EXT. COUNTRY ROAD - DAY

Decker's car moves down a long, open road.

INT. DECKER'S MOVING CAR - DECKER'S POV

looking down the open road THROUGH THE OUTSIDE REAR VIEW MIRROR, he sees no one behind him.

EXT. CLINTON HOLLOW MOTEL - NIGHT

Decker's car pulls into the motel and stops in front of his room. He gets out, looks around, and unties the steamship trunk.

INT. DECKER'S MOTEL ROOM - NIGHT

Decker drags the steamship trunk into his room. He draws the drapes shut before turning on the lights. Without haste, he opens the trunk and is repelled by the pungent, stale odor of decaying clothes. Decker removes clothing that was once stylish fifty years ago. He holds up a jacket with red and white awning stripes.

Beneath layers of old clothes, Decker finds a stack of old POSTCARDS tied together with twine and a HARDCOVER BOOK published in 1928, "NEW ENGLAND SEA CAPTAINS."

Under another layer of clothes, he finds an old GEOLOGICAL SURVEY MAP of Willshire County as well as a PENCIL SKETCH of an OLD NEW ENGLAND CHURCH.

DECKER

scrutinizes the map carefully but sees nothing unusual.

INT. DECKER'S MOTEL ROOM - NIGHT - HOURS LATER

Decker steps outside of his motel room and turns to shut the door. From behind, a SMASHING BLOW is delivered to the back of his head. Decker falls forward, face down, into his motel room.

(CONTINUED)

CONTINUED:

DECKER'S POV

lying on the floor in a semi-conscious state. His mind drifts through a collage of distorted sights and sounds. Decker sees and HEARS the sound of SHUFFLING FEET pass his blurred line of vision. The man's BOOTS focus clearly for a moment. And then, the TRUNK passes him in a hazy glare. Decker passes out, the SCREEN goes BLACK.

INT. DECKER'S MOTEL ROOM - NIGHT

DECKER'S POV

as his eyes start to focus. A blurred form gradually focuses into Carol's warm face.

CAROL

presses a damp towel to Decker's forehead.

CAROL
Matt, are you all right?

Still stunned by the blow, Decker remains motionless for a moment. Then he attempts to sit up.

CAROL
(continuing)
What happened?

DECKER
(sitting up)
Someone sapped me from behind when I was leaving...
(looking around)
Whoever it was, took the trunk.

CAROL
You found the steamship trunk that Nora bought?

DECKER
(rubbing his neck)
Yeah! She had put it into storage and I retrieved it this afternoon. Soon after, this black Trans Am tried to run me off the road but I got away. And then tonight...

Decker struggles to get up but Carol restrains him.

CAROL
Don't try to move now.

INT. DECKER'S MOTEL ROOM - LATER THAT NIGHT

No longer in a daze, Decker is up and moving about.

DECKER
Have you been following the news on these two hold-up men in the black Trans Am who have been sticking up gas stations and liquor stores?

CAROL
Sure. It's been in the headlines for weeks.

DECKER
A witness described what could have been a black Trans Am that ran Nora's car off the road. And it was a black Trans Am that attempted to run me off the road today. Unfortunately, I couldn't get a fix on the license plate.

CAROL
Could it be the same people?

DECKER
It sure is possible.

CAROL
(pause; and then)
Maggie came home early this morning after spending the night with Alex. She still won't tell me where he is...

Carol's apprehensive look does not escape Decker's detection.

DECKER
What else should I know?

CAROL
(hesitating)
... Maggie told me that Alex is planning to do something about his mother's murder.

DECKER
That's great... Carol, we've got to convince her to tell us where Alex is hiding before something terrible happens.

INT. DECKER'S MOVING CAR - NIGHT

Decker and Carol ride in silence for a while. Then...

CAROL
I'm sorry I sent you on that wild goose chase up to Northfield Farm.

DECKER
I met the foreman, Brad Hollis; he's a real charmer.

EXT. CAROL NELSON'S HOUSE - NIGHT

Decker parks his car in front of Carol's house. Getting out, he sees Maggie's car parked in the driveway. Carol walks towards the front door. When Decker does not follow her right away...

CAROL
Matt, are you coming?

Decker stands next to his open car trunk.

DECKER
I'll be right there. I'm looking for something.

INT. CAR TRUNK - NIGHT

Decker opens his attache case loaded with electronic equipment including boxes marked "detonating caps" and "mini detonator." He opens a box marked "Type B - Transmitter", takes it out, and closes the trunk.

EXT. DRIVEWAY - MAGGIE'S CAR

Decker walks over to Maggie's car and attaches the magnetized transmitter to the underside.

INT. CAROL NELSON'S HOUSE - LIVING ROOM - NIGHT

Decker and Carol stand over Maggie who is seated in a chair. They try to reason with her.

CAROL
Honey, please tell us where Alex is hiding?

MAGGIE
(adamantly)
Mom, I promised I wouldn't.

(CONTINUED)

CONTINUED:

DECKER
Maggie, don't you realize that Alex could be in great danger... It's important that I talk to him -- please, tell me where he is?

MAGGIE
(standing up)
For the last time, no.

Maggie attempts to leave the room but Decker grabs her by the arm. Forcefully, she tries to pull away.

DECKER
Would you at least go to him now and ask him to meet me somewhere... That's all I ask?

MAGGIE
(reluctantly)
... All right, but I go alone.

Decker looks at Carol and then nods in agreement.

EXT. CAROL NELSON'S HOUSE - NIGHT

Decker and Carol stand outside the front door and watch Maggie drive off. Once her TAIL LIGHTS disappear down the road, Decker walks towards his car.

CAROL
(walking behind him)
Where are you going?

DECKER
I'm gonna follow her.

CAROL
If she sees you, she won't go to Alex.

DECKER
Don't worry. I placed a transmitting device on her car. I can track her from two miles away.

Decker gets into his car. Carol opens the passenger's door and as she jumps in...

CAROL
I'm coming along and I don't want any arguments.

INT. DECKER'S MOVING CAR - NIGHT

Decker and Carol ride in silence. Decker monitors a hand-held receiving device. A digital signal FLASHES with a PULSING RED LIGHT. It soon FLASHES faster as Decker's car rounds a winding lakefront road.

DECKER
She's about two hundred yards ahead of us now.

EXT. LAKEFRONT ROAD - DECKER'S MOVING CAR

quietly glides along the lakefront road without headlights. A slight breeze forms a chop on the water's surface that shimmers in the soft moonlight.

INT. DECKER'S MOVING CAR - DECKER'S POV

looking at Maggie's car stop beneath a canopy of tall pine trees. She gets out and looks around. Assuming it is safe, she approaches a small bungalow and enters.

INT. BUNGALOW - NIGHT

Alex and Maggie are embracing when Decker opens the front door and enters with Carol right behind him. One light bulb, dangling from an open fixture, dimly illuminates the tiny bungalow.

With quick reflexes, Alex grabs his .357 Magnum from the nearby table and points it at Decker.

CAROL
(yells out)
Alex!

DECKER
(standing still)
... Alex... I'm your father.

Decker and Alex stare at each other for a long moment. Soon, the tension in Alex's face slowly dissolves. He gradually lowers the gun to his side. Maggie stands next to Alex and gives her mother a cold stare...

MAGGIE
(angrily)
You followed me.

CAROL
(to Maggie)
Honey, let's go outside.

(CONTINUED)

CONTINUED:

Maggie walks briskly past Carol and out the door. Carol looks at Decker and then exits the bungalow.

INT. BUNGALOW - NIGHT

Decker and Alex face each other in silence. The moment is awkward for both of them. And finally...

ALEX
Mom said that you died before I was born.

DECKER
... In one respect, your mother was right... Please understand one thing, Alex, until two days ago, I didn't know I had a son.

ALEX
What happened between you and Mom?

DECKER
(a difficult revelation)
... I loved your mother very much but because of my problems, I did things that hurt her. Eventually she left me and rightly so... Alex, I can't make excuses for the past -- nor can I change it. But I do know one thing, I want to get to know you... If you'll let me.

Alex looks coldly at his father. Without saying a word, he tries to walk past Decker with his gun in hand.

DECKER
(continuing)
Alex, I'll take that gun.

ALEX
(adamantly)
No way -- it's mine.

Decker grabs Alex and takes the gun away from him. Alex swings at him; his punch grazes off Decker's face.

ALEX
(continuing)
Give me that gun -- it's mine.

DECKER
No, you'll only get in trouble.

CONTINUED:

ALEX
(tearfully)
I'm gonna kill the son-of-a-b*#%h who killed Mom and you can't stop me!

Alex tries to leave but Decker grabs him by the arm.

DECKER
Hold it, Alex. We're gonna talk about this right now.

EXT. BUNGALOW - LATER THAT NIGHT

Alex exits the bungalow and heads down the lakefront road. Maggie quickly catches up to him.

Carrying Alex's handgun, Decker exits the bungalow. His anguished face reveals the outcome of meeting his son for the first time.

Decker stands next to Carol while he watches Alex and Maggie walk away together. He is devastated.

CAROL
... Matt, give him time. He'll come around.

DECKER'S POV

looking at Alex and Maggie walking along the lakefront road in the moonlight.

INT. DECKER'S MOVING CAR - NIGHT

CAROL
What else did Alex say about his mother's murder?

DECKER
The witness was right when she said there was a passenger riding with Nora -- it was Alex. He said it was a black Trans Am that ran them off the road. But he was unable see anyone inside the car because of the tinted glass.

CAROL
... Shouldn't you take him to the state police so he can make a statement?

(CONTINUED)

CONTINUED:

DECKER
No. He doesn't know enough to aid their investigation. And besides, considering what happened to me, it would be much safer for Alex to remain in hiding until the killer is caught. Now, I know one thing for sure -- there's a definite tie-in between Nora's murder, the steamship trunk, and the three million dollars supposedly buried in Willshire County. If I search for the money, I'm convinced that the killer will eventually reveal himself.

CAROL
But Matt, you don't have the trunk anymore -- where can you possibly start looking?

INT. DECKER'S MOTEL ROOM - NIGHT

Decker enters his motel room and draws the drapes closed. He reaches under the bed and pulls out a garment bag. He dumps the contents on the bed. It is the items from the steamship trunk: the postcards, the book on New England Sea Captains, the old geological survey map, and the pencil sketch of the old New England church.

Decker inspects each item but soon exhaustion takes over. Fully dressed, he lays back on the bed and quickly falls asleep.

INT. DECKER'S MOTEL ROOM - DAY

Decker comes out of the bathroom wiping excess shaving cream off his face. In the b.g., the TELEVISION BLATHERS away.

He sits on the edge of his bed and looks at the items from the steamship trunk. He picks up the book and thumbs through the pages. Then, he rubs his fingers over the front cover as well as the inside. He does the same to the book's back cover.

As Decker puts the book down, he feels a bulge in the book's spine. Using a pen knife, he slits the book's spine open along the edge and pulls it back. A small piece of paper falls to the floor. He picks it up.

(CONTINUED)

CONTINUED:

INSERT OF PAPER

shows three columns of handwritten numbers.

1st Col.	2nd Col.	3rd Col.
272R - SW	448R - NE	640R - W
3C - W	208R - S	300R - S
	60R - W	48R - E
	2C - S	

BACK TO SCENE

Decker picks up the telephone directory from under the night table. He thumbs through it, stops, and writes something down.

EXT. HOUSE - DAY

Decker RINGS the front door BELL. On the door, a sign: CLIFFORD BEVIS, SURVEYOR. A friendly man in his early sixties with a leathery complexion greets Decker.

Decker steps inside the house.

INT. SURVEYOR'S HOUSE - DEN - DAY

SMOKE from BEVIS' pipe SWIRLS into the air in WHITE, VAPOR-LIKE STREAMS as Bevis studies the piece of paper given to him by Decker. A pause and then...

BEVIS
Actually, it's quite simple. The chain and rod measurements, as well as the compass headings, are shown in abbreviated form.

DECKER
Chain and rod measurements?

BEVIS
In the old days, surveyors actually used a chain sixteen-and-a-half feet long to measure distance accurately. A rod, then, is sixty-six feet long -- the length of four chains. Just multiply the numbers in front of the chain or rod symbol by these factors. That will accurately determine the distance between each point.

(CONTINUED)

CONTINUED:

DECKER
But where do I start?

BEVIS
I can't tell you that. There's no starting point indicated on this piece of paper... By the way, where did you find it?

DECKER
In an old book...
(standing up)
Thanks for your time, Mr. Bevis.

INT. RAY'S DINER - DAY

Long after the early-morning crowd, Decker sits alone at the counter drinking a cup of coffee. He leaves some money on the counter, gets up, and walks out the door.

EXT. RAY'S DINER - PARKING LOT - DAY

Decker is getting into his car when the SOUND of a HIGH PERFORMANCE ENGINE attracts his attention. A black, late-model Trans Am with Massachusetts license plates passes the diner. The Trans Am pulls into a CONVENIENCE STORE about one hundred yards down the road.

EXT. RAY'S DINER - PARKING LOT - DECKER'S CAR

Decker retrieves his .38 special from his car. He pulls his shirttails out and tucks the gun into the waistband of his trousers. He crosses the highway and heads towards the convenience store.

EXT. CONVENIENCE STORE - DAY

From the corner of the convenience store, Decker looks at the BACK END of the Trans Am parked by the front door. The ENGINE RUMBLES. ROCK MUSIC THUNDERS from the car's RADIO. For a moment, Decker looks puzzled. The car does not have TINTED GLASS because he can see the driver through the rear window.

Decker pulls back from the corner. By his feet, he lifts the lid of a METAL GARBAGE PAIL and sorts through the debris. He picks up a spent PINT of MOON DOG VODKA. Then, he bends down and picks up a handful of pebbles.

INT. TRANS AM - A RATTY-LOOKING PUNK

with stringy hair looks anxiously around.

(CONTINUED)

CONTINUED:

Soon, the SOUND of something PINGING against his car draws the PUNK'S attention.

ANGLE ON DECKER

at the corner of the convenience store pitching pebbles at the Trans Am.

ANGLE ON THE TRANS AM

as the PUNK gets out and nervously looks around. His hand grips a handgun tucked into his jeans.

THE PUNK'S POV

of a man with his head tilted down, staggering towards him in a drunken stupor, mumbling incoherently. The man is DECKER. He is carrying a METAL GARBAGE PAIL LID in one hand and an empty PINT BOTTLE in the other. The PUNK is perplexed. He studies Decker carefully and then looks around -- more nervous than ever.

DECKER AND THE PUNK

Less than ten feet from each other, Decker looks up at the punk. As soon as they make eye contact, the PUNK reaches for his gun. But it is too late. In one forceful motion, Decker throws the GARBAGE PAIL LID like a FRISBEE. It strikes the PUNK in the forehead with a CLANG. The punk drops to the ground unconscious.

EXT. CONVENIENCE STORE - FRONT DOOR - DAY

With the garbage pail lid in hand, Decker moves quickly to the front door. A few seconds later, the SECOND PUNK exits the store carrying a GUN in one hand and a WAD of CASH in the other.

THE SECOND PUNK'S POV

looking at someone whose face is hidden behind a garbage pail lid. The punk stands there dumfounded -- his face registers, "what the hell is this?" Decker lowers the garbage pail lid and drops the punk with a sucker punch. At that very moment, the CAR RADIO PLAYS, "Another One Bites The Dust," by Queen.

INT. CONVENIENCE STORE - DAY

In the b.g., two local cops and three state troopers are taking statements from clerks, cashiers, and customers. Decker leans against the frozen food case and...

CONTINUED:

BRANFORD
(to Decker)
Is there anything else you'd like
to add to your statement?

DECKER
Nope, that's it, Lieutenant.

Decker's shirt opens enough to reveal the gun tucked in his pants to Branford for the first time.

BRANFORD
I'll take that handgun, Mr.
Decker. You are not licensed to
carry firearms in New Hampshire.
... You can pick it up when you
are ready to leave the state.

DECKER
(handing over gun)
If that's all?

BRANFORD
You're free to go...
(as Decker walks off)
You know, Mr. Decker, I find it
very strange that you haven't
asked me once about your missing
son -- unless, of course, you've
already located him yourself.

DECKER
Lieutenant, I didn't ask because I
assumed you would inform me if you
found him.

BRANFORD
If you have found your son, we
need to talk to him. He might
know something that would aid our
murder investigation.

Decker nods and walks off while Branford watches him.

EXT. BUNGALOW - DAY

Alex sits at a picnic table under a pine tree reading a book when Decker's car pulls in. Decker gets out and...

DECKER
Hi, Alex. How are you doing?

(CONTINUED)

CONTINUED:

Alex shrugs.

DECKER
(continuing)
Why don't we take a walk. I'd like to go over the things we discussed last night concerning your mother's -- murder.

EXT. LAKEFRONT ROAD - FROM A DISTANCE

we see Decker and Alex walk along the lakefront road. Whenever a car passes or a person walks by, Decker is very observant and turns Alex's face away from them.

EXT. BUNGALOW - DAY - HOURS LATER

Decker and Alex sit together at the picnic table.

DECKER
And that's everything you remember?

ALEX
... That's all of it.

DECKER
Tell me again about that telephone call your mother got concerning the steamship trunk.

ALEX
(reluctantly)
I answered the telephone. A man asked for Mom. He asked her if she would sell him the steamship trunk that she bought at the garage sale. When she said no, he became very angry and Mom hung up on him.

Decker remains silent in contemplation...

ALEX
(continuing)
... Do you think the police will find Mom's killer?

DECKER
(standing up)
If they don't, I promise you I will...

CONTINUED:

DECKER
(continuing)
What if I return after dark and pick you up -- we could have dinner with Maggie and her Mom at their home?

ALEX
That's all right. Maggie is coming here tonight.

DECKER
... Okay, I'll see you tomorrow. And please stay put.

Frustrated by his confinement, Alex just shrugs.

EXT. CAROL NELSON'S HOUSE - NIGHT

Decker's car pulls into the driveway. Getting out, he sees SMOKE BILLOWING from behind the house. He quickly rushes back there.

EXT. CAROL NELSON'S HOUSE - BACKYARD - DECKER

stands there, shakes his head, and chuckles.

THE BARBECUE GRILL

stands unattended. It is BLAZING away with FLAMES leaping for the sky and CLOUDS of SMOKE. On the grill, something has been burned beyond recognition.

CAROL

exits the back door with a plate and cooking utensils in hand. She sees Decker standing there.

DECKER
(looking at grill)
What is this, Bethlehem Steel?

CAROL
(embarrassed but also defensive)
Well... Who says that every woman has to be a good cook! Think you can do any better?

DECKER
(smiling)
Just give me a crack at your kitchen.

INT. CAROL NELSON'S HOUSE - KITCHEN - NIGHT

Decker stands in front of the stove tending a large skillet filled with meat and vegetables. From the spice rack, he selectively chooses condiments and sparingly seasons the meal.

Carol stands near Decker and watches him in amusement. He gestures for her to come closer.

DECKER
Let me show you some of my cooking techniques.

Very receptive, Carol stands in front of the stove with Decker close behind her. In a stirring motion, he gently guides Carol's hand on a wooden spoon.

DECKER
(continuing)
See -- there's nothing to it.

Carol turns her head and smiles at Decker.

DECKER
(continuing)
This next technique is my specialty.

Decker kisses Carol softly on the neck. It gives her the chills. She turns and faces Decker. He kisses her passionately and turns off the stove at the same time.

INT. BEDROOM - LATER THAT NIGHT

Moonlight filters through the sheer bedroom curtains. Under the sheets, Decker and Carol lie closely together. She gently combs his hair in place with her fingers.

CAROL
(sensually)
Who taught you to cook like that, Julia Child?

DECKER
No, it was actually James Beard.

Carol laughs.

CAROL
(cautiously)
... Matt, you're more than welcome to stay here. It would be a lot more comfortable than the motel.

(CONTINUED)

CONTINUED:

DECKER
Thanks. But until this thing is over, I don't want to put you or Maggie in any danger.

After a long silence, Decker slides out of bed and begins to get dressed.

CAROL
... Where are you going?

DECKER
Back to the motel. There are things I still need to do.

INT. LIVING ROOM - NIGHT

Carol, dressed in a bathrobe, sees Decker off.

CAROL
You know, you've become a big hero since you apprehended those two hold-up men.

DECKER
Yeah. For a while I thought they might have had something to do with Nora's murder because they were driving a black Trans Am -- but it didn't have tinted glass.

Carol kisses Decker. He heads out the front door...

CAROL
Matt... Don't worry about Alex. Just give him time to get to know you. He's been through a lot.

Decker smiles and leaves.

INT. DECKER'S MOTEL ROOM - NIGHT

Decker sits on his bed inspecting the items from the steamship trunk. He carefully looks through the stack of postcards -- one side, and then the other. He picks up the old geological survey map and holds it up to the light on the night table and sees nothing peculiar. He does the same to the pencil sketch of the old New England church.

Extremely tired, Decker puts everything aside and turns out the light.

THE SCREEN GOES BLACK.

FADE IN:

on a RINGING TELEPHONE sitting on a table. On the third RING, a delicate-looking hand picks it up.

INT. PRICE'S BOARDING HOUSE - DAY

PRICE
(on phone)
Hello?

INT. DECKER'S MOTEL ROOM - SAME TIME

Decker sits on the bed holding the telephone.

DECKER
(on phone)
Mrs. Price, this is Matt Decker. If you recall, I came to your home the other day. We discussed the steamship trunk that my ex-wife bought at your garage sale.

INTERCUT DECKER AND PRICE

PRICE
Oh, yes, Mr. Decker, I remember.

DECKER
Did anyone ever call you about that trunk?

PRICE
Why, yes. Two men called me about it the day after the article on the garage sale appeared in the newspaper. Both were very disappointed when I told them it was sold.

DECKER
Did these men identify themselves?

PRICE
No, they didn't. But they did ask me for the name of the person who bought it. I gave them Mrs. Decker's name and address -- did I do something wrong?

DECKER
No, you didn't, Mrs. Price. Thanks.

EXT. BARBERSHOP - MAIN STREET - DAY

Decker walks down the sidewalk and happens to glance into the BARBERSHOP WINDOW. He freezes in his tracks.

EXT. BARBERSHOP - DECKER'S POV

looking INTO the barbershop THROUGH THE WINDOW at a PAIR OF BOOTS on someone sitting in the barber's chair.

FLASHBACK

to the night when Decker was lying on the floor of his motel room. Those same boots passed his line of vision.

ANOTHER FLASHBACK

to the day he was at Northfield Farm. Brad Hollis was wearing those same boots.

INT. BARBERSHOP - ANGLE ON BRAD HOLLIS

sleeping soundly in the barber's chair while the barber cuts and trims his wavy head of hair.

INT. BARBERSHOP - DECKER

enters the barber shop and closes the door quietly. The barber is a small, compact man in his sixties with grey hair combed straight back over his forehead. A small mustache sits over a tight mouth.

BARBER
(friendly)
I'll be right with you, sir.

Decker moves to the chair and motions for the barber to step back. Totally puzzled, the barber backs away.

Decker taps Hollis on the shoulder. Hollis opens his eyes and sees Decker. Like a flash, Decker nails him with a right cross knocking him unconscious.

BARBER
(mortified; he covers his mouth with his hand)
Oh, my God!

Decker picks up a pair of ELECTRIC CLIPPERS and goes to work. We HEAR the CLIPPERS HUMMING away as we look at

THE BARBER

who cannot believe what he is seeing.

CONTINUED:

TWO SHOT

of Decker standing over Hollis who now has a PUNK HAIR CUT. Portions of Hollis' head have been clipped to the scalp with tufts of hair hanging over his face.

EXT. BARBERSHOP - DAY

Two young workmen look into the barbershop and see Hollis, still unconscious. They look in disbelief and step aside as Decker exits the barber shop.

ANGLE ON GEORGE PAXTON

standing on the sidewalk across the street.

EXT. MAIN STREET - PAXTON'S POV

of Decker walking out of the barbershop.

ANGLE ON GEORGE PAXTON

turning abruptly around and walking into a store.

EXT. NORTHFIELD FARM - DECKER'S MOVING CAR

passes through the entrance.

EXT. NORTHFIELD FARM - MAIN HOUSE - DAY

Decker gets out of his car and walks to the front door. He knocks three times. After no response, he walks around the side of the house.

Decker sees an elderly man tending a flower garden.

JUDGE WILLIAM J. TYLER

A modest figure in his early seventies with snow-white hair and brilliant eyes. There is about him an aura of intelligence, refinement and reserved dignity.

EXT. GARDEN - DAY

DECKER
(as he approaches)
Judge Tyler?

TYLER
(without stopping
or turning)
What can I do for you?

(CONTINUED)

CONTINUED:

DECKER
The name is Matt Decker. Two nights ago, I was knocked unconscious by your foreman, Brad Hollis...
(the Judge stops)
He took a steamship trunk away from me that once belonged to my ex-wife, Nora. She was murdered a little over a week ago.

TYLER
What does this have to do with me, Mr. Decker?

DECKER
That's what I'm here to find out.

Judge Tyler drops his tools and walks out of the garden.

DECKER
(continuing)
I believe my ex-wife was murdered over this trunk. It was once owned by "Cockeye" Eddie Malone -- you know the story, he supposedly buried three million dollars in cash in Willshire County.

TYLER
I'm familiar with this tall tale... If you have proof that Brad Hollis assaulted you and took this trunk, why don't you go to the police and press charges?

DECKER
Right now, my evidence is only circumstantial.

TYLER
I'm afraid, Mr. Decker, that I can't be of any help to you.

In the b.g., we HEAR a car door SLAM SHUT. Soon, Brad Hollis appears from around the side of the house wearing a HAT. Hollis sees Decker and seethes with anger. He moves quickly towards Decker. But...

TYLER
(firmly)
Brad!

(CONTINUED)

CONTINUED:

Hollis stops in his tracks and stares vehemently at Decker. Then, he looks at the Judge.

TYLER
(continuing; to Hollis)
Please wait for me in the house.

Decker and the Judge stand silent until Hollis enters the house through the rear entrance.

DECKER
(poised to leave)
It is my intention to find out who killed my ex-wife... And one last thing, my son, Alex -- God help anyone who attempts to harm him.

Decker looks at the Judge to confirm his intent and then walks o.c. The Judge looks troubled.

INT. DECKER'S MOTEL ROOM - DAY

Decker sits on the bed talking on the telephone.

DECKER
(on phone)
... T.J. Tyner please.

INT. 23RD PRECINCT - DETECTIVES' SQUAD ROOM - SAME TIME

Tyner is seated at his desk. Seated across from him is a knock-out hooker with a dynamite body.

TYNER
(on phone)
Homicide, Detective Tyner.

INTERCUT DECKER AND TYNER

DECKER
T.J. -- Matt Decker.

The hooker tantalizes Tyner by licking her lips and opening her blouse to play "peek-a-boob" with her ample breasts. Tyner's eyes bulge out of his head. He drops the TELEPHONE into a plate of CHOP SUEY sitting in front of him. It SPLASHES down and SPLATTERS all over him. The hooker smiles and says, "Bon appetit -- sucker!"

DECKER
(hearing only silence)
T.J., are you still there?

(CONTINUED)

CONTINUED:

TYNER
(wiping the chop suey off the phone and trying to talk)
Sorry, Lieutenant, I dropped the phone. What can I do for you?

DECKER
I need some research done.

INT. 23RD PRECINCT - DETECTIVES' SQUAD ROOM - LATER

TYNER
(on phone)
Okay, Lieutenant. I'll get right on it.

Tyner hangs up the telephone and shakes his head in exasperation. Over Tyner's shoulder, Detective Jack Murphy is looking into a file cabinet. Murphy pulls a folder, closes the file drawer, and walks away.

TYNER
(addressing the hooker)
Now, MS. RIDER, what can you tell me about Jack Frazer's murder?

INT. VARIETY STORE - DAY

At the cash register, Decker stands behind two middle-aged women who are buying a WILLSHIRE COUNTY TREASURE MAP from a counter display.

FIRST WOMAN
(to clerk)
Where do you think we should look on this trip?

CLERK
(confidentially)
I'd investigate the old railroad tracks and abandoned shacks near Mitter's Creek.

SECOND WOMAN
Thanks.
(to friend as they leave)
ALICE, let's go there first thing tomorrow morning.

CLERK
(to Decker)
Yes, sir?

CONTINUED:

Decker drops a newspaper and a dollar on the counter.

CLERK
(continuing)
This treasure nonsense is sure good for business...
(ringing the sale)
You'd be surprised by how many people are out looking for the three million dollars supposedly buried around here. Last year,
(laughing)
some fool fell down an old well shaft in Wheatley Meadows. He weighed three hundred pounds! They had to haul his fat a*# out of there with a block and tackle.

Decker smiles at the clerk and leaves.

INT. DECKER'S MOTEL ROOM - DAY

In the b.g., the TELEVISION BLATHERS away while Decker stands over the bed looking down at the four articles from the steamship trunk.

Decker inspects the articles again but sees nothing unusual.

INT. CAROL NELSON'S HOUSE - KITCHEN - EVENING

Decker helps Carol clean up the kitchen. Maggie enters and kisses her Mom goodbye. Carol looks surprised. Maggie rarely kisses her mom without being coaxed.

MAGGIE
Goodnight, Mom -- Mr. Decker.

CAROL
Are you going to see Alex?

MAGGIE
After I stop at Karen's house.

As Maggie walks out of the kitchen...

DECKER
Maggie, please be careful.

MAGGIE
(cheerfully)
Don't worry -- I will.

EXT. ROAD - EVENING (TWILIGHT)

Decker and Carol walk hand-in-hand up a deserted dirt road. After a long silence...

CAROL
What was your marriage to Nora like?

DECKER
... At first, it was great. But problems soon developed. And understand one thing, I blame no one but myself for the things that happened... God knows, she was more tolerant of me than anyone had a right to expect.

CAROL
... Did your problem with alcohol have something to do with it?

Decker unconsciously grips Carol's hand tighter. Knowing she has hit a sensitive nerve...

CAROL
(continuing)
... What do you think of New Hampshire?

DECKER
(smiling at Carol)
That was a tactful way of changing the subject.

CAROL
Seriously, I want to know?

DECKER
I like it a lot... But maybe you have something to do with it.

Decker kisses Carol. They reach the top of the hill and disappear down the other side in the glowing dusk.

INT. DECKER'S MOTEL ROOM - DAY

Decker rummages through his suitcase and soon hears...

TELEVISION (o.s.)
(WEATHERMAN'S VOICE)
The forecast for today calls for a gradual warming with temperatures
(MORE)

CONTINUED:

TELEVISION (o.s.)
(WEATHERMAN'S VOICE, Contd.)
in the mid-eighties. Now, let's take a look at an overlay of our weather map and see what's in store for the region during the next couple of days.

Something the weatherman says causes Decker to stop dead in his tracks. He picks up the geological survey map and studies it. Then, he picks up the pencil sketch of the church on the tissue-like paper. The sketch has a distinct horizontal line.

Decker lines up the horizontal line on the sketch over the horizontal boundary of the geological survey map. He moves the sketch back and forth across the map until the spire on the church steeple points directly at an intersection marked, HUXLEY CROSSROADS.

Decker sits down with a note pad and pencil. He begins to convert the chain and rod statistics into precise distances by each compass heading. He picks up his notes and heads out the door.

INT. BROWN'S HARDWARE STORE - DAY

Decker walks through sections of the hardware store. He picks up a pick axe, a shovel, a coil of heavy-duty rope, and a lantern. At the cash register.

CLERK
Will that be all, sir?

Decker nods "yes."

INT. DEXTER BROWN'S OFFICE - DEXTER BROWN

works at his desk in front of a one-way mirror facing the cash registers. He looks up and sees Decker.

ONE-WAY MIRROR - DEXTER BROWN'S POV

of Decker making his purchase and walking out the door.

BACK TO BROWN

picking up the telephone.

BROWN (on phone)
... I thought you'd like to know that Matt Decker just left here... And guess what, he bought a number of interesting items...

EXT. BUNGALOW - DAY

Decker gets out of his car and sees Alex standing near the lake skipping rocks across the surface.

DECKER
Hi, Alex.

ALEX
... I'm getting tired of staying here and doing nothing.

DECKER
I understand -- but please be patient. Until your mother's killer is apprehended, it's not safe for you to be moving around.

Alex drops a rock he is holding and turns to his father.

DECKER
(continuing)
Hopefully, it will all be over in the next day or two... Tonight, I'm making a move that should bring me closer to the killer.

EXT. LAKEFRONT ROAD - LATER THAT DAY - DECKER AND ALEX

walk together along the lakefront road. Alex's hard veneer in dealing with his father is breaking down.

ALEX
When I'm twenty-one, I'm going to apply for a position as a conservation officer with the Fish and Game Department.

DECKER
For someone who enjoys the outdoors so much, that's great... By the way, I think Maggie is a fine girl.

ALEX
(smiling)
... What do you think of her Mom?

Standing by the car...

DECKER
I think you already know the answer to that question...
(MORE)

(CONTINUED)

CONTINUED:

DECKER (Contd.)
After tonight, things should
really bust loose.

Decker slides into the front seat of his car.

ALEX
... Dad, please be careful.

Decker gets out of his car and hugs Alex tightly.
Without any reservations, Alex embraces his father.

DECKER
(pause; and then)
Alex... We've lost a lot of time.
But as soon as this thing is over
-- we'll make up for it.

EXT. CAROL NELSON'S HOUSE - NIGHT

Carol follows Decker out of the house and to his car.
The FULL MOON reaches its apex in the clear night sky
and softly illuminates the landscape.

Carol appears to be apprehensive.

DECKER
(sensing her concern)
... Don't worry, everything will
be all right.

As if she had the chills, Carol crosses her arms across
her chest and hunches her shoulders together.

CAROL
Matt, please be careful... It's a
night of the crimson moon.

DECKER
Crimson moon?

CAROL
My husband believed that at
certain times of the year, like
tonight, the moon basked in a
crimson color. As a hunter, he
believed that it gave night
predators exceptionally heightened
skills. It gave them the ability
to stalk their prey without being
detected until -- it was too late.

(CONTINUED)

CONTINUED:

DECKER
Don't worry, I can take care of myself.

CAROL
... Matt -- I love you.

Decker embraces Carol tightly.

DECKER
Until now, I never thought I'd be able to say those words again -- but I love you too.

Quickly, Decker gets into his car and drives off.

EXT. HUXLEY CROSSROADS - NIGHT

A WORLD WAR I MONUMENT

stands solitary guard in the center island of the intersection as Decker's car PULLS INTO VIEW.

INT. DECKER'S MOVING CAR - NIGHT

On the seat, next to the pad with all the map calculations, Decker picks up the compass. He turns it until the needle points SOUTH WEST. He drives slowly and approaches one of the intersecting roads.

DECKER'S POV OF STREET SIGN - BLACK TOWER ROAD

A SERIES OF CUTS...

THE TAIL LIGHTS

of Decker's car disappear down Black Tower Road.

THE COMPASS

held in Decker's hand is illuminated by the dim dashboard lights.

DECKER

looks down the road and then at...

THE ODOMETER

as the numbers roll over.

EXT. OPEN FIELDS

glowing in the brilliant moonlight.

EXT. DECKER'S MOVING CAR

glides silently through the night.

EXT. NORTHFIELD CEMETERY - NIGHT

Decker's car PULLS INTO VIEW. The cemetery is surrounded by a stone wall. A wrought iron gate bridges the entrance with NORTHFIELD CEMETERY across the top.

Decker stands by his car. He looks up and down the dirt road but it is deserted. With compass in hand, he enters the cemetery counting his paces.

Moonlight casts eerie shadows on old tombstones dating back to the late seventeen hundreds.

A PEN LIGHT reveals the compass needle pointing SOUTH EAST.

Decker's mouth moves as he counts the paces to himself. He passes tombstone after tombstone until he reaches the stone wall bordering the back of the cemetery. He pauses and then steps over the wall.

EXT. BACK OF CEMETERY - NIGHT

He stops in his tracks and looks down. With his hand, he brushes away decaying leaves and twigs covering the soft earth below his feet. He finds a six-inch square piece of marble embedded in the ground. There is no writing on it but it is clearly a marker of some kind.

EXT. CEMETERY - AT THE CAR - DECKER

retrieves the tools and the lantern from the car trunk.

EXT. BACK OF CEMETERY - FROM A DISTANCE

we see Decker's silhouette in front of the dark woods. The bright moonlight filters through the surrounding trees.

Decker strikes with the pick axe and digs with the shovel at a steady pace.

LATER THAT NIGHT - DECKER

stands in a deep hole swinging a pick axe.

His pick axe strikes something solid. He picks up the lantern from the edge of the hole and lowers it to his feet. With his hand, he wipes away a layer of dirt and finds a LARGE METAL BOX.

(CONTINUED)

CONTINUED:

Feverishly, Decker removes the dirt from the top portion and finds a clasp-type hinge. He flips the clasp back and opens the top -- the box is EMPTY.

DECKER

looks disgusted. His work was for nothing.

EXT. BACK OF CEMETERY - NIGHT

When Decker finishes filling the hole back up, he senses something wrong. He pauses and looks around. The sound of a HIGH-POWERED RIFLE CRACKS the dead silence of night. A bullet RICOCHETS off the stone wall, inches from where he stands.

Decker dives for cover behind the stone wall. He moves down the protective barrier and pulls out Alex's .357 Magnum. Twenty feet from the hole, Decker carefully peers over the jagged rock formation.

THE CEMETERY

looks gloomy with moonlight filtering through small open corridors of the dense oak trees. With a light breeze, eerie shadows take on moving forms around the headstones.

EXT. BACK OF CEMETERY - DECKER

senses the danger is not over and lowers his head behind the stone wall. At that precise moment, another shot CRACKS LOUDLY. The bullet PINGS off the stone wall inches from where his head was.

Adrenaline pumping, Decker takes a deep breath and leaps over the stone wall INTO the cemetery. At the same time, he FIRES three decisive SHOTS towards a shadowy figure standing near the front entrance. The figure drops low.

EXT. CEMETERY - DECKER

cautiously moves towards the front entrance using the headstones as a shield. He HEARS the SOUND of a CAR ENGINE in a TORTUOUS WHINE. Then, the SOUND of TIRES SPITTING up stones from the dirt road as the car makes a fast getaway.

EXT. CEMETERY - DIRT ROAD - DECKER

runs out into the dirt road in time to see the faint glow of distant tail lights in a cloud of dust.

INT. RAY'S DINER - DAY

The diner is packed with tradesmen eating hearty breakfasts and engaging in boisterous conversations. Decker sits next to a young worker at the counter. Soon, the empty seat to his right is taken by Lt. Branford.

DECKER
Lieutenant.

BRANFORD
Good morning, Mr. Decker.
(to the waitress)
I'll have a cup of coffee and a bran muffin...
(to Decker)
Someone reported shots being fired late last night on Black Tower Road -- near Northfield Cemetery. You didn't happen to be out that way last night?

DECKER
I don't like to go out during the full moon period -- too many whackos and loonies are active then.

BRANFORD
(sipping his coffee)
... I understand you gave Brad Hollis one hell of a haircut.

Ignoring the remark, Decker gets up to leave.

DECKER
Have a nice day, Lieutenant.

BRANFORD
Mr. Decker... I know you're involved in something -- but nothing that I can prove right now. If it has anything to do with your ex-wife's murder, you'll be seeing scenic New Hampshire from a cellblock window.

Decker looks at Branford, acknowledging his remark. He leaves some money on the counter and exits the diner.

EXT. NORTH COUNTRY REALTY OFFICE - DAY

Decker walks into frame and heads towards the front door. He looks into the office and enters.

INT. NORTH COUNTRY REALTY OFFICE - DAY

Decker sees two people. A secretary on the telephone and a tall, lanky man in his late forties dressed like a nightmare -- checkered slacks, striped shirt, and a Madras sport coat.

CHASE
(friendly)
Good morning, I'm HAROLD CHASE,
can I help you?

DECKER
I'm looking for Carol Nelson.

Carol steps out of her office in back and calls out...

CAROL
Matt, down here.

Passing Harold Chase, Decker rolls his eyes. Carol picks up on his mockery of Chase and smiles.

INT. CAROL'S OFFICE - DAY

Decker is no sooner in her office when Carol wraps her arms around his neck and kisses him passionately.

DECKER
(smiling)
What did you have for breakfast,
thirty cc's of spanish fly?

CAROL
No, I'm just glad to see you...
So, what happened last night?

DECKER
Not much! I dug up an empty box
behind Northfield Cemetery... I
think the whole thing about the
buried money is one giant hoax.
(pause; and then)
Carol, what can you tell me about
Judge Tyler?

CAROL
The Judge? He is probably one of
the wealthiest men in the state.
Northfield Farm is more than seven
hundred acres and--

The TELEPHONE RINGS.

(CONTINUED)

CONTINUED:

CAROL
(continuing)
Excuse me.
(on phone)
Yes, Jackie?... Put him on....
Where are you?... What?...
(temper rising)
Look, Charlie, I told you that
your car needed servicing...
Never mind the but... All right,
give me the directions...
(taking notes)
I'll take care of it.
(hanging up)
What an idiot!

Decker smiles. Carol is slightly embarrassed about losing her temper.

CAROL
I know, I should learn to control
my temper...
(more relaxed)
I'm sorry, I've got to run over to
Clayton; we've got a young couple
there waiting to see a house.

INT. NORTH COUNTRY REALTY OFFICE - DAY

Decker and Carol walk out of her office together. Decker walks past Harold Chase who is standing by his desk with a cup of coffee in hand.

DECKER
(to Chase with
a BIG smile)
Love that jacket.

CHASE
(really flattered)
Gee, thanks.

EXT. HUXLEY CROSSROADS - DAY

Decker's car pulls away from the center island of the intersection and passes a sign, WHEATLEY ROAD.

INT. DECKER'S MOVING CAR - DAY

Decker looks down at the compass in his hand. It is pointing NORTH EAST.

INT. DECKER'S MOVING CAR - DECKER'S POV

of the odometer as the numbers roll over.

DECKER

checks his notes on the seat.

DECKER'S POV

of the dirt road flanked by stone walls, huge trees, and vast open fields. In the far b.g., dense woods.

EXT. DIRT ROAD - DECKER'S CAR

comes to rest on the side of the deserted dirt road. He gets out and looks around. No signs of life anywhere.

At the trunk of his car, Decker takes out the shovel and pick axe and leans them against the rear bumper.

He soon HEARS the SOUND of a HIGH-PERFORMANCE ENGINE coming his way. He moves to the other side of the car and picks up the .357 Magnum from the front seat.

EXT. DIRT ROAD - AROUND THE BEND

a full-sized sedan ROARS towards him. Seeing that it is not the black Trans Am, Decker hides the gun.

EXT. DIRT ROAD - THE SEDAN

comes to a SCREECHING HALT next to Decker. He quickly assesses the passengers as four, wise-a*# punks in their late twenties -- high on beer.

PUNK
(passenger's seat;
to Decker)
Hey, man, can you tell us where
the Raven's Nest is?

DECKER
(moving closer)
Sorry, guys, I'm like you, a
stranger in these parts.

A big, loud-mouth punk in the back seat holding a beer speaks up...

BIG PUNK
Hey, a*#hole, then what are you
doing out here -- looking for
Cockeye's buried money?

(CONTINUED)

CONTINUED:

Decker leans against the car and looks in.

DECKER
(calm but deliberate
to the big punk)
You'd look pretty stupid trying to
eat corn on the cob with no teeth!

The nervous punk addresses BILLY, the driver...

NERVOUS PUNK
Hey, Billy, let's get out of here.

Decker stands back. The sedan pulls away in a cloud of dust and disappears around a bend in the dirt road. Decker picks up his tools and steps over the stone wall bordering the dirt road.

EXT. OPEN FIELD - DAY

Decker tramples a path through the tall rye grass glistening in the afternoon sun. He checks his compass bearings. His mouth moves as he counts the paces.

EXT. DIRT ROAD - THE SEDAN

carrying the four punks slides to a stop on the road.

INT. PARKED SEDAN - DAY

The big punk in the back seat puts his hand on the driver's shoulder...

BIG PUNK
I think we should go back and see
what that guy is up to.

BILLY
(skeptically)
I don't know...

NERVOUS PUNK
I don't think we should mess with
that guy.

The big intimidating punk turns to the nervous one...

BIG PUNK
Look, that guy is up to something
-- you saw the pick axe and the
shovel. We should check him out,
you know, follow him...

(CONTINUED)

CONTINUED:

The three other punks are afraid to reply.

BIG PUNK (Contd.)
(pause; and then)
He's one guy -- there's four of us...
(pushing the driver's shoulder very hard)
What are you, some chicken-s*#t candy a*#?

EXT. DIRT ROAD - THE SEDAN

spins around in a cloud of dust, heads back towards Decker, and a whole lot of trouble.

EXT. OPEN FIELD - DAY

Decker reaches the top of an elevated ridge in the open field. He looks at his compass and is about to continue when he sees in the distance...

THE FOUR PUNKS

following his footsteps in the trampled rye grass.

Decker shakes his head and looks ahead to a large oak tree at the edge of the field. He moves swiftly and continues to count his paces.

EXT. THE OAK TREE - FROM A DISTANCE

we see the four punks follow Decker's tracks. They stop under the oak tree.

EXT. THE OAK TREE - CLOSER ANGLE

The four punks stand together under the oak tree.

BILLY
Hold it, guys, I've got to take a breather.

IN THE TREE - DECKER

is suspended above the four punks. On a broken branch, he holds a DEADLY HORNETS' NEST. It is BUZZING loudly. Decker looks nervous.

IN THE TREE - DECKER'S POV

looking down at the four punks. Then...

EXT. THE OAK TREE - ANGLE ON THE FOUR PUNKS

They are about to move when the hornets' nest hits the ground with a BIG THUD and splits open.

BILLY
Holy s*#t!

Before they can blink, the hornets relentlessly attack the four punks. Flailing their arms and screaming obscenities, the punks turn and run.

IN THE TREE - DECKER'S POV

looking at the four punks running down the open field waving their arms frantically and SCREAMING like lunatics. Decker mutters to himself, "a*#holes."

EXT. DENSE WOODS - DECKER

looks at his compass and counts paces as he walks into a dark, dense pine tree woods that borders the back of the open field.

Decker's feet sink slightly in the soft pine-needle carpet beneath the shaded canopy. At the other end of the dark, dense woods, he walks into an open field that steeply inclines.

EXT. OPEN FIELD - DAY

At the top of a knoll, Decker sees a group of abandoned cabins basking in the afternoon sun. The wood has been weathered and bleached from years of exposure to the sun and the harsh New England climate.

He counts his paces to the end of a cabin and looks down at the compass. He turns, faces another direction, counts off ten paces and stops. Decker works his foot through the scruffy wild grass. He makes a wider circle until his foot hits something solid.

Decker bends down and pulls the grass away from another marker like the one he found behind the Northfield Cemetery stone wall. Without delay, he begins digging.

EXT. OLD CABINS - FROM A DISTANCE

we see Decker standing in a deep hole shoveling dirt.

LATER - IN THE HOLE - DECKER

bends over and wipes away a layer of dirt. He uncovers a HUMAN SKELETON. Carefully, he digs around the remains until he finds the skull with a bullet hole dead center.

INT. DECKER'S MOVING CAR - HIS POV - NIGHT

approaching Carol Nelson's house. Maggie passes in her car and waves to him.

INT. CAROL NELSON'S HOUSE - LIVING ROOM - NIGHT

Decker watches the news program on the television while Carol talks to him from the kitchen.

CAROL (o.s.)
Matt, another club soda?

DECKER
No thanks.

THE TELEVISION - ON SCREEN

A NEWSMAN stands off the highway with a microphone in hand. In the b.g., a state trooper observes a tow truck pulling a car up from a steep ditch.

TELEVISION
(NEWSMAN; on camera)
Tonight, a one-car accident has taken the life of a thirty-eight year old man on the state highway just north of Clinton Hollow.
(MORE)

The NEWS CAMERA moves closer to the car as it is pulled on to the side of the highway. It is clearly a BLACK TRANS AM with TINTED GLASS.

DECKER'S REACTION - SEEING THE CAR

He moves to the edge of his chair. Carol enters the room and is about to speak when Decker gestures for her to be quiet. She stands next to his chair.

TELEVISION
(NEWSMAN; Continuing)
The name of the man has not yet been released pending notification of family. We will update this story on the late-night edition of the news -- this is Mark Tanner for KNED TV.

DECKER
(getting up from chair)
I'm going to run to the state police barracks and find out who was driving that car.

CONTINUED:

CAROL
I'll come with you.

DECKER
(giving her a quick kiss)
Stay here, I'll see you tomorrow.

EXT. HIGHWAY - DECKER'S MOVING CAR

approaches a sign: NEW HAMPSHIRE STATE POLICE - TROOP B BARRACKS.

INT. CAROL NELSON'S HOUSE - KITCHEN - NIGHT

Carol wipes off the kitchen counter top. Soon, the TELEPHONE RINGS. She picks it up and...

CAROL
(on phone)
Hello?

MAGGIE (v.o.)
(trembling)
Maaa -- Mom.

CAROL
(alarmed)
Maggie, are you all right?

MAGGIE (v.o.)
Mom, someone has kidnaped Alex.

CAROL
Honey, what are you talking about?

INT. NH STATE POLICE BARRACKS - FRONT DESK - NIGHT

Decker enters the barracks. On duty at the front desk is SERGEANT FALLEN, a rugged man in his early thirties.

FALLEN
(to Decker)
Yes, sir?

Decker flashes his NYPD detective's shield. The Sergeant looks at it, unimpressed.

DECKER
Sergeant, can you tell who was killed in that black Trans Am tonight?

(CONTINUED)

CONTINUED:

FALLEN
I'd have to know why you want to know.

DECKER
How about professional courtesy?

The Sergeant pauses. Then, he picks up a clipboard. Folding the pages over, he reads...

FALLEN
Here it is. The driver killed in that car was LEROY QUILL, age thirty-eight. Four previous arrests, one conviction for assault -- he served eighteen months in the state prison.

DECKER
Does he have any family -- or how about his friends?

FALLEN
(reading more)
... Here's something. According to the coroner's preliminary statement, it is quite possible that Quill was killed earlier this evening by a blow to the head -- and his body dumped in the car later -- giving the impression that he died as a result of the automobile accident.

DECKER
That's very interesting... But Sergeant, what about family and friends?

FALLEN
(reading the report)
He's divorced and lives alone in a boarding house outside of Warren. He has a sister in Chicago.
(looking at Decker)
I know he used to hang out at the Trapper's Bar up in Warren. It's a rough place frequented by bikers and all sorts of lowlifes.

The sergeant writes down a few things on a piece of paper and hands it to Decker.

(CONTINUED)

CONTINUED:

DECKER
Thanks, Sergeant.

The TELEPHONE RINGS. The Sergeant answers it and acknowledges Decker with a wave of his hand.

INT. DECKER'S MOTEL ROOM - NIGHT

Decker enters his motel room to a RINGING TELEPHONE.

DECKER
(on phone)
Hello?

INT. CAROL NELSON'S HOUSE - LIVING ROOM - SAME TIME

Carol is on the telephone. Maggie is close by wiping tears from her eyes.

CAROL
(on phone)
Matt... Alex has been kidnaped!

INTERCUT DECKER AND CAROL

DECKER

is stunned. The words cut like a knife.

DECKER
... Carol, are you sure?

CAROL
When Maggie arrived at the bungalow, Alex was gone. She found a note addressed to you.

Decker does not respond, he is in a daze.

CAROL
(continuing)
Matt, are you still there?

DECKER
... Read the note.

CAROL
It says, "Decker, I have your son. I am willing to trade his life for the three million dollars you have or soon will have.
(MORE)

(CONTINUED)

CONTINUED:

CAROL (Contd.)
Any attempt to make this a police matter and he will die. When you are ready to trade, leave a message on the bulletin board at the Clinton Hollow Supermarket. Put the message on a piece of paper, fold it up and place it behind the enclosed business card. The bulletin board will be checked every morning between eight and nine a.m. by someone other than myself. If you attempt to follow the pickup man or involve the police, Alex will die."

DECKER
(emotionally exhausted)
... I'll be right over.

INT. CAROL NELSON'S HOUSE - LIVING ROOM - NIGHT

The headlights from Decker's car FLASH across the living room as he pulls into the driveway. Then, the SOUND of a CAR DOOR as it SLAMS shut.

Decker enters the house to find Carol sitting by herself in the living room, clutching the note in her hand. She quickly rises and embraces Decker.

DECKER
(holding Carol tightly)
... Where's Maggie?

CAROL
I gave her a mild sedative and put her to bed.

Decker takes the note and sits down. After reading it, he stares down at the floor; almost mesmerized.

DECKER

is totally destroyed and emotionally stretched to the limit. His new life suddenly dangles by a thin thread.

Almost in a daze, Decker walks into the dining room while Carol watches him.

INT. DINING ROOM - DECKER

stands in front of the liquor cabinet.

CONTINUED:

CAROL (o.s.)
Matt, are you all right?

Decker does not respond. He opens the cabinet door and picks up a bottle of SCOTCH. With a blank expression on his face, he just stares at it.

INT. LIVING ROOM - CLOSE ON CAROL

She looks pensive and frightened. She knows Decker has a problem with alcohol. She is not sure of what he will do and, for that matter, what she might do.

INT. DINING ROOM - DECKER

stares at the bottle of Scotch and rubs his neck. Then, he walks into the kitchen with the bottle.

INT. KITCHEN - NIGHT

Carol enters the kitchen and stands silently just inside of the doorway. She watches Decker take a glass out of the cabinet and pour a drink. She quickly moves towards Decker and...

CAROL
(softly; but firmly)
Matt, don't do it.

Decker raises the glass for a drink but Carol knocks it out of his hand. He turns for another glass. Carol puts her hands on the bottle. She struggles to get it away from Decker but his grip is too powerful.

Decker shoves Carol across the kitchen. She slams into the counter. DISHES on the edge of the counter CRASH to the floor and SHATTER into pieces.

Carol charges Decker full force. She is crying and throwing punches at him with all her might.

CAROL
(yelling loudly)
NOOOooo!

Carol grabs the bottle again but this time, she knocks it out of Decker's hand. It SMASHES into pieces on the floor. Decker turns away from Carol and leans over the counter feeling both pain and shame. Carol sobs quietly behind him.

After a long moment, Decker turns to Carol with tears in his eyes. They hold each other tightly for a long time without saying a word.

INT. DINING ROOM - LATER THAT NIGHT

Decker and Carol sit across from each other. Decker puts down the cup of coffee, stands up, and begins...

DECKER
... My father was an alcoholic... When I started drinking, I thought I could handle it better than him... My drinking affected more than my marriage -- it cost the life of my best friend and partner, Jack Dryer... Before I was forced to take professional help by the department, there were days when I shouldn't have been working. I wasn't drunk -- but I was still recovering from a previous binge. My judgment and my abilities were impaired... My responses were slow -- there was no sense of responsibility attached to what I was doing... Because of this, my partner had to die during a routine arrest... While I was exonerated, I know I caused Jack's death...

Carol gets up and stands in front of Decker.

CAROL
Matt, you made a mistake a long time ago and you've been paying for it ever since... Nothing can change what happened... It's time to start living again. Don't let your life slip away from you...

DECKER
... My life?... It started over when I found out I had a son -- and met you. And now, someone is trying to snatch it away from me.

Carol and Decker embrace each other tightly.

INT. DECKER'S MOTEL ROOM - DAY

Decker answers a KNOCK on the door. The motel manager hands him a Federal Express envelope.

MOTEL MGR.
Mr. Decker, this package just arrived for you.

(CONTINUED)

CONTINUED:

DECKER
(taking it)
Thanks.

Decker opens the package and sees a note from Tyner.

INSERT OF NOTE

It reads, "Matt, here's all the information I could find -- hope it will help." Signed, T.J.

BACK TO SCENE

Decker sorts through the enclosures. He glances over a newspaper article. Suddenly, he reacts to something he reads. He folds up the newspaper article and puts it into his pocket. Like a flash, he is out the door.

EXT. NORTHFIELD FARM - MAIN HOUSE - DAY

Decker knocks on the front door of the main house. A servant opens the door.

DECKER
I'd like to see the Judge.

SERVANT
Judge Tyler is in the barn.

EXT. BARN - DAY

Decker approaches the barn. The doors are closed. He is about to open the side door when he HEARS the Judge and Hollis arguing. Decker stands silent and listens.

HOLLIS (v.o.)
(defensively)
I'm telling you, Judge, there's no way Decker can tie you into this thing -- he has no proof. And Dexter Brown knows nothing -- all he did was keep me informed of Decker's activities.

TYLER (v.o.)
Unfortunately, Brad, I don't share your optimism.

INT. BARN - DAY

Decker swings open the side door and levels the gun at the Judge and Hollis. Both of them look surprised.

(CONTINUED)

CONTINUED:

Decker moves behind Hollis who is still wearing a hat. He puts the barrel of the gun up to Hollis' head.

DECKER
(threatening tone)
Where's Alex?

HOLLIS
(unnerved, stammering)
I -- I don't know.

Decker COCKS the hammer back -- Hollis flinches.

DECKER
This is the last time I'm gonna ask you -- where's Alex?

TYLER
Mr. Decker, we don't know where your son is... Please -- give me a chance to explain.

Decker still holds the cocked gun against Hollis' head.

DECKER
(looking at the Judge)
Are you going to deny that you hired Leroy Quill to run me off the road the day I picked up the steamship trunk -- or that Hollis didn't sap me and take the trunk from me later -- or shoot at me the night I was in Northfield Cemetery?

TYLER
Mr. Decker, please lower your gun and I'll explain everything.

Slowly, Decker releases the cocked hammer.

DECKER
(to Hollis)
Stand very still.

Decker stands behind Hollis but looks at the Judge.

TYLER
First of all, Mr. Decker, I don't know any Leroy Quill. But I did have Brad take the trunk away from
(MORE)

CONTINUED:

TYLER (Contd.)
you for a very good reason. Also, the night he shot at you was only an attempt to scare you off.

DECKER
I find that hard to believe since the bullets were only inches from my head.

TYLER
Brad is an expert marksman -- if he intended to kill you, he would have done so on the first shot.

DECKER
Where's my son?

TYLER
Honestly, we don't know.

Decker pulls out the folded-up copy of a newspaper article from his pocket and hands it to the Judge. The Judge puts on his glasses and reads. Soon, he lowers the paper and almost looks relieved.

DECKER
(to Judge Tyler)
Are you going to deny that your real name is Jake Styler? -- And that you were Eddie Malone's unknown accomplice in the heist of three million dollars?

TYLER
No ... I'd like you to take a ride with me and Brad. There's something I want to show you. It will explain everything.

DECKER
(pause; and then)
All right, Judge, but Hollis drives.

Decker motions for Hollis to walk in front of him as they exit the barn.

EXT. BARN - DAY

Hollis gets behind the wheel of a station wagon. It has a decal on the door, NORTHFIELD FARM. Decker and the Judge get in and sit behind Hollis.

EXT. NORTHFIELD FARM - MOVING STATION WAGON

slowly passes the fields where workers are busy tending their chores.

INT. MOVING STATION WAGON - DAY

TYLER
(to Decker)
I was twenty years old and just another reckless kid on the New York City streets. When Eddie and I pulled that heist, we had no idea who we were ripping off and how much money was involved... After we realized we hit Louie Lepke, Eddie, Johnny Sacks, our driver, and I came to New Hampshire to hide out. In the late thirties, New Hampshire was a primitive wilderness. We thought it would be safe...
(MORE)

EXT. HIGHWAY - MOVING STATION WAGON

swiftly covers the two-lane highway passing the scenic countryside.

TYLER (v.o.)
(continuing; to Decker)
Malone buried the money in two locations. He gave me ten thousand dollars plus a map to my share. Scared crazy, Sacks called Lepke's people and cut a deal for himself by turning us in. Eddie found out in time to take care of Sacks but -- he died the next day in a shoot-out with Lepke's killers. I was already in Canada.

DECKER (v.o.)
For your information, Judge, Malone made a map showing three locations. At the second spot, I found a skeleton with a bullet hole through the skull.

INT. MOVING STATION WAGON - DAY

DECKER
(continuing)
How long did you stay in Canada?

(CONTINUED)

CONTINUED:

TYLER

Four years. I returned to New Hampshire not knowing if my share of the money would really be behind Northfield Cemetery. To my surprise, it was. I liked the area so much I decided to stay. I assumed a new identity and made real estate investments over the years. After I became a respected member of the community, I ran for public office. For more than thirty years I was a county judge.

EXT. NORTHFIELD NURSING HOME - DAY

The Judge's station wagon passes through two cement columns. A brass plaque on one column reads:

NORTHFIELD NURSING HOME

The station wagon passes the massive front lawn. The property is manicured to perfection. Near the main building, workers tend magnificent flower gardens. Senior citizens sit on benches, basking in the sun while nurses assist invalid patients.

EXT. NORTHFIELD NURSING HOME - DAY

Decker, Hollis, and Judge Tyler get out of the car and enter the main building. Nurses affectionately greet Judge Tyler as he passes. He waves and smiles back.

INT. NORTHFIELD NURSING HOME - LOBBY

Decker and Judge Tyler enter the lobby with Hollis walking in front of them.

It is busy with visiting relatives. A worker conscientiously mops the floor.

At the front desk, the receptionist, MILDRED MAYFIELD, comes to attention at the sight of the Judge.

MAYFIELD

Judge Tyler!

TYLER

Hi, Mildred. We're going to take a stroll around the facility.

They walk down the main corridor with Hollis in front.

INT. MAIN CORRIDOR - DAY

A nurse, ANN PRESTON, exits a patient's room and...

PRESTON
Good afternoon, Judge Tyler. How are you doing?

TYLER
Just fine, Ann.

The Judge smiles and continues walking with Decker.

TYLER
Mr. Decker, this nursing home cares for destitute senior citizens -- people who need help and should be allowed to live out their lives with dignity... This is why I attempted to stop your investigation.

DECKER
Judge, I don't understand the connection?

TYLER
If it became public knowledge that this home was built on stolen money or from the profits of stolen money, it could be destroyed -- as well as the benefits it provides for senior citizens. Exposing me would only expose the facility to possible scandal and ruin -- and that would be the greatest crime of all.

They walk in silence to the lobby and exit the building.

INT. MOVING STATION WAGON - DAY

Decker sits next to the Judge in the back seat while Hollis drives. Decker relaxes his aggressive posture in dealing with Judge Tyler and Brad Hollis.

TYLER
When I die, twenty percent of my estate will go to my daughter and grandchildren in Minnesota.
(MORE)

CONTINUED:

TYLER (Contd.)
And for twenty years of faithful service, Brad will receive two hundred acres of farmland. The balance of my estate will be placed in trust for the Northfield Nursing Home. It will be large enough to allow for the home's maintenance and expansion.

EXT. NORTHFIELD FARM - MAIN HOUSE - DAY

The Judge's car stops in front of the main house. They get out and enter the house.

INT. MAIN HOUSE - THE STUDY - DAY

Decker and Judge Tyler are alone in the study. Decker looks out the study window with only one thought in mind, Alex, his son. He turns to Judge Tyler and...

DECKER
Judge, someone has kidnaped my son. He's already killed my ex-wife and, more than likely, his accomplice. Now he wants to trade Alex's life for the three million dollars buried by Malone.

TYLER
Have you considered going to the police?

DECKER
It's too risky. The police have no leads on the killer... If the killer thinks that I have involved the police in my son's kidnaping, he's likely to kill Alex!

TYLER
Have you checked out the third location yet?

DECKER
No, not yet! Think Malone's share could still be there?

TYLER
If his hiding spot has remained undiscovered, it should be
(MORE)

(CONTINUED)

CONTINUED:

TYLER (Contd.)
there... Mr. Decker, most of my assets are real estate holdings and stocks. If it becomes necessary, I could probably raise five hundred thousand dollars in cash within a week.

DECKER
Thanks, Judge, but I don't think the killer will give me that kind of time... I'm going to check out this Leroy Quill and see if I can find out who he was working with.

Decker heads towards the door, the Judge follows.

EXT. HIGHWAY - DECKER'S MOVING CAR

passes a highway sign: TOWN OF WARREN - 3 MILES

EXT. BAYLOR'S BOARDING HOUSE - DAY

Decker's car stops in front of a dilapidated boarding house. The sign over the front door reads:

BAYLOR'S BOARDING HOUSE

Decker gets out, walks to the front door, and enters.

INT. BAYLOR'S BOARDING HOUSE - DAY

Decker stands in the hallway looking at names scribbled above the row of mailbox compartments.

A door CREAKS open a crack. A nervous-looking woman dressed in a bathrobe with a cigarette dangling from her lips suspiciously eyes Decker.

WOMAN
(curtly)
What do you want?

Decker approaches the door. She peers out at him.

DECKER
I want to see Leroy Quill's room?

Cautiously, she peeks out at Decker.

WOMAN
Are you the police?

(CONTINUED)

CONTINUED:

Decker quickly flashes his NYPD shield. After a moment, the woman hands Decker a key.

WOMAN
It's the second door on the left at the top of the stairs.

With that comment, the woman SLAMS her door shut and secures it with a SLIDING BOLT.

INT. QUILL'S APARTMENT - LIVING ROOM - DAY

Decker enters the first-class, seedy hovel. An old stuffed couch and chair look like a large dog had taken big bites out of the padding. A coffee table with the edge scarred by cigarette burns is covered with empty beer cans and porno magazines.

Decker searches through the piles of garbage around the room. He picks up any piece of paper with writing on it and inspects it carefully. He finds nothing important.

INT. KITCHEN - DAY

The walls are heavily stained with grease. The sink is filled with dirty dishes. Decker opens the refrigerator door. Two shelves are filled with beer. A putrid piece of cheese with a fuzzy green mold sits on a plate. Decker shakes his head and closes the door.

INT. BEDROOM - DAY

The furniture is old and beat-up looking. More porno magazines lie on the floor near the bed. Loose change, papers, and a matchbook lay on top of a dresser. After sifting through the papers, Decker picks up the matches.

CLOSE ON MATCHBOOK COVER

It reads, THE TRAPPER'S BAR.

EXT. THE TRAPPER'S BAR - DAY

A shabby-looking building. Parked in front, a few Harley-Davidsons and beat-up pickup trucks and old cars ravaged by rust and neglect. Decker heads for the door.

INT. TRAPPER'S BAR - DAY

Decker enters the smokey, dimly-lit bar. Bone-cutting HEAVY-METAL MUSIC THUNDERS from a JUKE BOX in the corner of the room.

(CONTINUED)

CONTINUED:

The clientele is definitely not the social elite. It is an assortment of lowlifes with long hair, shaggy beards, and sleeveless shirts displaying tattooed arms.

The collection of misfits look at Decker with obvious contempt as he walks up to the corner of the bar. From the other end, the bartender gives him a cursory glance. Six bruisers standing together at the bar stare at him with critical eyes.

The bartender finally approaches Decker. In his mid-thirties, he is scruffy looking with mustache and two days' growth on his face. A LARGE SCAR tracks from his left ear to the corner of his mouth. The bartender does not speak; he just lifts his chin up as to gesture, "what do you want?"

DECKER

What can you tell me about Leroy Quill?

The bartender looks away from Decker and towards a man at the other end of the bar. The man is not visible -- Decker's view of him is blocked by other men standing at the bar.

From the other end of the bar, a man moves around the thugs standing between him and Decker. He is still not quite visible.

DECKER'S REACTION

when he sees the man. He straightens up and his face clearly registers, "Oh s*#t."

THE MAN - SLY RANKIN

is easily six-four with wide shoulders and narrow hips. A tight sleeveless shirt displays bulging chest muscles and massive arms. He is completely bald with a Fu Manchu mustache and has a SKULL and CROSSBONES earring. Everyone clearly gives him room to pass. RANKIN moves like a man who knows no fear and has few challengers. Decker is no fool -- he knows immediately he is in deep s*#t. Rankin stands next to Decker with an intimidating presence and addresses him in a deep, raspy voice...

RANKIN

Hey man, why are you asking questions about Leroy -- he died yesterday?

(CONTINUED)

CONTINUED:

DECKER
(leaning casually
against the bar)
He bought some Girl Scout cookies
from my little sister and forgot
to pay for them.

As he spoke, Decker realized he made a big mistake.

RANKIN
(in a low voice)
F*#%in' wise guy.

Rankin grabs Decker's shoulders with his powerful hands and begins to squeeze. Decker cannot believe the strength of the man's hands as he starts to sink towards the floor in excruciating pain.

Decker tries to break Rankin's grip but no dice. He throws a power punch into Rankin's stomach -- it is as hard as a rock. He attempts to knee Rankin's groin but Rankin blocks Decker's move with the side of his leg.

Decker is now on his knees, his face twisted in agony.

RANKIN
(to the bar crowd)
This guy's a real candy a*#.

Like a sack of potatoes, Rankin flings Decker across the room. Decker crashes over a small table and hits the floor. Slowly, Decker gets up to his feet rubbing his shoulders with both hands. Rankin moves casually towards him like a cat playing with a mouse.

Rankin tries to grab Decker but he steps sideways and throws a punch to Rankin's face. It lands full force with SMASHING IMPACT. Unfortunately, it has no effect on Rankin other than making him more angry.

Rankin spins around quickly and delivers the back of his fist to the center of Decker's chest. It hits with a loud THUD making everyone cringe. Decker flies backwards and crashes into a table.

B.G. VOICES
(calling out)
Hey Sly, give the guy a chance --
give him a gun.

When are you gonna stop playing
with him, Sly, and finish him off?

(CONTINUED)

CONTINUED:

B.G. VOICES (Contd.)
(calling out)
Hey mister, you can't win when
you're fighting a f*#%in' machine.

Rankin turns his head towards one of the thugs. Decker, still gasping from the blow, does not waste the moment. He goes for a sixty-yard field goal. With full force, he delivers his right foot to Rankin's nuts. Rankin doubles over and drops to the floor.

With tremendous willpower, Rankin attempts to get up. He looks at Decker, his face contorted in pain and anger. Decker kicks another field goal but this time, to Rankin's stomach. The force of the blow expels the wind from Rankin's lungs and flips him over on his back. He is finally unconscious. Decker, still recovering from the assault, staggers over to a chair and drops down.

B.G. VOICES
(calling out)
Mister, that was incredible.

Jesus, did you see that?

S*#t, I don't believe it.

Decker sits at a table rubbing the back of his neck with his right hand. Rankin is moving slowly on the floor, GROANING in agony. In this macho environment, Decker has earned the respect of the rugged crowd.

A small, wiry man with a beer in hand approaches. Big ears jut out from a scruffy, angular face with tufts of hair sticking out from his head. The man squints at Decker with beady little eyes.

HORSEFLY
Hey, man. They call me Horsefly.
That was some job you did on
Rankin.

Decker moves his head back and forth in an attempt to stretch the kinks out of his neck.

DECKER
... I tell you what, I wouldn't
want to try that again.

Horsefly takes a seat at Decker's table and leans towards him. Discreetly in a quiet voice...

(CONTINUED)

CONTINUED:

HORSEFLY
What do you want to know about Leroy Quill?

DECKER
(leaning towards him)
I want to know who he hung out with and what he was into?

HORSEFLY
(pause; and then)
I knew Leroy fairly well. He told me he had something going that would set him up for life.

DECKER
Did he tell you what it was?

HORSEFLY
No. He'd just sit there and grin.

DECKER
Look, Horsefly, it's important. Who was he working with?

HORSEFLY
Hey, man, I don't know -- but I'm sure it ain't no one from this place.

DECKER
Why do you say that?

HORSEFLY
Because Leroy was here almost every night. On a couple occasions, he told me he had to leave and meet someone important.

DECKER
Do you know where he went?

HORSEFLY
I'm sorry, man, he never said.

DECKER
(standing up)
Horsefly, would you come outside for a minute?

HORSEFLY
(a little uncertain)
... All right.

EXT. THE TRAPPER'S BAR - DAY

Decker and Horsefly walk out of the bar together. They pass two rough-looking characters heading inside.

DECKER
Without going through the formalities of acquiring a permit, how can I get my hands on some explosives?

HORSEFLY
(BIG SMILE)
You're talkin' to the man who can make it happen.

EXT. CAROL NELSON'S HOUSE - NIGHT

Decker's car pulls into the driveway. He gets out and walks to the front door where Carol anxiously waits for him. Carol goes to kiss Decker and sees that his face is slightly bruised.

INT. CAROL NELSON'S HOUSE - LIVING ROOM - NIGHT

CAROL
(entering the house)
Matt, what happened to your face?

DECKER
Nothing.

CAROL
Nothing? Let me clean it up.

INT. BEDROOM - NIGHT

Decker sits on the edge of the bed. Carol stands over him and tends to his cuts and bruises.

DECKER
... Where's Maggie?

CAROL
(dabbing his face with a soft cloth)
Stop squirming... She's staying at her friend's house. So, what happened today?

INT. DINING ROOM - LATER THAT NIGHT

Decker and Carol sit across from each other at the dining room table talking over a cup of coffee.

(CONTINUED)

CONTINUED:

CAROL
That's amazing... You really like Judge Tyler, don't you?

DECKER
Considering what he's doing for other people, you can't help but admire him.

CAROL
Since your investigation of Leroy Quill turned out to be a dead end, are you going to the police now?

DECKER
(standing up)
Only as a last resort... There's something I must do first.

INT. DECKER'S MOVING CAR - HIS POV - NIGHT

pulling into the Huxley Crossroad intersection.

DECKER'S CAR

parked next to the center island.

THE ODOMETER - DECKER'S POV

checking the reading.

THE COMPASS

held in Decker's hand reflects in the soft light from the dashboard. The direction needle points due WEST.

EXT. STREET - DECKER'S MOVING CAR

pulls around the island and heads out Miller Creek Road.

EXT. DECKER'S MOVING CAR - TAIL LIGHTS

glow brightly but gradually fade out of sight as the car drives off into the dark night.

EXT. DESOLATE ROAD - DECKER'S CAR

is parked off the road. He stands over the open trunk.

INT. CAR TRUNK - DECKER & HIS EQUIPMENT

are softly illuminated by the trunk light. The shovel, pick axe, rope, lantern, attache case, and a box marked "EXPLOSIVES - HANDLE WITH CARE," are all visible.

EXT. DESOLATE ROAD - NIGHT

Decker lights the lantern and closes the car trunk. He looks at the compass and turns it until the direction needle is pointing NORTH WEST. He walks into the dense woods near the car and gradually fades into the night.

EXT. CLINTON HOLLOW MOTEL - DAY

Decker closes the motel door. He puts his luggage in the trunk, gets into his car, and drives away.

EXT. STREET - AROUND THE CORNER - A SEDAN

is parked in the distance so it is too far away to distinguish who is behind the wheel.

INT. SEDAN - DRIVER'S POV

looking at his hand holding a RECEIVING DEVICE similar to the one that Decker used to track Maggie's car. The DIGITAL LIGHT FLASHES RED with a PULSING beat.

INT. SEDAN - DRIVER'S POV

looking at Decker's car pass and head towards town.

INT. CLINTON HOLLOW SUPERMARKET - DAY

Decker stands in front of the store's bulletin board. He looks at his wrist watch.

CLOSE ON WATCH FACE - It is 6:58 a.m.

BACK TO SCENE

Decker waits for a woman pushing a grocery carriage to pass. Then, he takes out the business card and a folded-up note from his pocket. He puts the note behind the card and pins it to the board with a thumbtack. Without looking around, he walks out of the supermarket.

EXT. STREET - DECKER'S MOVING CAR

swings up Norwood Street from the highway.

EXT. CAROL NELSON'S HOUSE - DAY

Decker gets out of his car and walks to the front door.

INT. CAROL NELSON'S HOUSE - KITCHEN - DAY

CAROL

Coffee?

(CONTINUED)

CONTINUED:

DECKER

Sure.

Carol pours the coffee. Maggie enters through the back door. Both Carol and Decker are surprised to see her.

CAROL

Maggie! What are you doing here? I thought we agreed that you would stay at Karen's house until this thing is over?

MAGGIE

Mom, I'm tired of just waiting around --

(to Decker)

What's going on?

DECKER

(pause; and then)

I'm meeting with the kidnaper this morning.

Both Carol and Maggie seem surprised.

CAROL

But what about the money?

DECKER

No questions -- I've worked up a game plan and we need to go over it in detail.

EXT. CAROL NELSON'S HOUSE - DAY

Decker stands by his car and kisses Carol goodbye. She holds him tightly in her arms.

CAROL

Matt... come back to us safely with Alex.

Maggie walks up to Decker and kisses him on the cheek. She then stands close to her mother who puts a comforting arm around her. Standing together, they watch Decker drive off.

EXT. DESOLATED ROAD - DECKER'S PARKED CAR - DAY

Decker opens the car trunk and takes out just the rope. He closes the trunk and without looking around, he walks into the dense woods bordering the road.

EXT. WOODS - DAY

Decker walks with deliberation through a dense corridor of thick pine trees. The shaded forest is dark, cool, and has an ominous aura. He still does not look around to see if he is being followed -- he just keeps walking.

INT. CAROL NELSON'S HOUSE - LIVING ROOM - DAY

Carol is on the telephone. Maggie stands near by.

CAROL
(on phone)
That's right, Lt. Branford, I can't tell you any more than that until you get here.

EXT. OPEN FIELD - DAY

Decker exits the dense woods and follows a well-worn path through an open field. The rope, looped around his shoulder, swings as he walks.

EXT. NARROW PATH - DAY

The open field turns to a narrow path flanked by two ridges covered with small trees. In the distance, a clearing is evident.

EXT. DEADMAN'S QUARRY - DAY

Decker follows the narrow path past an OPEN PRECIPICE near the upper ledge of Deadman's Quarry. He moves to the edge of the quarry and looks out over the basin area filled with dark, green water. Thick woods surround the outer rim of the quarry providing ideal cover for someone hiding in wait.

FROM ACROSS THE QUARRY - ON THE OTHER SIDE

we see Decker stand on the edge of the rim. The quarry's chiseled banks are straight and stand fifty feet high from the water below. Decker turns and heads back to...

THE OPEN PRECIPICE

where he belays a rope to a tree and lowers himself down the jagged edge into the deep pocket below.

LOOKING DOWN INTO THE PRECIPICE

as Decker descends. Small pools of water at the bottom FLICKER from the activity of water bugs.

AT THE BOTTOM OF THE PRECIPICE

Decker's feet touch the slime-covered rocks.

LOOKING DOWN INTO THE PRECIPICE

we see Decker disappear underneath a rock ledge.

INT. CAROL NELSON'S HOUSE - LIVING ROOM - DAY

Lt. Branford looks out the living room window and then turns to face Carol who is seated in a chair. Maggie is poised next to her. Two state troopers stand erect like granite statues...

BRANFORD
Mrs. Nelson, the sooner you tell me where Decker is, the faster I can help him!

Carol does not speak, she just glances at her wrist watch.

EXT. DEADMAN'S QUARRY - LOOKING DOWN INTO THE PRECIPICE

From under the rock ledge, Decker appears dragging a LARGE METAL BOX -- it is similar to the one he found behind Northfield Cemetery. He ties the box to the rope he climbed down on.

AT THE BOTTOM OF THE PRECIPICE - DECKER

HEARS approaching FOOTSTEPS coming from ABOVE. He pulls out the .357 Magnum and takes a shooting stance with both hands on the gun. He points the weapon up, towards the rim of the precipice.

DECKER'S POV - LOOKING UP

A figure moves towards the edge and looks down at him.

ANGLE ON JACK MURPHY

the detective from Decker's division.

DECKER'S POV

looking up at Murphy.

DECKER
(screaming; ready to shoot)
Murphy, you son-of-a-b*#%h!

DECKER'S POV

Murphy thrusts his empty hands forward.

ANGLE ON MURPHY

MURPHY
(yelling)
Matt, don't shoot, I can explain.

DECKER

His arms tremble from holding the gun overhead.

DECKER
Let's hear it -- fast and simple.

MURPHY

stands on the rim of the precipice with his arms extended. He stands frozen.

INT. CAROL NELSON'S HOUSE - LIVING ROOM - DAY

BRANFORD
Mrs. Nelson, the longer you delay in telling us where Decker is --

CAROL
(interrupting as she gets up from her chair)
Lieutenant, he is at Deadman's Quarry -- do you know where it is?

BRANFORD
(annoyed; walking towards the door)
Let's go before it is too late.

EXT. DEADMAN'S QUARRY - DAY

INTERCUT DECKER AND MURPHY

Various ANGLES as they speak; their POV of each other.

MURPHY
When you and Nora broke up nineteen years ago, I kept in touch with her all this time.

DECKER
You son-of-a-b*#%h, you knew I had a son and wouldn't tell me?

MURPHY
Matt -- please. Nora made me promise not to say anything to you
(MORE)

CONTINUED:

MURPHY (Contd.)
about Alex... She was very bitter over the way her marriage ended. Because of your drinking problems, she felt that you were unfit as a father. Believe me, I tried to convince her that it was unfair to both Alex and you but -- she wouldn't change her mind.

DECKER
You still haven't explained why you're here.

MURPHY
After Nora was murdered, Alex called and asked me to help him find her killer. When he told me that he finally met you, I asked him to tell you about me but he said no. At the time -- he didn't know you or trust you.

DECKER
How did you know where I was?

MURPHY
I bugged your car with a transmitter.

Decker lowers his gun and tucks it into his trousers. He grabs hold of the rope and...

DECKER
I'm coming up -- just stay where I can see you.

Arm over arm, Decker pulls himself up the rope. When he is twenty feet from the top...

MURPHY
Matt, I've been up here for the past two days checking out some leads. I've got a pretty good idea who killed Nora and kid--

DECKER'S POV

looking up at Murphy. Before Murphy can finish what he is saying, a HIGH-POWERED HANDGUN EXPLODES LOUDLY and ECHOES in the quarry. Murphy's body drops over the edge of the precipice barely missing Decker on the way down to the bottom.

HANGING ON THE ROPE - DECKER

takes the .357 Magnum out and holds it with one hand while he grips the rope with the other.

At the SOUND of APPROACHING FOOTSTEPS, Decker cocks the hammer. It CLICKS into firing position.

DECKER'S POV

looking up at the edge of the precipice. Soon, Alex appears on the edge with his hands tied behind his back. Shielded by Alex's body, Decker cannot see who stands behind him -- but he does see a .357 Magnum pointed at Alex's head. The man turns and slowly reveals himself.

ANGLE ON GUS GILSUM

the staff writer from the Concord Chronicle. We saw him interviewed on Howard Clayton's television show and his picture displayed in his newspaper column.

Gilsum is no longer the soft-spoken, pleasant-mannered writer we saw interviewed on television. He is clearly a crazed killer consumed by greed.

ANGLE ON GILSUM

GILSUM
(keeping Alex between Decker and himself)
Drop the gun, Decker, or I'll kill the boy.

ANGLE ON DECKER

dropping the gun without hesitation. It bounces off the rocks below and into the water.

GILSUM AND ALEX

move back from the edge of the precipice.

GILSUM
Do you have the money?

DECKER
-- I do.

GILSUM
Where is it?

DECKER
It's in a box tied to this rope.

(CONTINUED)

CONTINUED:

GILSUM
(pause; and then)
All right, climb up here. And remember one thing, any funny business and your son dies.

GILSUM'S POV

of Decker climbing up the rope.

GILSUM (Contd.)
I've been searching for this money for ten years. I knew the story about Malone was true.

EXT. HIGHWAY - STATE POLICE CARS

move swiftly down the desolated dirt road kicking up clouds of dust.

EXT. THE EDGE OF THE PRECIPICE - DAY

Decker climbs to the top and sees a bruise on Alex's head. He wants to strike out at Gilsum but knows he cannot risk it.

DECKER
Alex, are you all right?

GILSUM
(cautiously keeping Alex between them)
Never mind that. Just haul that box up here.

Gilsum notices Decker straining to haul the box up. Heavy with money, Gilsum figures, as he smiles insanely.

DECKER
(pulling the rope up)
Why did you kill Nora?

GILSUM
I wanted to buy the trunk from her but she was stubborn -- she wouldn't sell it to me. I searched her house that morning and when I didn't find it, I thought she might have had it with her. So, I followed her out of town and tried to force her car off the road...

(CONTINUED)

CONTINUED:

Decker struggles to lift the box up to the edge of the precipice. Still very cautious, Gilsum keeps Alex between Decker and himself.

GILSUM
(continuing)
Drag that box over here.

DECKER
(dragging the box)
What about Leroy Quill?

GILSUM
(very anxious to get his hands on the money)
Quill was a fool. I was driving his car the day we drove the boy's mother off the road. He was in as deep as I was. But when I decided to take your son in exchange for the money, Quill got cold feet -- so... I had no choice.

Gilsum points with his gun to the quarry's rim.

GILSUM
(continuing; to Decker)
Move that box over there.

Decker drags the heavy box to ten feet from the edge.

GILSUM
(continuing)
All right, leave the box there and move towards the edge -- backwards -- and keep your hands away from your body.

Looking over his shoulder, Decker walks backwards with his hands away from his body. Standing on the edge, he looks down to the water-filled basin fifty feet below.

Finally, Gilsum releases Alex. Decker hugs him tightly without saying a word.

GILSUM

drops to one knee with his gun trained on Decker, his face twisted with greed. He looks demented. Anxiously, Gilsum fumbles with the clasp on top of the metal box.

Decker tries to untie Alex's hands but...

(CONTINUED)

CONTINUED:

GILSUM
(looking up)
Leave his hands tied.

Decker stops untying Alex's hands. He stands still until Gilsum looks back to the metal box. Gilsum flips the lid open and slowly lowers his gun at the sight of

THE OPEN BOX

filled with hundred dollar bills.

GILSUM

is mesmerized by the sight of all that money.

DECKER

retrieves a small explosive detonator from his back pocket like the one he used before. With Gilsum caught off guard, Decker makes his move. He quickly grabs Alex, turns, and jumps off the edge of the quarry.

GILSUM

looks up but it is too late. Decker and Alex are gone. He rises to his feet but...

IN MID-FALL - DECKER

detonates the explosive charges hidden below the shallow layer of money. Decker and Alex plummet to the waters below as the metal box and Gilsum are blown to smithereens in a THUNDEROUS ROAR.

IN THE WATER

Decker grabs a hold of Alex and swims to a spot where he can hang on to the side and untie Alex's hands. Soon, they HEAR the SQUAWK from a POLICE RADIO.

A STATE TROOPER

stands on the edge of the quarry rim holding a two-way radio in his hand.

THE STATE TROOPER'S POV

looking down at Decker and Alex clinging to the edge of the quarry in the water.

ANGLE ON STATE TROOPER

talking into two-way radio. Other troopers approach.

CONTINUED:

TROOPER
(clutching two-way radio)
This is unit two. All units report to sector six.
(he turns to another approaching trooper)
Bring that rope over here.

EXT. DEADMAN'S QUARRY - THE UPPER RIM - DAY

Lt. Branford, Carol and Maggie stand together on the edge. Two troopers assist Alex as he climbs the rope to the top. Decker is right behind him.

Carol and Maggie joyfully embrace Alex. When Decker appears on top of the rim, he receives the same warm greeting from both of them.

Lt. Branford looks at a depression in the ground where the metal box and Gilsum once stood. Troopers find bits of money on the ground and stuck to leaves in the trees.

BRANFORD
(to Decker)
I'll need your statement.
(firmly)
-- And I want all of it!

Jack Murphy's body is pulled up to the edge of the precipice by a team of troopers. Seeing it, Alex begins to cry. Decker puts a comforting arm around him.

BRANFORD
(to Decker)
What's the story on the money?

Decker walks over to the far end of the precipice and pulls on a rope hidden in the bushes. From the dark recesses of the precipice, he pulls up a BULGING DUFFEL BAG. He drags it to Branford's feet. Everyone moves close as Decker pulls back the zipper and reveals...

THE DUFFEL BAG

filled with twenty, fifty, and hundred dollar bills.

B.G. VOICES
(TROOPERS)
Good God, will you look at that.

How much is there?

(CONTINUED)

CONTINUED:

Carol hangs onto Decker's arm while Alex has his arm around Maggie's waist and kisses her forehead.

Branford looks at the duffel bag filled with money and shakes his head in disbelief.

BRANFORD
(to Decker)
Any idea how much money is in that bag?

DECKER
(pause; and then)
I'd probably guess about one-and-a-half million dollars.

B.G. VOICE
(TROOPER)
Holy gees!

BRANFORD
Is that all of it? I thought there was supposed to be three million dollars?

DECKER
(very low-keyed)
That's it, Lieutenant, the story was slightly exaggerated.

Branford looks at the money and then at Decker.

BRANFORD
(pause; and then)
Mr. Decker, I assume, after an investigation, you'll probably be one wealthy person.

Decker smiles and walks away from the quarry with his arm around Carol. Right behind them, Alex and Maggie.

AERIAL VIEW OF DEADMAN'S QUARRY

as everyone walks away from the rim. The dark, greenish water below glistens in the late morning sun. The mystery of "Cockeye" Eddie Malone's missing millions is finally over -- fifty years after it began. And, most importantly, Matt Decker has found a new life...

-- THE END --

ORDER FORM

MICHAEL WIESE
PO Box 406
Westport, CT 06881

Please send the following:

Quantity		*Price*	*Sub-Total*
____	THE INDEPENDENT FILM AND VIDEOMAKERS GUIDE	$ 16.95	= ________
____	FILM AND VIDEO BUDGETS	16.95	= ________
____	HOME VIDEO: PRODUCING FOR THE HOME MARKET	16.95	= ________
____	FADE IN: THE SCREENWRITING PROCESS	16.95	= ________
____	HOLLYWOOD GIFT CATALOG	5.95	= ________
____	GOIN' HOLLYWOOD: THE MOVIE-MAKING GAME	34.95	= ________
COMING SOON:			
____	FILM AND VIDEO MARKETING ***(Do not order until Feb. 1989)***	16.95	= ________
		SUBTOTAL	________
		DISCOUNT -	________
		SHIPPING (See below) +	________
		CT RESIDENTS add 7.5% SALES TAX +	________
		TOTAL : $	________

I am enclosing $______. Check or money order payable to *Michael Wiese.*

Name:____

Address:____

City:______________________________State:_________Zip:______

Telephone: (____)________________

SHIPPING: $2.00/one book
$3.50/two books
$4.00/three books
+$1.00 each book thereafter
(Example, Six books =$6.00)

Except Hollywood Gift Catalog
$.75/one book
.50 each book thereafter
(Example: Five books= $2.75)

Except Goin' Hollywood
Add $5.00 shipping/handling per game.

DISCOUNTS: 20% 3 copies or more
30% 5 copies or more
40% 10 copies or more
44% 25 copies or more

FOREIGN ORDERS Must be Prepaid:
Add $4.00 each via surface mail.
Add $7.00 each via air mail.

(All prices subject to change without notice.)